Machine Learning on Commodity Tiny Devices

This book aims at the tiny machine learning (TinyML) software and hardware synergy for edge intelligence applications. This book presents on-device learning techniques covering model-level neural network design, algorithm-level training optimization and hardware-level instruction acceleration.

Analyzing the limitations of conventional in-cloud computing would reveal that on-device learning is a promising research direction to meet the requirements of edge intelligence applications. As to the cutting-edge research of TinyML, implementing a high-efficiency learning framework and enabling system-level acceleration is one of the most fundamental issues. This book presents a comprehensive discussion of the latest research progress and provides system-level insights on designing TinyML frameworks, including neural network design, training algorithm optimization and domain-specific hardware acceleration. It identifies the main challenges when deploying TinyML tasks in the real world and guides the researchers to deploy a reliable learning system.

This book will be of interest to students and scholars in the field of edge intelligence, especially to those with sufficient professional Edge AI skills. It will also be an excellent guide for researchers to implement high-performance TinyML systems.

Song Guo is a Full Professor leading the Edge Intelligence Lab and Research Group of Networking and Mobile Computing at the Hong Kong Polytechnic University. Professor Guo is a Fellow of the Canadian Academy of Engineering, Fellow of the IEEE, Fellow of the AAIA and Clarivate Highly Cited Researcher.

Qihua Zhou is a PhD student with the Department of Computing at the Hong Kong Polytechnic University. His research interests include distributed AI systems, large-scale parallel processing, TinyML systems and domain-specific accelerators.

Machine Learning on Commodity Tiny Devices

Theory and Practice

Song Guo and Qihua Zhou

CRC Press
Taylor & Francis Group
Boca Raton London New York

CRC Press is an imprint of the
Taylor & Francis Group, an **informa** business

First edition published 2023
by CRC Press
6000 Broken Sound Parkway NW, Suite 300, Boca Raton, FL 33487-2742

and by CRC Press
4 Park Square, Milton Park, Abingdon, Oxon, OX14 4RN

CRC Press is an imprint of Taylor & Francis Group, LLC

© 2023 Song Guo and Qihua Zhou

ISBN: 978-1-032-37423-9 (hbk)
ISBN: 978-1-032-37426-0 (pbk)
ISBN: 978-1-003-34022-5 (ebk)

DOI: 10.1201/9781003340225

Typeset in CMR10 font
by KnowledgeWorks Global Ltd.

Publisher's note: This book has been prepared from camera-ready copy provided by the authors.

Contents

List of Figures

List of Tables

CHAPTER 1

Introduction

1.1 WHAT IS MACHINE LEARNING ON DEVICES?

In recent years, modern AI-oriented applications, such as computer vision [350, 449], natural language processing [94], big data analytics [376] and automatic robotic processing [496], have all benefited greatly from the use of machine learning (ML) techniques. For practical purposes, many of these applications rely on large-scale datasets for model training in the cloud environment, which necessitates a great demand for computing resources [568].

While several in-cloud learning systems have been developed, they often fall short of the rising trend of enabling edge-intelligent perception to function on tiny devices by just utilizing personal data [58, 548]. It is possible to group the primary disadvantages of in-cloud learning into three categories in this situation. First, in-cloud computing often face the concerns of privacy and security. The sensitive information of users, such as intermediate training results and model parameters, is at risk of being intercepted and revealed to the cloud carrier since they must be sent over the network and kept there [594]. Second, the in-cloud learning is designed to aggregate results from many different devices in a data-parallel way, rather than offering personalized models for each user [521]. It cannot provide individualized models for users in the same way that traditional training methods can. Third, it is feasible to run the application processing on cloud servers, but data transfer may take an extremely long time, particularly in a bandwidth-constrained environment, to provide the final output to the user. The real-time model updating will be hindered, and the processing throughput will be reduced as a result of this high delay [132].

The emergence of on-device learning, which conducts the whole machine learning process by user devices, has been seen as a great outcome to deal with the constraints of the in-cloud learning paradigm [522]. Thus, edge devices are often used for on-device learning applications and such a learning paradigm is also commonly referred to as "edge intelligence". Also, on-device learning mainly focuses on producing a high-quality individualized model in a resource-constrained platform, such as the TensorFlow Lite or PyTorch Mobile.

The co-design of training-level algorithms and system-level implementation is required to achieve these objectives. However, we need to overcome various issues in practice. First, edge devices often have a limited amount of user data [445], which may

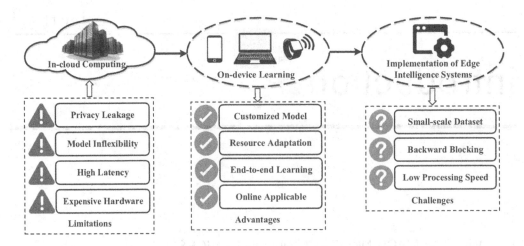

Figure 1.1 Edge intelligence on tiny devices: From in-cloud computing to on-device learning.

lead to the overfitting of models [445]. Second, because not all neurons or layers can be stored on devices, backward propagation for model updates may be hindered [112]. Also, considering the devices' inability to run at full speed for an extended period of time, the operating system usually limits the maximum processing speed. This results in slower processors and a shorter battery life. The demonstration for moving from in-cloud to on-device learning is highlighted in Figure 1.1, and we also discuss some of the obstacles that may arise during system deployment. We refer to the relevant research topic as tiny machine learning (TinyML) systems in this chapter.

As a result, it is often difficult to implement a high-performance TinyML system. We need to dive into the fundamental architecture design and framework implementation, standing in the perspective of system implementation in a full stack, which contains the scope of algorithm-level training coordination, model-level computation acceleration and data-level feature perception. For the most part, enhancing edge intelligence applications requires coordinating algorithmic training and speeding up computing at the model level. On-device learning software is built on these factors, where the most important performance criteria (*e.g.,* memory footprint, processing speed and prediction accuracy) are measured for the implementation of the lower-level device hardware. Data-level feature perception follows the criteria of the learning software and exploits domain-specific acceleration to completely increase the system efficiency. For the design of a desired TinyML system, this combination of software and hardware synergy provides a roadmap to overcome device heterogeneity and resource limits, which are the keys to performance improvement.

Currently available solutions make the implicit assumption that the cluster is homogeneous, which is not true in many real-world situations. Prior methods to handle heterogeneity often primarily prioritized the contributions from fast workers and minimized the contributions of slow workers, resulting in the constraints of workload imbalance and computing inefficiency. Alleviating the restrictions of limited resources and reducing computational costs is a promising way to speed up on-device learning applications. For on-device learning, we demonstrate that the 8-bit fixed-point (INT8) quantization can be used in both forward and backward propagations in the dense neural networks. Utilizing hardware acceleration while maintaining training quality at each layer is essential for a successful quantization-aware training approach. Fixed-point processing on a mobile device requires a different approach to off-the-shelf quantization techniques. According to relevant researches, the INT8 training paradigm, which optimizes the calculation of the forward and backward propagations, may be used to address these constraints.

Actually, there have been many artificially created or NAS-based approaches to save computational cost. However, these methods are mainly designed for on-device inference and cannot develop models to support continuous analytics. This issue can be solved by dividing models between devices and the cloud, which is suitable for model evolving. By capturing the spatial connections between channels, previous researches discover that compressing each pixel along with all the channels in a structured manner can provide a much larger traffic reduction over traditional quantization methods. Considering the key challenges of reducing traffic size for transmitting feature maps, this kind of compression is a fundamental direction to improve the efficiency TinyML training.

Overall, building an efficient TinyML system requires the co-design of device collaboration, computational acceleration and communication saving, which corresponds to the three research points of (1) heterogeneity-aware parameter server, (2) INT8 quantization-aware training and (3) communication-efficient split learning, respectively.

1.2 ON-DEVICE LEARNING AND TINYML SYSTEMS

ML approaches have seen a remarkable rise in popularity over the last decade [94,350]. The power of ML derives from the model training procedure on large-scale datasets, depending on the deployment in powerful cloud servers to fulfill the resource-hungry requirements of data-intensive processing [431,435,568]. Due to the significant latency and privacy leakage of the in-cloud computing paradigm [382,436], it is often difficult to generate personalized models [132]. As shown in Figure 1.2, the on-device learning paradigm is rapidly developing to address the constraints and drawbacks of in-cloud learning [59,381,623,624], which manages the end-to-end learning procedure mainly on edge devices [58,548], such as mobile and IoT equipment [522]. As a result, on-device training is generally constrained by the device's limited processing and memory resources [629]. The key to developing on-device learning systems is to overcome resource restrictions.

1.2.1 Property of On-Device Learning

For the most part, the term *on-device learning* refers to the use of machine learning (ML) applications and the model training process directly on the device itself [522].

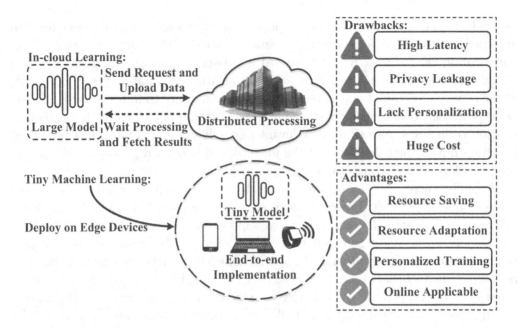

Figure 1.2 A new trend to build a high-performance TinyML system: Evolving from the traditional in-cloud learning to the swift on-device learning.

On-device learning is sometimes referred to as *edge learning* or *edge intelligence* since it is essentially related to the development of edge and mobile devices [629].

The on-device learning applications may confront the problems of costly computing primitives, restricted memory capacity and constrained I/O bandwidth in the real-world situation of edge devices [379]. In addition, because of the high volume of network traffic generated during training, communication costs become an important consideration when learning applications are implemented in a great number of edge devices [218]. Because of this, on-device learning systems are generally hampered by resource constraints, which require minimizing computational overhead, increasing hardware efficiency and reducing energy costs [151].

1.2.2 Objectives of TinyML Systems

For the purpose of developing a high-performance TinyML system, it is necessary to have a deep understanding of why we need on-device learning and what benefits on-device learning may provide. The following are the aims of on-device learning, summarized in four aspects.

Resource Saving. As a result of the limited resources available on edge devices, a high-efficiency on-device learning system must minimize the use of these resources by reducing overhead at the hardware level, communication traffic at the network level and energy consumption at the device level. Therefore, on-device learning requires a significant amount of resources to be saved [631].

Personalized Model. Traditional distributed ML systems on the cloud cannot be used to develop learning frameworks for on-device apps since they are entirely dependent on the local data of the users they are designed for. To avoid this, on-device learning should give a variety of models tailored to the user's preferences, i.e. different users will have various models depending on their demands [132].

Privacy Protection. The data privacy must be strictly maintained since the training phase only occurs on the edge devices and the final model includes sensitive information about user preferences [382]. All training data should be saved and accessed only by the user, with no data being shared with other computers unless absolutely required.

Online Learning. In order to keep the individual model up to date, systems should be able to manage the learning process online and progressively retrain the model according to the most recent user data [436].

Summary. The co-design of learning algorithms and system implementation is critical to the success of the above four properties. We will discuss them in the following text.

1.3 CHALLENGES FOR REALISTIC IMPLEMENTATION

The implementation of high-performance frameworks in a practical situation is not trivial, even while on-device learning offers promising benefits for deploying current ML apps at the edge. We will outline the most pressing issues in the field of on-device learning and the design of matching systems below.

Insufficient User Data. Traditional distributed ML does not have adequate training data for edge devices because of privacy concerns, hence the models cannot be trained using edge devices' training dataset. For example, the few-shot learning with little user data can be used here [445]. In general, small-scale training datasets make it difficult to create a model with excellent generalization. Conventional training approaches, on the other hand, are not applicable to on-device learning. As a result, the systems must be able to extract high-level semantics from a small-scale dataset in order to achieve this attribute.

Backward Propagation Blocking. The most important stage in calculating gradients and making model parameter updates is called backward propagation. It is possible, however, that the chain-rule based gradient computation may become stuck in certain levels and prevent backward propagation to the following layers. For example, only the FC: Fully-connected; Conv: convolutional layers may participate in the gradient computation when utilizing the Core ML framework on an iPhone, whereas weights based on batch normalization, embeddings, bias and scaling operations are unable to be modified. Model architectures based on LSTM: Long Short-term Memory; GRU: Gated Recurrent Unit; RNN: Recurrent Neural Network are not widely supported either. As a result, when using mobile devices for on-device learning, the systems must include additional layers and model features. This target is strongly connected to the hardware implementation on various edge platforms, including the elements of embedded memory, computational primitives, low-level instructions and communication schemes.

Limited Peak Speed. Edge devices, such as cell phones, are not designed to operate at full speed for long periods of time to complete a job, unlike cloud servers. Because of this, it takes a long time for a model's training method to reach convergence. The CPU cooling mechanism will be activated to prevent the expensive hardware from being overheated. In order to reduce the temperature of on-device hardware, the most frequent method is to decrease the CPU clock frequency, which will significantly degrade the processing speed. Also, the battery life of smartphones and tablets will be shortened if they are continuously used at maximum speed [521]. Consequently, it is necessary to more efficiently manage the restricted resources while running learning applications on devices, where reducing model size and simplifying arithmetic operations are two crucial stages. For speeding up computing, the model compression and data quantization are both promising techniques to address this issue.

1.4 PROBLEM STATEMENT OF BUILDING TINYML SYSTEMS

Eliminating resource limits is a critical premise in implementing TinyML systems. Conventional model compression techniques, such as Low-rank Decomposition [286, 573, 574, 604], Model Pruning [116, 178, 185, 188] and Network Sparsification [22, 186, 377] are inappropriate because they are optimized for large-scale training tasks and do not adequately capture the characteristics of microscopic on-device learning. Fortunately, prior research indicates that neural networks are often implemented in the full accuracy of the 32-bit floating-point (FP32) format [179], and thus high-precision representation of model parameters is not essentially needed [360]. It is possible to express parameters with less accuracy while maintaining the network's overall quality. According to previous studies (*Sec.* 2.1.4) that handle CNN training in the 8-bit fixed-point (INT8) format [34], developing a fully INT8 quantization-aware training system for on-device learning will be a fruitful endeavor.

Existing quantization methods, on the other hand, can only be used for on-device training due to the following limitations:

- They cannot support generic networks without specific structure design [346, 444, 563].

- They cannot make the gradient calibration fit on-device resource restrictions in the backward pass [324, 631].

- They cannot enable hardware-level INT8 acceleration during the training phase [89, 239, 487, 541].

- They cannot be applied to the training process [35, 59, 255, 360, 401].

As a result, we need an INT8 training approach that works on devices directly and covers both forward and backward passes. In order to achieve the goal of INT8 on-device learning, we must first address the following issues:

- Maintaining model quality when using INT8 quantization-aware training,

- Making the system simple to use and compatible with multiple platforms,

- Simplifying the computational procedure and significantly increasing processing speed on devices,

- Alleviating system overhead, such as reducing memory footprint and I/O bandwidth utilization.

We can accomplish these goals with the collaborative construction of neural network constructors and 8-bit training engines.

1.5 DEPLOYMENT PROSPECTS AND DOWNSTREAM APPLICATIONS

With the three research directions stated above, we provide the insights gained by implementing edge intelligence in real-world situations. In addition, the software and hardware synergy of all of the techniques provides implementation details to handle the issues associated with the construction of high-performance learning systems. Besides analyzing various on-device learning strategies, we will discuss the system performance when different methods are used, as well as highlight possible research areas that can be used to implement on-device learning applications in the future.

1.5.1 Evaluation Metrics for Practical Methods

On-device learning is often used on embedded systems or mobile devices, where object identification and image categorization are two important applications. We thus concentrate on the complexity and performance of these applications when using the various methodologies listed in this book.

Because neural networks are often used to implement on-device learning applications, limiting the complexity of neural networks will have a significant influence on the overall efficiency of the system. In this section, we primarily analyze the following seven fundamental metrics.

- Memory footprint.

- Training speed.

- Energy consumption.

- Inference latency.

- Arithmetic operation overhead.

- Model size.

- Model quality.

With regard to the image classification applications in particular, we need to preserve the model quality and prediction accuracy. Meanwhile, we need to improve the performance in metrics of the Mean Average Precision (mAP) and Intersection over Union (IoU), in the context of objective detection applications. It is clear that the overall system performance can be effectively improved with different methods in diverse aspects. We will discuss the details of these methods in the following chapters of this book.

1.5.2 Intelligent Medical Diagnosis

Intelligent medical diagnostic applications based on edge and mobile devices have emerged as a popular research issue in recent years. For example, some academics are concentrating on utilizing a single photograph of the human body to diagnose surgery. On the basis of pattern extraction methodologies, it is feasible to evaluate medical pictures at the user's end by applying on-device learning approaches, which can provide a significant amount of convenience to users during illness screening. Furthermore, on-device learning algorithms can automatically diagnose scoliosis on a mobile phone, where sensitive information about the user data will not be sent to the cloud, therefore protecting the user's privacy to the greatest extent possible. It is a promising trend that makes use of on-device learning techniques for intelligent monitoring and analysis of sports rehabilitation, which can fulfill the online needs of mobile phones. As a result, on-device learning is a potential strategy for addressing the key problem of privacy leakage while also providing real-time processing capability for medical diagnostics.

1.5.3 AI-Enhanced Motion Tracking

In light of the high real-time demands placed on motion tracking applications, particularly in the capture of arm movement, running and sports, it is natural to employ on-device learning techniques to improve the motion tracking quality, including improving the detection accuracy and providing stronger robustness of motion capture. Also, by using on-device learning techniques, it is possible to create a more lightweight model on user devices, while ensuring real-time capacity and high-level accuracy in the process. In certain cutting-edge studies, for example, smart watches are utilized to accurately measure an individual's arm motion in a real-time situation [352]. This is in order to integrate learning-based arm motion tracking for human activity detection. By capturing the motion trace of the human postures, the industry may then use on-device learning methods to identify numerous body gestures and comprehend the corresponding activities, which are common in human everyday life (*e.g.*, walking, sleeping, sitting and driving). On the other hand, as compared to traditional statistical analysis, activities tracking employing on-device learning may provide various users with intelligent health monitoring and individualized health analysis. A broad variety of social applications, such as natural user interfaces, motion-based virtual reality, sports and training analytics, may also benefit from the approaches used for on-device learning. In summary, on-device learning represents a significant step forward in meeting the real-time requirements of AI-enhanced motion tracking, and it has the potential to substantially improve the human interaction experience.

1.5.4 Domain-Specific Acceleration Chips

A variety of modern AI-oriented tasks, where the system performance is often constrained by the restricted hardware resources, can benefit from the use of on-device learning approaches. The development of domain-specific artificial intelligence processors for task acceleration is thus a viable research topic for enhancing the computational capability. In order to directly assist developers in optimizing the training process without requiring extensive code modifications, these AI chips can be designed from the perspectives of model compression, few-shot learning, quantization-ware training, memory management and low-level instructions. For example, in order to accelerate sparse tensor operations by encoding the components in low precision, NVIDIA: Nvidia Corporation, commonly known as Nvidia, is an American multinational technology company incorporated in Delaware and based in Santa Clara, California. https://www.nvidia.com/en-us/ presented the Ampere architecture [23], which is designed to facilitate quantization-aware training on the INT8/INT4 format. Furthermore, these chips can be incorporated in edge devices to deliver more powerful computing primitives for users. Designing the *Application-specific Integrated Circuit* (ASIC) [79] on the basis of actual needs of on-device learning is a promising way to satisfy the requirements. For example, we can use model fine-tuning approaches to improve the detection of human faces on mobile phones, allowing them to recognize people faster. Therefore, the creation of domain-specific chips has emerged as a popular open research issue. The acceleration of on-device processing will bring significant advantages for the TinyML systems in the future.

1.6   THE SCOPE AND ORGANIZATION OF THIS BOOK

In this section, we discuss the scope and organization of this book. An overview of organization is shown in Figure 1.3. Specifically, we first introduce the fundamentals about tiny machine learning and edge intelligence, including the rise of on-device learning, typical training algorithms, basic parameter synchronization mechanism, multi-client learning paradigm and evaluation platforms (in Chapter 2). Then, we present the preliminary theory to help the readers understand the elements of modern neural networks, the basis of convergence order and the rationale of model optimization (in Chapter 3). Based on this preliminary knowledge, we discuss the design of tiny machine learning methods in four aspects: Model-level design of computation acceleration and communication saving (in Chapter 4), hardware-level design of neural engine and tensor accelerators (in Chapter 5), infrastructure-level design of serverless computing and decentralized learning (in Chapter 6) and system-level design of standalone and cluster coordination (in Chapter 7). With the understanding of the four-aspect design, we present the implementation of realistic downstream tasks, including the image-based visual perception (in Chapter 8) and video-based real-time processing (in Chapter 9). Finally, we also discuss the privacy, security, robustness and trustworthiness concerns in tiny machine learning systems (in Chapter 10). Apart from the discussion of algorithms, theory and framework, we also provide the practice tutorials to guide the readers to better understand the rationale of machine learning techniques, including image classification via convolutional neural networks, distributed training of federated learning and real-time mobile human pose tracking.

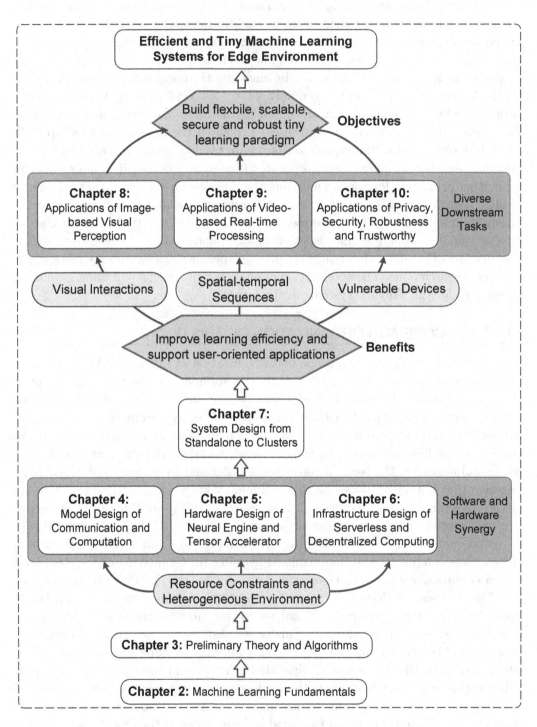

Figure 1.3 The scope and organization of this book.

CHAPTER 2

Fundamentals: On-device Learning Paradigm

There are many commodity machine learning (ML) applications that are deployed on the cloud to take advantage of parallel processing. A cloud computing architecture, however, cannot meet the needs of edge intelligence scenarios, such as generating individualized models that preserve privacy, reacting to real-time activities, and conserving resources. With the emergence of on-device learning, which puts the whole ML process on the user's device and eliminates the need for the cloud, the drawbacks of traditional in-cloud computing can be well addressed. Although on-device learning has numerous benefits, a high-efficiency on-device learning system still confronts several serious obstacles, such as a lack of adequate user training data, backward propagation blockage and a restricted peak processing speed. We will give a complete review of the most recent research achievements in terms of on-device learning system implementation and the corresponding acceleration. We also identify prospective optimization from a system view, with large improvement space. On-device learning strategies, such as neural network model design, algorithm training optimization and hardware instruction acceleration, are investigated in this book. These techniques show how software and hardware synergy can improve on-device learning performance and accuracy. We believe that this book will motivate the readers understand the importance of edge intelligence and further advance the development of this field.

2.1 MOTIVATION

Beginning with the drawbacks of typical cloud-based learning and the origins of on-device learning paradigm, we explain how the two differ. Through quantization-aware training, we will show how to use on-device learning in real-world applications, and why it is preferable to other model compression approaches. A case study is also presented to illustrate how INT8-based training on devices improves performance, and the restrictions of current quantization approaches are discussed.

DOI: 10.1201/9781003340225-2

2.1.1 Drawbacks of In-Cloud Learning

The pipeline of building machine learning models requires a large amount of data and processing power. This means that many traditional machine learning (ML) applications need costly machine clusters and distributed processing to handle the implementation in the cloud environment. When using an in-cloud learning paradigm like this, the user's personal information may be exposed to untrustworthy parties. As a more severe matter, the high latency for retrieving inference results may slow down the learning process. Due to the training property of global model, such as Federated Learning (FL) [382], it is difficult to create models that are customized for each individual user [58].

2.1.2 Rise of On-Device Learning

The on-device learning, which conducts the whole ML procedure on devices directly, is on the increase as a result of the fast expansion in device processing capability and memory volume. This overcomes the restrictions of in-cloud learning. Face ID [510], Apple's solution for individualized facial recognition on mobile devices, is a good example. Here, we will go over the basics of what on-device learning is and why it is important.

Definition. All model training and inference procedures are handled on the user devices, with no requirement for data exchange with other machines. This is called as on-device learning. Edge Intelligence may also be applied to edge devices, such as IoT and mobile devices, where on-device learning can also be applied for this purpose [629].

Major Objectives. We summarize the major objectives of the system implementation for on-device learning tasks as follows.

- **Resource Saving.** With limited processing capability [281], memory space [212, 337] and I/O bandwidth [379], on-device hardware is typically hampered by the resource constrained environment. Consequently, the key to on-device learning is to minimize the system overhead.

- **Model Quality.** The learning algorithm should be able to maintain a constant convergence efficiency, with the same accuracy and generalization capabilities as the in-cloud training schemes [381].

- **Personalized Training.** In order to satisfy the needs of individual users, rather than providing a generic model for common applications, the training approach should only utilize data from the user devices [132].

- **End-to-end Implementation.** Since new user data is always being collected, trained models should be kept up to current at all times. As a result, the whole learning process must be carried out on user devices [78].

From the above analysis, we will use these four essential factors to guide the architecture design and efficiency optimization of a desired on-device learning system.

2.1.3 Bit Precision and Data Quantization

Compressing model size and reducing computing burden are critical when using on-device learning in real-world applications because of the limited resources available on smartphones. On-device learning differs from the large-scale training tasks for which typical compression approaches like Low-rank Decomposition [286, 573, 574, 604], Model Pruning [116, 178, 185, 188] or Network Sparsification [22, 186, 377] are usually adopted. To this end, data quantization is a potential solution to address this challenge.

Definition. The goal of quantization is to reduce the amount of precision needed to represent data, such as when converting a 32-bit floating-point number (FP32) to an 8-bit fixed-point number (INT8). Two key steps in the quantization process are outlined below.

Major Operations. We summarize the major objectives of data operations as follows.

- **Number Discretization.** Floating-point numbers to integers is a typical procedure that maps from a "continuous" domain to discrete values. The quantization level refers to how many discrete values there are in a data set. It's usual practice to divide the original domain into numerous intervals and represent the numbers in each interval by the center point [360]. With the help of number discretization, we may narrow the range of possible values for a given number and simplify its representation.

- **Domain Transformation.** The most important step is to reduce the range of values from a large representation range to a smaller one, for example from 32 bits to 8 bits. There are two ways to define the "width" of a step in the transformation process: Uniform or non-uniform manners [255]. Non-uniform transformation provides more bit accuracy than uniform transformation, but it is more hardware-friendly. The goal of domain transformation is to reduce the number of bits required to store each real number in a fixed-point format.

Deployment. Tensor arithmetic is commonly implemented in FP32 or FP64 format in existing ML frameworks to provide high numerical accuracy. However, prior research has shown that most neural networks are over-parameterized, and a high-precision representation of model parameters is not essential [360]. A reduced bit accuracy can be maintained without lowering the overall network quality. Moreover, IoT devices that lack floating-point processing units are unable to perform floating-point operations, which are more costly than fixed-point operations. Therefore, our objective is to reduce model parameters from FP32 to INT8 format and conduct the training operation on mobile devices.

Summary. The following features of data quantization are summarized: The first benefit is that it allows to optimize models at the bit level, which reduces memory footprint and speeds up tensor multiplication operations. On-device learning systems with limited resources benefit from this. Second, quantization is more compatible with general-purpose hardware (*e.g.,* CPUs and GPUs) as well as specialized chips (*e.g.,* FPGAs), making it suitable for the implementation in cutting-edge applications.

Table 2.1 Model quality and processing speed when adopting INT8 and FP32 value formats during the training.

	Forward Pass (ms)	Backward Pass (ms)	Per-iteration Time (ms)	Parameter Memory (MB)	Model Accuracy
FP32	96.75	141.23	238.07	19.15	97.6%
INT8	55.37	68.36	124.51	9.37	96.1%
Comparison	1.75×	2.06×	1.91×	2.04×	−1.50%

2.1.4 Potential Gains

The use of data quantization in model training can reduce hardware overhead and speed up processing. With a case study, we demonstrate the possible benefits by presenting an example. In this work, a three-layer CNN using the MNIST database of handwritten digits. http://yann.lecun.com/exdb/mnist/ dataset [105] is trained on the Huawei Atlas 200DK platform [265] with 20 epochs for image classification. Using an INT8 format, we quantize the mini-batch input, weights and gradients of convolutional layers and examine the system's performance in terms of arithmetic efficiency, memory footprint and I/O bandwidth. Table 2.1 shows that INT8-based quantization-aware training may efficiently reduce system overhead while without sacrificing model quality. Here comes a question: Is it possible to get the same degree of training performance with INT8 operations for ubiquitous on-device learning applications, such as image classification? A lightweight INT8 training system will help us reach this goal.

2.1.5 Why Not Existing Quantization Methods?

Existing quantization approaches are inadequate for on-device learning systems because of the following drawbacks.

- **Cannot apply to training process.** For the most part, most quantization approaches are developed for inference, where quantization is utilized in the forward pass based on a pre-trained model in order to speed up prediction speed [35, 59, 255, 360, 401]. These approaches cannot be employed in training because they do not solve the difficulties of computing gradients on discretized parameters and reducing the error gap after convolutional processes.

- **Cannot support generic networks without specific structure design.** The binary [563], ternary [346] and XNOR [444] networks are all representative approaches that attempt to quantify parameters with very low bit accuracy. However, they have been particularly created and need fundamental network changes. Therefore, they are not suited for training generic networks.

- **Cannot enable hardware-level INT8 acceleration in training phase.** Fake Quantization [239], a technique developed by Google for evaluating quantization, leverages INT8-based numerical information for parameter encoding while packaging results in FP32 format for tensor arithmetic. The tensors are quantized and dequantized prior to arithmetic operations in the succeeding procedures [89,487,541]. Due to the lack of hardware-level capability of fixed-point computing, this paradigm is unable to radically enhance processing speed or shrink memory footprint.

- **Cannot make the gradient calibration in backward pass fit on-device resource restrictions.** It's been popular to look at quantization-aware training using an 8-bit system recently. INT8 training was proposed by Zhu *et al.* [631] to cover both forward and backward passes at the same time. Note that the backward pass derivative computation of model parameters and intermediate tensors has not been refined, the fake quantization paradigm still remains in vlaue storage. Also, backward quantization significantly impacts the training efficiency since the backward pass commonly dominates the per-iteration time.

Summary. Consequently, our goal is to develop an INT8 quantization approach that can be used to train neural networks directly on mobile devices.

2.2 BASIC TRAINING ALGORITHMS

We will begin by introducing the relevant gradient descent methods. This is followed by a discussion of Deep Learning (DL) paradigm, which use neural networks to extract knowledge.

2.2.1 Stochastic Gradient Descent

Algorithm 1 Stochastic Gradient Descent

    Input: Training dataset $\mathbb{X}$
    Output: Updated model parameters w_T

1: **procedure** SGD(Training dataset $\mathbb{X}$)
2:     Initialize the model parameters;
3:     **for** $t = 0, 1, \cdots, T - 1$ **do**
4:         Randomly select a sample $x_{i,t}$ from $\mathbb{X}$;
5:         Calculate the loss function based on $x_{i,t}$;
6:         Calculate the gradients $\nabla f_{i,t}(w_t)$ of Eq. (2.2);
7:         Update the model parameters by using Eq. (2.1);
8:     **end for**
9:     **return** the latest model parameters w_T;
10: **end procedure**

Model optimization, which tries to minimize the loss function that assesses the estimated values and ground-truth values, is required in this iterative training scheme in order to speed up the processing time. For this, the *Stochastic Gradient Descent* (SGD) [452] is often used. Note that the training data is randomly sampled in SGD.

Thus, the corresponding update rule can be formulated as:

$$w_{t+1} = w_t - \eta_t \nabla f_{i,t}(w_t), \tag{2.1}$$

where i is the data index of the random sampling in the t-th iteration and η_t is the *learning rate* in current iteration. The idea of learning rate is comparable to the step length of several optimization techniques (*e.g.*, the *Steepest Descent* and the *Newton's* method). Note that $f_{i,t}(w_t)$ is the value the loss function $\mathcal{L}$, which reflects the gap between prediction based on $x_{i,t}$ and ground-truth label $y_{i,t}$. Besides, $R(w_t)$ is the regularization term for shrinking the large ones inside model parameters w_t.

$$f_{i,t}(w_t) = \mathcal{L}(w_t; x_{i,t}; y_{i,t}) + R(w_t). \tag{2.2}$$

On top of this formulation, we will present the algorithm of SGD via Algorithm 1.

Based on the SGD method, the experienced loss function can be transferred to the average value of the sampling loss function. It is possible to get an unbiased estimate of the standard gradients computed by all the data since SGD uses bootstrapping, which refers to as random sampling with replacement. Therefore, we have:

$$\mathbb{E}[\nabla f_{i_t}(w_t)] \leftarrow \nabla f(w_t). \tag{2.3}$$

SGD, on the other hand, only selects one instance from the entire dataset, which reduces the computing burden. As a result, the SGD algorithm is a logical choice for model training.

2.2.2 Mini-Batch Stochastic Gradient Descent

Algorithm 2 Mini-batch Stochastic Gradient Descent

    Input: Training dataset $\mathbb{X}$
    Output: Updated model parameters w_T

1: **procedure** SGD(Training dataset $\mathbb{X}$)
2:     Initialize the model parameters;
3:     **for** $t = 0, 1, \cdots, T - 1$ **do**
4:         Randomly select a mini-batch of samples B_t from $\mathbb{X}$;
5:         Calculate the loss function based on B_t;
6:         Calculate the gradients by using Eq. (2.4);
7:         Update the model parameters by using Eq. (2.5);
8:     **end for**
9:     **return** the latest model parameters w_T;
10: **end procedure**

Mini-batch Stochastic Gradient Descent (Mini-batch SGD) is a variant of the conventional SGD, which is frequently utilized in current machine learning applications to minimize gradient estimation variance. Mini-batch SGD uses a batch of data instead of one training sample to calculate loss functions and gradients in each iteration,

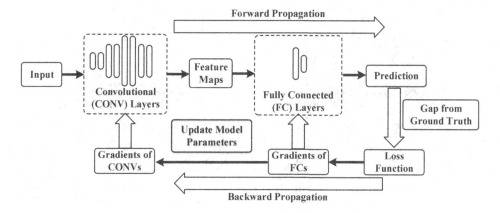

Figure 2.1 The workflow of neural network training.

which is usually described as:

$$\nabla f_{B_t}(w_t) = \frac{1}{|B_t|} \sum_{i \in B_t} \nabla f_i(w_t), \tag{2.4}$$

A critical hyper-parameter for training effectiveness and convergence speed is *batch size* B_t [313], which determines how many samples are included in each batch. Accordingly, the update policy can be formulated as:

$$w_{t+1} = w_t - \eta_t \nabla f_{B_t}(w_t), \tag{2.5}$$

where η_t is the learning rate of the batch. The Mini-batch SGD method is summarized in Algorithm 2 to further illustrate its rationale.

2.2.3 Training of Neural Networks

Gradient descent optimization is the theoretically guaranteed way to minimize the loss function in model training, as previously stated. As part of this article, we will analyze the reasoning behind training neural networks for deep learning applications. Training data, which are often on a huge scale, are the premise for neural network training. The key/value pairs in the neural network models can be used to represent these patterns and knowledge.

Here, Figure 2.1 depicts the process of training a neural network. Two phases, *i.e., forward propagation* (FP) and *backward propagation* (BP), are used to represent each training iteration. The convolutional (CONV) layers provide feature maps of data samples, and the fully connected (FC) layers construct the prediction in the FP stage by pipelining the intermediate outputs layer by layer. Using the loss function, we can determine how accurate our predictions are compared to the actual labels. SGD-based algorithms are often used in the BP stage to minimize loss function based on current data samples and create gradients for all parameters. We can proceed with the training by beginning a new iteration once the model has been updated with the gradients.

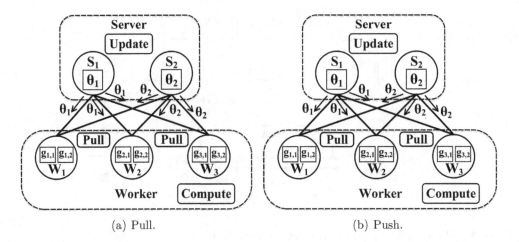

(a) Pull.   (b) Push.

Figure 2.2 The workflow of a distributed DL training task in a parameter server system.

2.3 PARAMETER SYNCHRONIZATION FOR DISTRIBUTED TRAINING

2.3.1 Parameter Server Paradigm

Distributed DL training problems need decoupling processing from communication. Using a data-parallel method is a typical approach, which involves doing local parameter pruning across several machines and combining their intermediate gradients at a logical central root for global model updating. The rise of the Parameter Server (PS) architecture [5, 88, 98, 206, 213, 230, 244, 578], where workers compute the gradients of parameters and the server updates the global model, is inspired by this straightforward distributed training paradigm.

Figure 2.2 illustrates the usual pipeline of a parameter server system, which includes two servers (S_1 and S_2) and three workers (W_1, W_2 and W_3). To get to model convergence, a DL training job typically performs several rounds of reducing the parameter until it is reached. Therefore, one iteration serves as the training procedure's primary execution time unit. Here, W_1 is used as an example to show the process, and the other two workers follow a similar manner. In each iteration, W_1 *pulls* the most recent model parameters from three servers at the start of each iteration. Because various elements of the model may be kept on different servers, W_1 must get them from the appropriate servers (*e.g.*, θ_1 from S_1 and θ_2 from S_2) in order to use the full model. To *compute* the gradients ($g_{1,1}$ and $g_{1,2}$), W_1 uses its sub-dataset and local forward computation to set the parameters of the neural network model. It then *pushes* the gradients to two servers, S_1 and S_2, by sending separate sections of the gradients to each. When all partial gradients from separate works are merged together, the servers *update* the global model parameters (such as S_1 merging the values of the three partial gradients, *i.e.*, $g_{1,1}$, $g_{2,1}$ and $g_{3,1}$, to generate the parameter θ_1). Once the current epoch is complete, DL continues the remaining repetitions of these four steps. In order to preserve trimming parameters, the task handler will re-partition the dataset and execute a new epoch.

2.3.2 Parameter Synchronization Pace

Parameter synchronization in data-parallel training is done after the gradient calculation of layer weights is completed. Preliminary research has focused on using the distributed *stochastic gradient descent* (SGD) method, which can be used in both synchronous and non-synchronous systems. The *Bulk Synchronous Parallel* (BSP) [373, 546, 604] is a common synchronous architecture that offers consistent consistency control and assures steady training convergence. In the case of BSP, the *straggler* [193, 244], the slowest worker, potentially lead to time waste. Oppositely, *Asynchronous Parallel* (ASP) [5, 106, 416], a standard asynchronous technique, overcomes this problem by simply eliminating the imposed barrier synchronization at the conclusion of each round. Delay error and poor convergence efficiency are also problems if accumulating a huge *staleness* [73] error in ASP. Therefore, it comes the *Stale Synchronous Parallel* (SSP) [98, 206, 552, 612], a fusion of BSP and ASP, which makes a trade-off between iteration speed and efficiency in convergence by using a delay-bounded threshold to restrict worker iteration staleness and time waste.

2.3.3 Heterogeneity-Aware Distributed Training

To ensure the performance of parameter server systems in a heterogeneous environment, which is common in real-world clusters, many prior works have been proposed to ensure that the network conditions and compute capacity of the clusters to be homogeneous [69, 244]. In order to create a parameter server that is heterogeneity-aware, Jiang *et al.* [244] dynamically controlled the learning rate while taking delay information into account. Chen *et al.* improved the training degradation of heterogeneity by adjusting the training batch size for each worker to fit their computational capabilities. Tandon *et al.* devised the gradient coding approach to give redundancy in calculations and may be expanded to deal with stragglers and heterogeneity. Chen *et al.* [73] handled synchronization with backup workers and deleted over-stale updates to prevent model conflicts.

Some academics have recently concentrated on the hybrid synchronization approaches by controlling the cluster in groups [182, 279]. These approaches, however, may have the following drawbacks: If the group strategy is dynamically determined at runtime, it may not execute well in a heterogeneous computing environment with diverse computational primitives, since the underlying hardware has to be configured differently for each group. As a result, we still need an unified technique to intelligently create the grouping strategy and automatically manage hybrid synchronization for diverse distributed training circumstances.

Current solutions to heterogeneity fall into two broad categories: (1) Shifting workloads from slow to fast devices (*e.g.,* Chen *et al.* [69] and Tandon *et al.* [504]); (2) emphasizing the importance of fast workers' training as a top priority (*e.g.,* Jiang *et al.* [244] and Chen *et al.* [73]). By relying on fast workers for the bulk of their distributed training, these systems ensure that iteration progress is not slowed or errors are introduced, *i.e.,* training workloads can be handled in an almost homogenous cluster without the participation of slow workers. There are two drawbacks to these approaches: first, the computation capacity of slow workers is underestimated, and

Table 2.2 Training and test accuracy under different consumed time in PS(3, 12), running image classification on Alexnet [273] with MNIST [290] dataset.

Scheme	Training Accuracy	Iteration Count	Completion Time (s)	Training Accuracy	Iteration Count	Completion Time (s)
SSP	95.83%	900	303.613	95.11%	700	294.464
SSP	96.60%	1080	459.572	96.03%	880	372.193
SSP	97.02%	1700	731.341	97.07%	1420	609.167
SSP	98.08%	4000	1666.239	98.06%	3940	1642.339
Hybrid	95.18%	650	239.054	95.56%	550	200.951
Hybrid	96.13%	950	352.323	96.19%	840	309.304
Hybrid	97.12%	1620	604.196	97.10%	1350	503.675
Hybrid	98.27%	3950	1477.046	98.02%	2740	1020.277

second, the workload imbalance can occur if the training contribution of fast workers is overestimated. These drawbacks should be taken into consideration when using these solutions. Therefore, developing a new architecture for heterogeneous parameter server is needed to alleviate the aforementioned constraints.

2.4 MULTI-CLIENT ON-DEVICE LEARNING

2.4.1 Preliminary Experiments

In spite of the PS cluster's heterogeneity, our experiments show that there is still some correlation and similarity between the training behaviours of different workers. Training convergence under normal conditions diverse vastly, when workers with varied processing capabilities (eg CPU and GPUs) have an analogous-level per iteration time for the same batch size (*i.e.,* no stragglers). To better manage the PS cluster, we can take advantage of this tendency by treating workers similarly. As a result, we're concerned about whether or not it will be possible to teach the PS cluster's workers if they are divided up into groups with equal iteration times. This synchronization of parameters at the group level is the foundation for the distributed model training.

Workers inside a group may utilize the BSP method since we manually partition the cluster into four groups based on this criteria. As a result, we adopt the SSP scheme within groups because of the substantial differences in per-iteration duration between workers in various groups. Generally, PS(p, q) is a convenient way to refer to a PS cluster, where p and q are the server and worker amounts, respectively. Hybrid is also the term given to the group-based synchronization technique.

2.4.2 Observations

2.4.2.1 Training Convergence Efficiency

PS(3, 12) has been used to conduct exploratory experiments to examine the training convergence efficiency under two systems (SSP and Hybrid), where the results are shown in Table 2.2. In comparison to the SSP method, this group-based approach uses less time while maintaining the same level of training and testing accuracy. A

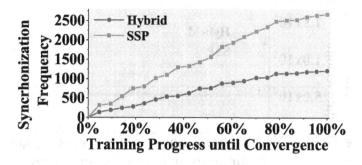

Figure 2.3 The accumulation of synchronization frequency counted on the server side in PS(4, 16) under SSP and Hybrid group-based schemes.

group-based synchronization technique shows promise benefits in these first studies, which calls for further investigation.

2.4.2.2 Synchronization Frequency

Here, we shall thoroughly examine this hybrid synchronization as the group-based approach accelerates. With the same number of workers, we manually modify group numbers in PS (4, 16). Employing a hyper-thread approach on workers with multi-core CPUs, we can replicate the BSP process for groups of workers by using the training function of a worker in a group for each core in the worker's CPU. As a result, the workers use multiprocessing to manage intra-group BSP and follow SSP with other workers.

When the staleness threshold counted on the server is surpassed, as illustrated in Figure 2.3, we record the accumulative emergence number. Workers' iteration efficiency varies widely and the staleness threshold (an essential hyper-parameter in SSP) is more easily reached when the accumulated emergence number is high. Synchronization frequency is a term we use to describe this phenomenon. We found that the number of workers in a group has a considerable influence on the frequency of synchronization. A larger synchronization frequency means that the training process will be greatly hindered because of the enforced synchronization waiting for slow workers.

A high staleness threshold may be used to mitigate this issue. However, this will lead to more inconsistencies between workers and additional delays that would degrade training convergence. As a result, it is possible to lower synchronization frequency without increasing the threshold for staleness. We need to employ group division to increase the convergence efficiency of distributed training.

2.4.2.3 Communication Traffic

In a distributed training environment, the volume of communication traffic is a critical parameter. As to the tensor of gradients, it is reasonable to combine the gradients obtained by various members of a team. The tensor size sent between the groups and the server may be effectively reduced using this element-wise aggregation. This also

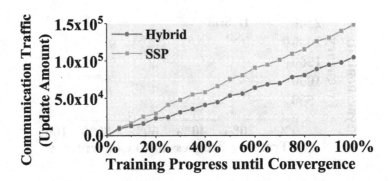

Figure 2.4 The accumulation of communication traffic (*i.e.,* the amount of updates counted on the server side) in PS(4, 16) under SSP and Hybrid group-based schemes.

eases the burden on the logical central server and alleviates bandwidth constraints that have been a performance barrier. Communication traffic is visually compared in Figure 2.4, where we see that the Hybrid method generates much less traffic than does the original SSP technique.

2.4.3 Summary

As shown by these findings, group-based synchronization is worth further investigation for its possible advantages and motivations.

2.5 DEVELOPING KITS AND EVALUATION PLATFORMS

2.5.1 Devices

To match the on-device learning environment, this book chooses two kinds of commodity devices: (1) NVIDIA Jetson Xavier [266] with dedicated INT8 neuron chips, and (2) HUAWEI Atlas 200DK [265] with Ascend 310 AI processors [125]. All these devices are operated with the Ubuntu 18.04 LTS system with GNU/Linux 4.15.0-118-generic kernel.

2.5.2 Benchmarks

Major benchmarks are visual tasks based on the training of AlexNet [276], VGG11 [482], ResNet18 [198] and MobileNet-V1 [212], with the CIFAR-10 (CF) [272] and Fashion MNIST (FM) [567] datasets. By default, we set batch size as 100 and use the Adam [263] optimizer. Indeed, we can employ more advanced networks and optimizers for complex applications.

2.5.3 Pipeline

Pre-training and backbone fine-tuning on NVIDIA GPUs is a typical pipeline, followed by downstream task inference on the same devices. We are particularly interested in optimizing three kinds of matrix instructions, namely dot product, broadcast, and addition, to meet the on-device execution environment, which is provided by the lightweight Pybind [421] and Eigen [511] toolkit. As a result of this hybrid architecture, the inference can be used on most commodity edge devices.

2.6 CHAPTER SUMMARY

It is becoming increasingly common to move the learning process from the cloud to the device itself, driven by the needs of new ML applications in edge intelligence circumstances. One of the most important concerns in the cutting-edge study of on-device learning is the implementation of a high-efficiency learning framework and the facilitation of system-level acceleration. Taking this into consideration, we take an in-depth look at the most recent developments in the field and identify prospective avenues for further study and development. Model-level computing acceleration, algorithm-level training coordination, and data-level feature perception are all discussed in this chapter to show where research is headed. Edge intelligence applications may benefit from a high-performance TinyML system that can be used to integrate on-device learning methods into the realistic downstream tasks.

2.5 CHAPTER SUMMARY

CHAPTER 3

Preliminary: Theories and Algorithms

Various neural network architectures have attained remarkable achievements in many downstream tasks, such as ResNet [198], VGG [482] in computer vision, Recurrent Neural Networks (RNNs) [490], and Long Short-Term Memory (LSTM) networks [207] in natural language processing. Although these architectures have proved to be effective in the past few decades, they are computationally and memory intensive at the same time. To deploy complicated neural networks on resource-limited platforms, tiny ML aims to *compress* them by reducing memory overhead and adapting hardware acceleration on embedded systems.

3.1 ELEMENTS OF NEURAL NETWORKS

3.1.1 Fully Connected Network

Fully connected networks are the most widespread architecture, which is mathematically equivalent to a matrix (parameters) - vector (input) multiplication $y = Wx + b$. The equation also refers to as Multiply-Accumulate (MAC). This operation will repeat many times for large matrix-vector multiplications (often occur in huge networks). Once all calculations complete, the accumulated values are feed-forward to the next layer.

There are three kinds of methods to accelerate the Multiply-Accumulate (MAC) operation:

- Reducing the dimension of both input data and parameters, and designing deeper but narrower networks.

- Using pruning strategy to reduce redundancy in a high-dimensional fully connected network.

- Using quantization strategy to transfer FP32 weights and activation into low bit-width integers, such as INT8 [400].

DOI: 10.1201/9781003340225-3

3.1.2 Convolutional Neural Network

Tiny convolutional neural networks focus on lightweight convolutional filters. Existing channel-wise pruning and quantization strategies for fully connected networks can also be applied to convolutional neural networks.

Inspired by the previous work that explicitly assigns different precisions to different layers, [65] proposed a typical group-wise mixed-precision quantization method. 4-Bit power-of-two and fixed quantization methods are selected for insensitive filters. Lower bit-width (such as 2 bit) leads to significant performance loss. 8-bit fixed precision is suitable for sensitive filters to boost accuracy. Especially, the power-of-two scheme is not applied to sizeable bit-width quantization due to its intrinsic rigid resolution issue.

A more significant portion of filters that are assigned to the 4-bit power-of-two scheme can speed up the inference due to high hardware adaptability. However, it is harmful to the accuracy at the same time. Thus, there is a trade-off between lightweight. In general, the performance degradation can be mitigated by applying large bit-width (e.g., 8-bit fixed precision) to a small portion of filters.

3.1.3 Attention-Based Neural Network

RNNs have prevailed in various kinds of natural language processing tasks for a long time, benefiting from their sequence modeling ability [497]. However, it is difficult for RNNs to co-process multiple sequences due to the temporal coupling. Recently, a few researches have proved that RNN may not be a fundamental architecture to approach state-of-the-art performance. For example, convolution-based architectures can be an alternative to capture the local context information [149]. However, it is deficient in modeling the critical long-range relationship in sequential tasks.

As a promising paradigm, attention mechanisms have the ability to model global-context information through calculating pairwise correlation, which is used in conjunction with RNN in early-stage [429]. Nowadays, attention mechanisms become an essential architecture of gripping sequence modeling in numerous downstream tasks.

As shown in equation (3.1), attention mechanisms can be regarded as a mapping from a query as well as a set of key-value pairs to an output, where the vectors query, keys and values are denoted as Q, K and V, respectively. The output can be conceived as a weighted sum of the values V, and the softmax function constitutes the assigned weight. In particular, the dot-product attention (i.e., QK^T) is scaled by the dimension of query and keys d_k, which can smooth the gradient of the softmax function when the dot-product attention value becomes large [529].

$$\text{Attention}(Q, K, V) = \text{softmax}\left(\frac{QK^T}{\sqrt{d_k}}\right) V \qquad (3.1)$$

By utilizing the above attention mechanisms, Transformer [529] is able to approach state-of-the-art performance by simply stacking the self-attention architecture. Inspired by this pioneering work, many variants of the transformer have been proposed [87, 433, 491]. All these work attempt to improve the performance of the

Table 3.1 Complexity of three kinds of neural networks architecture.

Neural Networks Architecture	Complexity per Layer	Sequential Operations	Maximum Path Length
Attention	$O(N^2d)$	$O(1)$	$O(1)$
Convolution	$O(kNd^2)$	$O(1)$	$O(\log_k N)$
Recurrent	$O(Nd^2)$	$O(N)$	$O(N)$

transformer or migrate it to various downstream tasks. It is still a challenge to deploy computation-intensive attention-based neural networks on mobile devices.

The attention function computes pairwise dot-product between each query and key vectors to model both local-context and global-context relationships. Despite its effectiveness, it is difficult for mobile devices and embedded systems to bear the corresponding massive computation overhead. For each attention layer, let N denotes the length of input vectors (e.g., number of pixels in image and length of tokens in language processing, etc.). Variable d is the dimension of features. The computing complexity of the query-key production is N^2d. For vision tasks, N can be extremely large (e.g., high-quality images and videos). In normal neural network architectures such as ResNet, the computing complexity of fully connected and convolution operations increases linearly with respect to the number of input elements, while the computing complexity of attention-based operation grows quadratically with respect to the number of input elements.

As listed in Table 3.1 [529], an attention layer computes a weighted output of all elements, where the computing complexity and the number of sequential operations are $O(N^2d)$ and $O(1)$, respectively. For a convolution layer, a convolution kernel traverses the entire sequence as a sliding window. Thus, the maximum sliding path length is $O(\log_k N)$, where k denotes the kernel size. For natural language processing tasks, the length of sentences N is usually smaller than its representative feature dimension d. In such cases, the attention layer is faster than convolution as well as recurrent layers in terms of computational complexity. While for vision tasks, the number of input elements N can be much larger than d. As a result, the computation of the attention module will overwhelm the other two architectures.

3.2 MODEL-ORIENTED OPTIMIZATION ALGORITHMS

3.2.1 Tiny Transformer

Transformer has become the mainstream model architecture in natural language processing (e.g., semantic analysis and statement generation). However, it consumes massive computations to accomplish satisfactory performance. Thus, it is not suitable for resource-constrained mobile devices in respect of both hardware (e.g., limited battery power) and software (e.g., computation capability of CPU).

To address the dilemma, there are two common attempts. The first is to modify the model directly to make it lightweight. A linear projection layer can be applied before the attention layer to decrease the number of channels and recover the channel

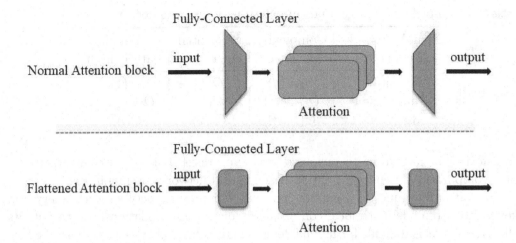

Figure 3.1 Flattened bottleneck of transformer blocks.

dimension afterward. As shown in figure 3.1, for each attention module in the normal Transformer architecture, the channel dimension is reduced by four times compared with that of the fully connected module. Similarly, convolution and recurrent operations are combined to capture long-range dependencies in videos. The constructed non-local neural network reduces the number of channels in half before connecting to the attention-like module [547]. Although the tiny attention module, as well as fully connected layer saves the computation overhead, nevertheless, fewer parameters also decrease the contexts capture ability and lead to worse network performance. The harmness could be more serious for natural language processing tasks since attention modules are responsible for capturing long-range contexts (unlike vision tasks where convolutions take the role by conducting a series of sliding window operations).

For language processing tasks, the sequential length of the statement N is usually small (e.g., 20–30 elements in common cases). Each transformer block is composed of an attention module, followed by a fully connected layer. For the whole transformer block, the Mult-Adds would be $O(4Nd^2 + N^2d)$ (for the attention module) plus $O(8Nd^2)$ (for the fully connected layer). Given a relatively short input, the bottleneck design may not achieve an appropriate trade-off between computation and accuracy on 1D attention. For each transformer block, the linear projection operation consumes massive computation, which is not preferable since the self-attention operation actually captures global contexts. Thus, the reduction in computational overhead caused by decreasing the dimension of the attention module is compromised by the large fully connected layer.

Although large-capacity models may have some redundancy, their performance generally exceeds that of lightweight models. However, due to the resource and power constraints, redundancy cannot be tolerated when these complicated models are deployed on mobile devices. Simply reducing the dimension of the attention module cannot achieve satisfactory performance. In general, the attention modules are responsible for capturing both global and local information, which not only requires

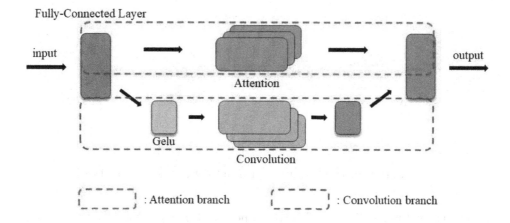

Figure 3.2 Long-short range attention.

a relatively large representative dimension but also introduces massive computation overhead. Thus, a few researchers turn to combining attention mechanisms with convolution. Specialized context capturing, instead of having one module for tasks, may lead to a more efficient model architecture.

Wu *et al.* [566] proposed a lite Transform framework to capture global and local information separately, named Long-Short Range Attention (LSRA). As shown in Figure 3.2, LSRA divides the original attention module into two branches. The top branch is a standard self-attention operation, which captures long-range information. The bottom branch models short-range contexts by convolutions. The input is firstly embedded by a fully connected layer. Instead of supplying the same embeddings to both branches, it is separated into two parts along the channel dimension. Both results of the two branches will be concatenated by the following linear projection operation. Since the channel dimension of the top attention module reduces in half due to the split of input, this design can decrease the overall computation by two times. For the right branch, convolution has been demonstrated to capture local information efficiently. To further decrease the overhead, the standard convolution can be replaced with a light version [561], which consists of depth-wise separable convolution and full-connected layers.

In addition to the parallel combination method, there are also many works that adopt the serial mode to design the hybrid neural network model. [164] proposed a hybrid architecture named LeViT by combining useful components in convolutional networks and normal transformers, where multiple convolutional layers are mainly used for image preprocessing. The effectiveness of this design comes from the following considerations: Vision Transformers (ViT) [117] utilizes a large convolution kernel (16x16) with the same size of stride as the patch extractor. While in convolutional architectures, the convolutional kernels overlap considerably, which the spatial smoothness comes. For normal attention blocks, there is no overlap. Thus, the smoothness modeling relies on data augmentation.

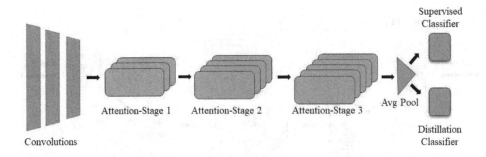

Figure 3.3 Block diagram of the hybrid neural network architecture LeViT.

As shown in Figure 3.3, LeViT utilizes normal 3×3 convolutions to embed the input raw images, which replaces the linear projection layer in ViT [117]. For the main body of the architecture, LeViT adopts the design of ResNet [199], which divides the attention block-stacking into three stages and reduces the resolution with a small computation overhead in the first two stages. When the activation map feeds forward from the first to the third stage of LeViT, the resolution keeps shrinking, and the number of attention heads increases from 4 to 8 to enhance the information capture ability. Referring to the design in DeiT [517], LeViT keeps both the distillation classifier and the supervised classifier, which enables efficient model training via knowledge distillation.

3.2.2 Quantization Strategy for Transformer

In addition to designing efficient models, quantizing transformers directly without modifying the architecture is also a promising approach to realizing tiny transformers. However, there are two main challenges when applying quantization to transformers:

- Quantization introduces additional noise in the neural network, which can lead to a severe performance drop and even crush the network.

- Compared with convolutional neural networks, transformers have unique quantization issues: High dynamic activation ranges that are difficult to represent with a low bit integer [46].

It was experimentally proved that existing 8-bit post-training quantization methods result in significant performance degradation for transformers, and numerous ablation studies have been done to find the corresponding bottleneck [46]. Different ranges of activation tensors lead to a mismatch in the residual connections. Especially, those mismatched tensors are regarded as distinct attention patterns. Based on these observation, Bondarenko *et al.* [46] proposed two kinds of transformer-oriented quantization methods, as shown in Figure 3.4.

The first is mixed precision post-training quantization. Since different parameters in transformers are not equally sensitive to the quantization noise, choosing different bit-width for different blocks can make the model lightweight while minimizing the

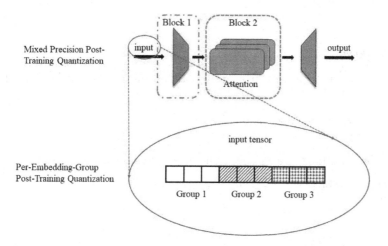

Figure 3.4 Two kinds of quantization strategies for transformers.

impact of extra noise. Specifically, higher bit-width 16-bit is allocated to highly sensitive blocks, such as the residual sum connection after the fully connected network.

The second is per-embedding-group post-training quantization. This is a finer-grained quantization method than mixed precision. Specifically, mixed precision post-training quantization divides transformers into several blocks. In comparison, group-wise embedding post-training quantization separates different elements in one tensor into groups, which increases the quantization granularity.

3.3 PRACTICE ON SIMPLE CONVOLUTIONAL NEURAL NETWORKS

Here, we give an practice example in Python and guide the readers to conduct image classification by using convolutional neural network (CNN). The readers will learn how to create, train and evaluate the CNN model. All the procedures are developed with PyTorch.

3.3.1 PyTorch Installation

PyTorch is an open source machine learning library, used for applications such as computer vision and natural language processing, primarily developed by Facebook's AI Research lab. Please install it via following command.

3.3.1.1 On macOS

Please open the terminal, and install PyTorch via following command.

```
1 $ conda install pytorch torchvision torchaudio -c pytorch
```

Then test the installation and check the torch version number, such as 1.10.

```
1 $ python -c "import torch; print(torch.__version__)"
2 1.10.0
```

3.3.1.2 On Windows

Please open the anaconda prompt from Start menu, and install PyTorch via following command.

```
1 (base) C:\Users\%USERNAME%> conda install pytorch torchvision torchaudio
     cpuonly -c pytorch
```

Then test the installation and check the torch version number, such as 1.10.

```
1 (base) C:\Users\%USERNAME%> python -c "import torch; print(torch.
     __version__)"
2 1.10.0
```

3.3.2 CIFAR-10 Dataset

For the tutorial of this practice, we will use the CIFAR10 dataset. As shown in Figure 3.5, the CIFAR-10 dataset consists of 60,000 32×32 colour images in 10 classes, with 6000 images per class. There are 50,000 training images and 10000 test images. The images in CIFAR-10 are of size $3 \times 32 \times 32$, *i.e.*, 3-channel color images of 32×32 pixels in size. Note that PyTorch take channels as first dimension by convention. This convention is different from other platform such as Pillow, Matlab, skimage, etc. They all put channels at last dimension.

Figure 3.5 CIFAR-10 Dataset.

We can load CIFAR-10 from `torchvision`. It may take several minutes to download the dataset.

```
1 from torchvision.datasets import CIFAR10 from torchvision.transforms
     import ToTensor
2 trainset = CIFAR10(root='./data', train=True, download=True, transform=
     ToTensor())
3 testset = CIFAR10(root='./data', train=False, download=True, transform=
     ToTensor())
```

The dataset consists of two parts. One is train set, another one is test set. Usually, we train our model (CNN) on train set, and test the model on test set.

- **Train:** Show CNN images, and tell it which classes they belong to. In such a way, we can teach it to distinguish different classes.

- **Test:** Show CNN images, and ask it which classes they belong to. In such a way, we can test how well the CNN learns.

`trainset.classes` contains the all class names in order.

```
1 trainset.classes
2 # ['airplane', 'automobile', 'bird', 'cat', 'deer', 'dog', 'frog', 'horse
     ', 'ship', 'truck']
```

Train set contains 50,000 images. Let's get the first image in train set, and show it.

```
1 len(trainset) # 50000 images
2 image, label = trainset[0] # get first image and its class id
3 image.shape # 3 x 32 x 32
4 imshow(image) # 'imshow' is in cifar10.py
5 trainset.classes[label] # 'frog'
```

We can see that the image is of shape, which means it has channels, and pixels.

The PyTorch `cifar10.py` script already contains all code to load the dataset. Therefore, we only need to:

```
1 from dataset import load_cifar10, imshow
2 trainset, testset = load_cifar10()
```

Beside the dataset itself, we also need `DataLoader` objects to help us randomly load image batch by batch. Batch means a small collection of images. Here, we set `batch_size` to 4, so each batch contains 4 images.

```
1 from torch.utils.data import DataLoader
2 trainloader = DataLoader(trainset, batch_size=4, shuffle=True)
3 testloader = DataLoader(testset, batch_size=4, shuffle=False)
```

Then we may iterate over the `DataLoader`, to get batches until the dataset is exhausted.

```
1 for batch in trainloader:
2    images, labels = batch print(images.shape) # [4, 3, 32, 32]
3    print(labels.shape) # [4]
4    break
```

`images` is of shape [4, 3, 32, 32] , which means it contains 4 images, each has 3 channels, and is of size 32 × 32. `labels` contains 4 scalars, which are the class IDs of this batch.

3.3.3 Construction of CNN Model

Here, we implement a simple but famous CNN model, the LeNet-5. As shown in Figure 3.6, 5 means it contains 5 convolutional or fully connected layers.

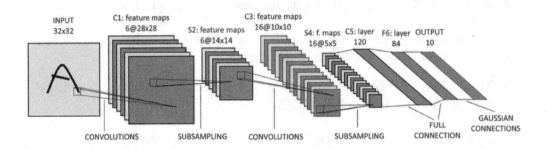

Figure 3.6 Architecture of LeNet-5.

A typical CNN consists of these kinds of layer, including convolutional layers, max pooling layers, and fully connected layers.

3.3.3.1 Convolutional Layers

Convolutional layers are usually the first several layers. They perform a convolution on the output of last layer to extract features from the image. As shown in Figure 3.7, a convolutional layer has three architecture parameters:

- kernel_size $h \times w$: the size of the convolutional kernel (also called the filter).

- in_channels: The number of input channels.

- out_channels: The number of output channels.

In this layer, beside the convolutional kernel K, we also have a bias added to each output channel. The formula for output is:

$$X' = K * X + b, \tag{3.2}$$

where $*$ stands for concolution, X and X' are input and output, respectively. The total number of trainable parameters in the convolutional layer is:

$$\underbrace{h \times w \times \text{in\_channels} \times \text{out\_channels}}_{\text{kernel}} + \underbrace{\text{out\_channels}}_{\text{bias}}. \tag{3.3}$$

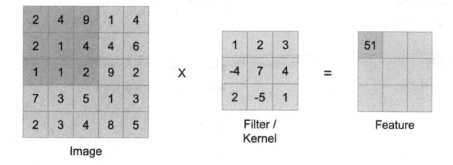

Figure 3.7 A convolutional layer.

The convolution is performed without padding by default, so image size will shrink after convolution. If input image size is $H \times W$ and the kernel size is $h \times w$, the output will be of size:

$$(H - h + 1) \times (W - w + 1). \tag{3.4}$$

Then we take channels and batch size into consideration, assume the input tensor has shape [batch_size, in_channels, H, W], then the output tensor will have shape

- Input shape: [batch_size, in_channels, H, W].

- Output shape: [batch_size, out_channels, H+1-h, W+1-w].

3.3.3.2 Activation Layers

The output of convolutional layer and fully connected layer is usually "activated", *i.e.,* transformed by a non-linear function, such as ReLU, sigmoid, tanh, etc. As shown in Figure 3.8, activation functions are all scalar function. They do not change the tensor shape, but only map each element into a new value. They usually contain no trainable parameters.

Here, we choose the most popular activation function that $\text{ReLU}(x) = \max(0, x)$.

Then, we demonstrate how to create the first convolutional layer of LeNet-5 by PyTorch. This layer has kernel size 5×5 and its output contains 6 channels. Its input is the original RGB images, so in_channels=3. The output is activated by ReLU (Original paper uses tanh).

```
import torch.nn as nn
# convolutional layer 1
conv_layer1 = nn.Sequential(
  nn.Conv2d(in_channels=3, out_channels=6, kernel_size=(5,5)),
  nn.ReLU(),
)
```

3.3.3.3 Pooling Layers

Pooling (also called subsmapling) usually follows a convolutional layer. There are two kinds of pooling layer — maximum pooling and average pooling. As shown in

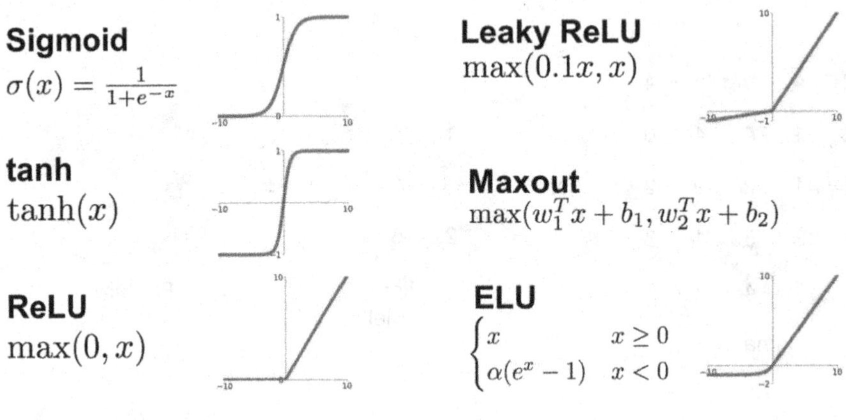

Sigmoid

$\sigma(x) = \frac{1}{1+e^{-x}}$

tanh

$\tanh(x)$

ReLU

$\max(0, x)$

Leaky ReLU

$\max(0.1x, x)$

Maxout

$\max(w_1^T x + b_1, w_2^T x + b_2)$

ELU

$\begin{cases} x & x \geq 0 \\ \alpha(e^x - 1) & x < 0 \end{cases}$

Figure 3.8 Different activation functions.

Figure 3.9, the maximum pooling computes the maximum of small local patches, while average pooling computes the average of small local patches.

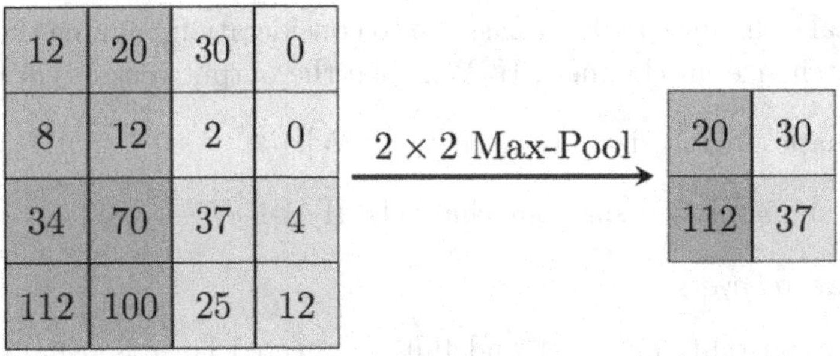

12	20	30	0
8	12	2	0
34	70	37	4
112	100	25	12

2×2 Max-Pool $\longrightarrow$

20	30
112	37

Figure 3.9 Max pooling with kernel size 2×2.

The kernel size of a pooling layer is the size of local patches. Assume the input image size is $H \times W$ and the kernel size is $h \times w$, the output size of pooling layer will be:

$$\frac{H}{h} \times \frac{W}{w}. \tag{3.5}$$

Then we take channels and batch size into consideration, the shapes of input tensor and output tensor are:

- input_shape: [batch_size, in_channels, H, W].

- output_shape: [batch_size, in_channels, H/h, W/w].

Pooling layers do not change the number of channels and do not contain any trainable parameters. This code snip demonstrates how to create a 2×2 max pooling layer.

```
1 max_pool = nn.MaxPool2d(kernel_size(2,2))
```

3.3.3.4 Fully Connected Layers

Fully connected (FC) layers are usually the last several layers. They take the features conv layers produced and output the final classification result. Before go into FC layers, we need to "flatten" the intermediate representation produced by convolutional layers. The output of CNN is a 4D tensor of shape [batch_size, channels, H, W]. After flattened, it becomes a 2D tensor of shape [batch_size, channels*H*W]. This 2D tensor is exactly what FC layers consumes as input.

As shown in Figure 3.10, a FC layer has two architecture parameter: The input features and output features.

- in_features: the number of input features.

- out_features: the number of output features.

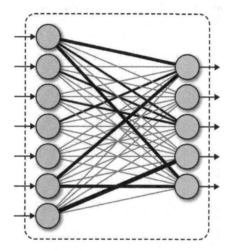

Figure 3.10 A FC layer with seven input features and five output features.

The input and output of FC layers are of shape:

- input_shape: [batch_size, in_features].

- output_shape: [batch_size, out_features].

The formula for output is:

$$X' = \theta X + b, \tag{3.6}$$

where θ is weight, and b is bias. As there is a weight between any input feature and any output feature, θ is in shape of in in_features × out_features. The number of biases is equal to the number of output features. Each output feature is added by a bias. In total, the number of trainable parameters in a FC layer is

$$\underbrace{\text{in\_features} \times \text{out\_features}}_{\text{weights}\theta} + \underbrace{\text{out\_features}}_{\text{bias}}. \tag{3.7}$$

This example shows how to create a FC layer in PyTorch. The created FC layer has 120 input features and 84 output features, and its output is activated by ReLU.

```
1 fc_layer = nn.Sequential(
2   nn.Linear(in_features=120, out_features=84),
3   nn.ReLU(),
4 )
```

The last layer of our CNN is a little bit special. First, it is not activated, *i.e.,* no ReLU. Second, its output features must be equal to the number of classes. Here, we have 10 classes in total, so its output features must be 10.

```
1 output_layer = nn.Linear(in_features=84, out_features=10)
```

3.3.3.5 Structure of LeNet-5

LeNet-5 is a simple but famous CNN model. Recall the structure mentioned in Figure 3.6, it contains a series of convolutional or fully connected layers. Here, we choose it as our CNN model. The layers of LeNet-5 are summarized as:

```
1 0. Input image: 3x32x32
2
3 1. Conv layer:
4    kernel_size: 5x5
5    in_channels: 3
6    out_channels: 6
7    activation: ReLU
8
9 2. Max pooling:
10   kernel_size: 2x2
11
12 3. Conv layer:
13   kernel_size: 5x5
14   in_channels: 6
15   out_channels: 16
16   activation: ReLU
17
18 4. Max pooling:
19   kernel_size: 2x2
20
21 5. FC layer:
22   in_features: 16*5*5
23   out_features: 120
24   activation: ReLU
25
26 6. FC layer:
27   in_features: 120
28   out_features: 84
29   activation: ReLU
30
31 7. FC layer:
32   in_features: 84
33   out_features: 10 (number of classes)
```

We build the LeNet-5 by using PyTorch. First, we create the 2 convolutional layers:

```
1 import torch.nn as nn
2
3 # convolutional layer 1
4   onv_layer1 = nn.Sequential(
5   nn.Conv2d(in_channels=3, out_channels=6, kernel_size=(5,5)), nn.ReLU())
      ,
6 )
7
8 # convolutional layer 2
9   conv_layer2 = nn.Sequential(
10  nn.Conv2d(in_channels=6, out_channels=16, kernel_size=(5,5)), nn.ReLU()
      ),
11 )
```

Then, we create the 3 remaining fully connected layers:

```
1 # fully connected layer 1
2   fc_layer1 = nn.Sequential( nn.Linear(in_features=16*5*5, out_features
      =120),
3   nn.ReLU(),
4 )
5
6 # fully connected layer 2
7   fc_layer2 = nn.Sequential( nn.Linear(in_features=120, out_features=84),
8   nn.ReLU(),
9 )
10
11 # fully connected layer 3
12 fc_layer3 = nn.Linear(in_features=84, out_features=10)
```

Finally, we combine them together to build LeNet-5.

```
1 LeNet5 = nn.Sequential(
2   conv_layer1,
3   nn.MaxPool2d(kernel_size=(2,2)),
4   conv_layer2,
5   nn.MaxPool2d(kernel_size=(2,2)),
6   nn.Flatten(), # flatten
7   fc_layer1,
8   fc_layer2,
9   fc_layer3
10 )
```

3.3.4 Model Training

After creating the network, we will teach it how to distinguish images between different classes. Intuitively, the teaching is achieved by showing it the images in train set, and telling it which classes they belong to. The network will gradually learn the concepts, such as "bird", "cat", "dog", etc., just like how human children learn.

First, we import our model LeNet5 , and define the loss function and optimization method. Here, we use cross-entropy loss, which is designed for classification tasks. This loss measures how similar the prediction is to the correct answer (ground truth). The closer this prediction is to the correct one, the smaller this loss is. To minimize this loss, we need an optimizer. Here, we use stochastic gradient descent (SGD) method as optimizer.

```
1 from model import LeNet5
2 model = LeNet5
3
4 loss_fn = nn.CrossEntropyLoss()
5 optimizer = optim.SGD(model.parameters(), lr=0.001, momentum=0.9)
```

When training a network, the most important parameter is learning rate. In above example, learning rate `lr` is 0.001. To train model successfully, we need a proper learning rate. If learning rate is too small, the loss will converge very slowly. If learning rate is too big, loss may not converge at all.

Then we start training. The training usually takes minutes to hours. Once the program finishes looping over the dataset one time, it finishes one epoch. A successful train usually has multiple epochs. Following example trains the network for 10 epochs.

```
1 # training
2 num_epoch = 10
3 for epoch in range(num_epoch):
4     running_loss = 0.0
5     for i, batch in enumerate(trainloader, 0):
6     # get the images; batch is a list of [images, labels]
7     images, labels = batch
8
9     # zero the parameter gradients
10    optimizer.zero_grad()
11
12    # get prediction
13    outputs = model(images) # compute loss
14    loss = loss_fn(outputs, labels)
15
16    # reduce loss
17    loss.backward() optimizer.step()
18
19    # print statistics
20    running_loss += loss.item()
21    if i % 500 == 499: # print every 500 mini-batches
22       print('[%d, %5d] loss: %.3f' % (epoch + 1, i + 1, running_loss / 500)
          )
23       running_loss = 0.0
24
25 print('Finished Training')
```

3.3.5 Model Testing

After training, our model can classify images now. At first, we show it several images in test set to see if it can correctly recognize them.

```
1 dataiter = iter(testloader)
2 images, labels = dataiter.next()
3 predictions = model(images).argmax(1)
4
5 # show some prediction result
6 classes = trainset.classes
7 print('GroundTruth: ', ' '.join('%5s' % classes[i] for i in labels))
```

```
8 print('Prediction: ', ' '.join('%5s' % classes[i] for i in predictions))
    imshow(torchvision.utils.make_grid(images.cpu()))
```

Figure 3.11 shown the testing results of the trained model. Due to randomness, the results may be different.

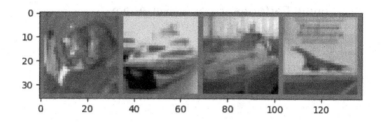

Figure 3.11   The testing results of the trained model.

```
1 GroundTruth: cat ship ship plane
2 Prediction: cat ship airplane airplane
```

Next, we will inspect how the model performs on the whole dataset.

```
1 @torch.no_grad()
2 def accuracy(model, data_loader):
3   model.eval()
4   correct, total = 0, 0
5   for batch in data_loader:
6     images, labels = batch
7     outputs = model(images)
8     _, predicted = torch.max(outputs.data, 1) total += labels.size(0)
9     correct += (predicted == labels).sum().item()
10  return correct / total
11
12 train_acc = accuracy(model, trainloader) # accuracy on train set
13 test_acc = accuracy(model, testloader) # accuracy on test set
14
15 print('Accuracy on the train set: %f %%' % (100 * train_acc))
16 print('Accuracy on the test set: %f %%' % (100 * test_acc))
```

The output is:

```
1 Accuracy on the train set: 72.17 %
2 Accuracy on the test set: 61.37 %
```

Since we trained for only 10 epochs, the accuracy is not very high. Finally, we can save our model to a file:

```
1 torch.save(LeNet5.state_dict(), 'model.pth')
```

3.3.6   GPU Acceleration

GPU acceleration plays an important role in reducing training time of CNNs. Modern CNNs usually contains tons of trainable parameters and are extremely computationally hungry. It takes hours to days or even weeks to training a perfect CNN model.

GPU acceleration technique could speed up training by 10–100 times, Figure 3.12 shows a typical GPU acceleration performance, over the traditional CPU. The acceleration is even more significant with large batch-size.

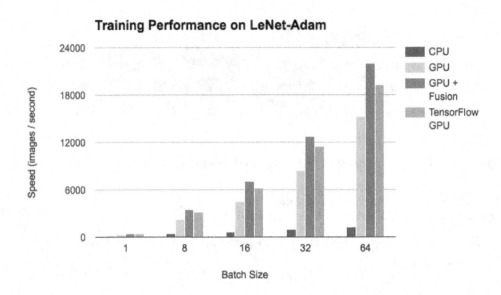

Figure 3.12 Typical GPU acceleration against CPU.

3.3.6.1 CUDA Installation

To get GPU acceleration, we need to have a machine with NVIDIA GPU equipped and have `cudatoolkit` installed. Please use following command to install `cudatoolkit`.

```
1 $ conda install cudatoolkit=11.3 -c pytorch
```

Then test the PyTorch environment to check the installation.

```
1 $ python -c "import torch; print(torch.cuda.is_available())" True
```

The expected output should be `True`.

3.3.6.2 Programming for GPU

We also need to modify the code to get GPU acceleration. Specifically, we need to move the model and data to GPU.

First, we need to move the model to GPU:

```
1 device = torch.device('cuda:0') # get the GPU No. 0
2 model = model.to(device) # move model to GPU
```

Then, we move data to GPU:

```
1 # get some image from loader
2 dataiter = iter(testloader) images,
```

```
3 labels = dataiter.next()
4
5 # move it to GPU
6 images = images.to(device)
7 labels = labels.to(device)
```

After that we get the prediction as usual, but the computation is done by GPU and is faster.

```
1 # get prediction as usual
2 predictions = model(images).argmax(1).detach()
3
4 # or perform one-step training when training the model
5 optimizer.zero_grad()
6 outputs = model(images)
7 loss = loss_fn(outputs, labels)
8 loss.backward()
9 optimizer.step()
```

Finally, we transfer the result back to CPU and print the result:

```
1 # transfer results back to CPU and so we can print it
2 predictions = predictions.cpu()
3 print(predictions)
```

However, above code only works on PCs with GPU. To let our code be able to work, no matter GPU is equipped or not, we usually define device as:

```
1 if torch.cuda.is_available():
2   # If GPU is available, use gpu
3   device = torch.device('cuda:0')
4 else:
5   # If not, use cpu
6   device = torch.device('cpu')
```

3.3.7   Load Pre-Trained CNNs

Besides training our own CNN from scratch, we can also use pre-trained networks in PyTorch Hub. Pre-trained models have two major advantages.

- These models were searched out and tested by previous researchers, and usually performs better than the one we train from scratch.

- All of them are already pre-trained for specific vision tasks, such as image classification, object detection, face recognition. Usually, we only need to fine-tune the model a little bit to fit the dataset. Some model may perfect fit the task without further training.

If your are interested in other CNN models, please visit https://pytorch. org/hub/research-models/compact for more information.

CHAPTER 4

Model-Level Design: Computation Acceleration and Communication Saving

Resources like computing power, memory storage, network and I/O bandwidth are commonly required by ML applications. When building large-scale ML systems in a distributed fashion, all of these characteristics may become the bottleneck. Research in recent years has focused on how to speed up machine learning, particularly in a resource-constrained scenario. This problem can be solved by using model compression technology. We will discuss the optimization of this topic from two perspectives: (1) Network architecture and (2) training algorithm.

4.1 OPTIMIZATION OF NETWORK ARCHITECTURE

Currently, the machine learning tasks usually generate enormous computational demands, which may easily exceed the device's memory, I/O bandwidth, network connection and data storage capacity.

Table 4.1 compares the resource costs of various neural networks when models are actually deployed. As a result, potential research areas for the deployment of on-device learning systems include improving network architectures and reducing model size. While typical in-cloud ML applications are usually free of the amount of energy spent during task execution, on-device learning applications need specific optimization of resource costs, because the small batteries of mobile devices make it impossible to run tasks continuously for lengthy periods of time.

As a result of all of these difficulties, researchers will be forced to develop new frameworks for on-device learning that will alleviate the implementation bottleneck. There are three ways to overcome the aforementioned challenges: (1) Network-aware parameter pruning, (2) knowledge distillation and (3) fine-tuning training, which we shall describe in this section. In order to lower the cost of hardware, these three factors can be used in model compression techniques.

DOI: 10.1201/9781003340225-4

Table 4.1 Resource cost of different neural networks.

Model	Image Scale	Memory Footprint (MB)	#GFLOP
AlexNet	227×227	232.39	0.716
SqueezeNet	224×224	4.98	0.828
MobileNet	224×224	16.03	0.568
DenseNet-201	224×224	76.89	3/97
VGG-16	224×224	527.95	15.68
VGG-19	224×224	547.35	19.81
GoogleNet	224×224	50.84	1.95
ResNet-18	224×224	44.62	1.98
ResNet-50	224×224	97.82	3.96
ResNet-101	224×224	171.39	7.64
ResNet-152	224×224	229.57	10.98
Inception-V3	299×299	90.62	5.62

4.1.1 Network-Aware Parameter Pruning

Complex neural networks with large mode sizes, parameter quantities, and matrix operations, which may rapidly surpass the mobile device's capabilities, are commonly required for current ML applications. Because of this, reducing the model computational cost is one of the most critical aspects of on-device learning acceleration and implementation. Reducing the model complexity of the neural network is an obvious approach, where the "elephant" models have been simplified using the parameter pruning approach.

4.1.1.1 Pruning Steps

The following basic phases are involved in the construction of parameter trimming algorithms. First, inspecting each neuron and calculating its contribution to the overall model's update significance allows us to determine whether or not it is possible to model compress the original neural network's sparsity. Second, we can then remove the trivial neuron weights and activations, as well as any others that contain insignificant parameters. Third, by re-training on the compressed model in layers, we can fine-tune it to better fit our objective function. We can also examine the sparsity of the model and keep removing superfluous parameters.

Properly estimating the sparsity of a network is the most critical stage. As a result, we shall begin by defining sparsity. Sparsity is a factor to determine whether or not a model has redundant parameters by analyzing the proportion of elements in the parameter tensors, which have zero or near-zero values and are often in the lowest possible rank. A sparse tensor is one that has a large number of zeros in its values. Otherwise, it is dense. It is logical to use the $L0$-normalization function to determine the total number of zero elements in the model.

Considering the entire parameter tensor $\mathbb{X}$ is comprised by a serious of layer-wise tensors $x_1, x_2, \cdots, x_l$. where l is the number of layers. The model sparsity can be calculated as follows:

$$\|\mathbb{X}\|_0 = |x_1|^0 + |x_2|^0 + \cdots |x_l|^0. \tag{4.1}$$

Under the control of $L0$-normalization, elements with exact value of zero will be marked as 1, otherwise 0. Therefore, one easy way to reflect the model sparsity s can be finally defined as: $s = \frac{\|\mathbb{X}\|_0}{|W|}$, where $|W|$ represents the total number of model parameters.

4.1.1.2 Pruning Strategy

Several elements are needed to consider while designing a pruning strategy. Of the many considerations, the most basic is choosing the granularity of pruning [356]. Fine-grained and coarse-grained pruning may be categorized as two distinct types of pruning. By assessing weights and activations in order, the fine-grained pruning is frequently based on processes that delete unnecessary neurons. When training deep models, this strategy has the potential to reduce model size while still requiring a significant amount of processing power to search through all of the input parameters. While this constraint is overcome by the fine-grained pruning, the coarse-grained pruning uses a group-wise inspection of the neuron importance to filter out unimportant neurons. Prune may thus significantly minimize the searching complexity and is simple to apply.

Additionally, the timing of pruning during training is critical. One-shot pruning is the simplest implementation of the pruning method since it only prunes the model once, shortly before training convergence one-shot pruning [295]. The iterative pruning is different from the one-shot pruning in that it selectively prunes the important neurons, eliminates the insignificant ones and reconstructs the network function by fine-tuning the compressed model again [201]. In this case, the beginning and end of the pruning process will have a substantial influence on the model training efficiency, which may be simultaneously adjusted using data quantization [184,632] and gradient sketch [238,455].

4.1.1.3 Pruning Metrics

Most pruning algorithms have four major issues that need to be addressed, including:

- Accurately measuring the training contribution of each neuron.

- Correctly determining which neurons can be removed from the model.

- Effectively re-tuning the compressed model after pruning.

- Making pruning operations online applicable in production scenarios.

In order to ensure the sparsity of the parameter tensors in neural networks, Han et al. [188] used the regularization remainder term in the model's loss function to define the training contribution of each neuron. It is easy to represent each neuron's contribution by setting the significance thresholds in advance so that neurons with modest values of parameters (e.g. weights and activations) can be eliminated from the model. It is possible that the theoretical assumption for inserting the regularization term may not hold in reality, causing the integrity of the network function blocks to be damaged and therefore distort the prediction results.

The second-order partial difference, based on *Taylor Series*, was presented by Dong et al. [116] in an effort to build an efficient pruning method. The authors then constructed an estimate to assess the contribution of each neuron to the loss function. Despite its simplicity, the calculation of the second-order Hession matrices would result in a significant amount of computational overhead, making it impractical for practical application. Rather than using the gradient approximation for the complete network model, it may be possible to limit it to a subset of the layers. This second-order based strategy may successfully minimize the model size without decreasing the model training quality or inference accuracy because of the linear convergence speed of the approximation error in each layer.

Moreover, Han et al. [184] proposed a comprehensive pipelining-aware pruning method for handling the subsequent model reconstruction and fine-grained re-tuning, based on three key stages: (1) Removing redundant neurons, (2) quantizing the weights and activation of a compressed model and (3) using Huffman coding to simplify data representation. A small memory footprint and high training accuracy may be achieved by following these three procedures.

As a final step, Guo et al. [178] used a combination of parameter reduction, network training and dynamically adjusting model structure to accomplish this target. Optimizing the loss function by sparsity-based regularization reduces the model size and reduces the amount of gradient computation required during the backward propagation stage, resulting in a more efficient implementation.

4.1.1.4 Summary

Consequently, it has been clearly proven that network-aware parameter pruning strategies can effectively minimize model size, lower computational costs and restrict memory footprint. We believe the on-device learning applications and frameworks can benefit from parameter reduction and improve the processing speed.

4.1.2 Knowledge Distillation

While model compression technologies, such as resampling, significantly alter the structure of the original neural networks, knowledge distillation offers the potential to produce a small model that performs the same function as its larger counterpart, without the need for manual adjustment of the loss function and update rule.

Knowledge distillation is all about training a little model, called the *student*, to mimic a larger model, called the *teacher*. The teacher-student scheme follows the concept of education. Student models are often shallow and simplistic, consisting of typical neural blocks in real-world implementations of the concepts (*e.g.,* FC and CONV layers). For example, the structure of ResNet18 can be approximated, by using a basic CNN network with five layers of training data [198]. Specifically, Breiman et al. [299] developed the concept of using a basic model to perform the same operations as several tree-based models. For neural networks, Bucila et al. [54] used this approach to design a knowledge distillation technique. As a result, Hinton et al. [205] expanded this strategy to a wider range of situations. Since Hinton's work is the foundation for the vast majority of extant knowledge distillation implementations, we will go through Hinton's theory in detail.

Students in this method are taught how to reduce the forward propagation loss function by using the teacher model's prediction probabilities. Hence this technique is called knowledge distillation. In the context of image classification, an important ML application, the teacher's expertise could be represented in the classification distribution of distinct labels, which is intimately linked to the softmax component at the end of the neural network. Because of this, the student model may use the teacher's loss function to update the loss function derived by the student itself. This is a natural notion of assisting the student to rapidly understand the "advanced" teacher's prediction abilities and can successfully speed up training convergence over the learning process from the beginning. This has some similarities to the key principles of *Transfer Learning* [425]. Knowledge distillation, on the other hand, involves the use of a pre-defined student model and the modification of the loss function.

4.1.2.1 Combination of Loss Functions

We cannot directly use the teacher model's vanilla loss function to extract knowledge, despite the fact that it is the crucial premise. For example, when the teacher model has been thoroughly trained with excellent prediction accuracy, the ground-truth label dominates the classification distribution, whereas other classes are almost zero after the softmax block [432]. It is impossible to provide the student with any more information over and beyond the vanilla loss function based on ground truth labels, even if the teacher's loss function is used. The temperature-based softmax function can be used to modify the initial logits from the FC layers and normalize the form of log probability. The temperature-based softmax can be described as:

$$p_i = \frac{\exp(z_i/T)}{\sum_j \exp(z_j/T)}, \tag{4.2}$$

where p_i is the classification probability of each class i and z is corresponding logits inside the softmax function.

Apart from that, T represents the temperature hyper-parameter used to regulate the output probability distribution. With a greater T, we obtain the typical softmax function, where a softer probability distribution means that the teacher model is able to convey better information to the student model, resulting in better learning outcomes for model quality. Teacher-to-student information transfer is only possible when the teacher's loss function, referred to as *dark knowledge* [526], can be used to forecast the student's future behavior. Transferring this dark knowledge from teacher to student is at the core of the distillation process.

Therefore, the core modification of the student's loss function (*i.e.*, overall loss) can be formulated as:

$$\begin{aligned}
\mathcal{L}\{x; w\} &= \alpha \cdot \mathcal{L}_s\{y, \sigma(z_s; T = 1)\} \\
&+ \beta \cdot \mathcal{L}_d\{\sigma(z_s; T = t), \sigma(z_d; T = t)\}, \tag{4.3}
\end{aligned}$$

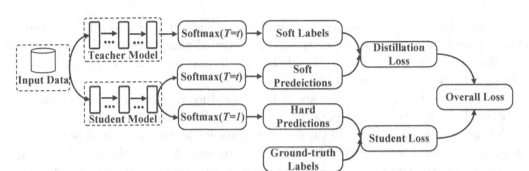

Figure 4.1 The workflow of knowledge distillation.

where x, y, w and σ represent the input data, ground-truth label, model parameters and the softmax block, respectively. Besides, z_s and z_d are the logits of the student and teacher, respectively. Note that the overall loss function $\mathcal{L}$ contains two parts: The student loss $\mathcal{L}_s$ and distillation loss the $\mathcal{L}_d$, under the control of the coefficient hyper-parameters α and β.

Here, Figure 4.1 depicts the process of knowledge distillation using these two loss functions in a more visual way. When $T = 1$ is satisfied, the student loss is the difference between the projected class and the ground-truth labels recorded in the dataset. Assuming that $T = t$ is true, we can utilize the distillation loss to determine the amount of dark knowledge a student has learnt from their teacher, which is also impacted by the internal temperature.

4.1.2.2 Tuning of Hyper-Parameters

The adjustment of t is an error-and-trial process that has a considerable influence on the distillation efficiency of the hyper-parameters *alpha* and *beta*. The temperature t is commonly set as $t \in [1, 20]$ in the implementation of previous methods [231, 453]. Lower temperatures are expected when the student model is much smaller than the instructor model. As the temperature rises, more information is lost in the distillation process, making it difficult for students to make sense of the intermediate features [598]. Even if a student model's genuine learning capacity is difficult to determine, additional study into how to adjust the temperature t is needed in the future.

The values of *alpha* and *beta*, on the other hand, need to be carefully selected since these hyper-parameters indicate the learning weight between the student loss and the distillation loss, which are from the ground-truth labels and the teacher experience, respectively [205]. It's common practice to put $\alpha + \beta = 1$, although *beta* might be much lower than *alpha*. Hyper-parameters may also be adjusted in a more flexible way, as some recent studies have discovered [508].

4.1.2.3 Usage of Model Training

In addition to adjusting the loss function and coefficient hyper-parameters, we can easily construct a lightweight student model that owns the same representation capacity as the sophisticated teacher model. Specifically, the data samples will be fed into the student and teacher models at the start of each round. The teacher's loss will be added to the student model's loss function after the forward propagation to generate the output prediction. Students will benefit from the teacher's knowledge and experience by following this pattern. A backward propagation is used in which the student model updates the model parameters by calculating gradients based on corrected loss. It is thus possible to forecast as accurately with the student model as with the teacher model. Student models are often trained on servers in advance to save computing time spent on knowledge distillation. Finally, this model can be used to run embedded learning applications, including smartphones, tablets and mobile sensors.

4.1.2.4 Summary

To further enhance neural network training, knowledge distillation can be integrated into existing model compression methods (*e.g.,* the network pruning and data quantization). In the forward propagation step, for example, Polino et al. [440] trained a quantized student model from a full-precision teacher. The distillation optimization and network pruning were both considered in the work of Theis et al. [513]. By applying knowledge distillation, Tann et al. [507] developed a hardware and software co-design for low-precision neural networks. With knowledge distillation techniques, it may overcome the problem of a large memory footprint and storage requirements by extracting a tiny student model with the same performance. Inference latency for on-device learning applications may be effectively reduced by using this method.

4.1.3 Model Fine-Tuning

The resource-constrained environment, where the device's CPU is not allowed to operate at full speed for a long period and the training data are limited, is the common implementation scenario for on-device learning applications. In addition, due to the device's limited memory capacity, not all neurons or layers can participate in the training process. In order to deal with on-device learning effectively, model structure and computational efficiency need to be carefully designed and optimized.

In order to meet this goal, it is possible to use transfer learning to fine-tune the model, which is illustrated in Figure 4.2. Using the transfer learning method, we first train a model on a large dataset (*e.g.,* ImageNet [108]) and then apply it to the on-device dataset using the model we developed. Next, we define a subset of layers that can be updated (the rest are frozen) and fine-tune these layers during the training process. Therefore, transfer learning and fine-tuning of partial layers are the most basic ideas for on-device learning. Following, we'll talk about these techniques.

4.1.3.1 Transfer Learning

In general, image classification [275] and object detection [315] have been extensively deployed in large-scale commodity clusters, but their effectiveness implicitly depends on the scale of the available training data, which has been pre-labeled for each

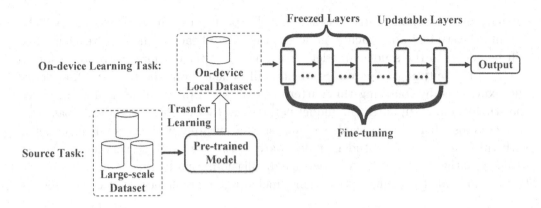

Figure 4.2 The workflow of model fine-tuning.

individual image. Nonetheless, this assumption cannot be met in the context of on-device learning, as we have already discussed before [222]. As a result, the use of transfer learning is a potential way to overcome this difficulty by employing the prediction knowledge from a bigger dataset, which is generally larger in data size. Note that the training procedures are described as using a different large-scale dataset as a source task, where the accompanying training data is labeled as to source datasets for convenience [425]. Because the model is pre-trained on the source dataset, transfer learning is powerful because it overcomes the constraint of inadequate on-device data by extracting new information.

Fine-tuning is one of the most promising strategies for addressing the criteria of on-device learning acceleration in transfer learning based approaches [132], which are employed in many visual computing situations, boosting attempts to develop more intelligent and adaptable algorithms [76, 148, 277]. For the pre-training of the model, we can utilize the ImageNet [108] dataset, which has a wealth of information regarding feature extraction and pattern placement for use in mobile learning applications. The key to speeding up training is to shorten the time it takes to update the model's parameters in each iteration of the process. Due to this, two types of fine-tuning methods are developed: (1) Updating only a portion of the network layers to reduce the computational overhead of matrix operation [359] and (2) updating all parameters while giving the pre-trained model's backbone blocks more importance [447], so as to better extract classification features from training data.

As a result, it is still restricted by the manual configuration that determines the hyper-parameters of how many layers may be updated and how the backbone network is designed. These hyper-parameters should be automatically controlled by a high-performance on-device learning system. There are two ways to accomplish this goal, *i.e.,* (1) layer-wise freezing and updating and (2) model-wise feature sharing.

4.1.3.2 Layer-Wise Freezing and Updating

Each neuron parameter can be fine-tuned via layer-wise freezing and updating. In most cases, the learning process necessitates the use of a pre-trained model that has been taught how to extract relevant features from a large-scale training dataset. Then, the model will be re-trained using the local dataset on the device. There are several advantages to using transfer learning instead of standard machine learning (ML) applications, which typically train from the start with random beginning parameters and need much more rounds to achieve convergence [270, 502].

In order to implement fine-tuning, we must first specify the freezing and updating layers. It is impossible to change the specifications of the freezing layers since they are fixed. Updatable payers, on the other hand, are the neural network's most active component, where parameters are continuously altered until training convergence. Here, we present a simple explanation of this pipeline. The frozen layers preserve information gleaned from large-scale source datasets, while the updatable layers build unique models from data stored locally on the device.

The decision of updating portions of the model instead of the full model is obtained based on the following knowledge, *i.e.,* training using small-scale on-device datasets, especially when supplemented by pre-training with source datasets, will inevitably lead to model over-fitting [589]. Therefore, only the final few layers of the pre-trained model can be changed, but the rest of the layers must be frozen to preserve the low-level features retrieved from the data [29]. However, the performance of on-device learning is still hindered by the fact that the hyper-parameters of how many layers should be frozen still rely on the empirical setup.

Nevertheless, because of their shallow network structures and inability to express the comprehensive parameterized details of original deep models, some compact models designed for mobile environments, such as ShuffleNet [613] and MobileNet [212], are not well adaptive to the fine-tuning method, due to the requirements of high-accuracy pre-trained models and numerous adjustment of diverse hyper-parameters. Therefore, model size and training quality must be balanced, and generalized techniques to automatically manage training configurations are clearly needed.

4.1.3.3 *Model-Wise Feature Sharing*

In addition to layer-by-layer fine-tuning, we can also use the complete pre-trained model's information in the on-device learning process. Sharing features across models by transferring matching parameters is reasonable since various on-device activities may have the same learning target. Sharing knowledge of feature extraction amongst models has been widely studied by many researchers [388]. Image classification applications often involve shallow models and less knowledge than other types of machine learning jobs [585]. Despite this, the models have been more complex and pose new difficulties for on-device learning. It is challenging to transfer information from deep models and apply it effectively when computational and memory resources are in a constrained environment. On-device learning is not compatible with the traditional learning paradigm, such as vanilla life-long learning. However, it is feasible to enhance this strategy by integrating model compression methods.

4.1.3.4 Summary

In order to overcome the difficulties of on-device learning, such as insufficient training data, limited processing resources and rigorous parameter update constraints, fine-tuning and transfer learning are both feasible methods. By eliminating model over-fitting caused by insufficient training data, this strategy may provide four benefits for on-device learning: (1) Saving in network training's computational burden, (2) eliminating model over-fitting, (3) improving the overall training speed and (4) generating personalized models.

4.1.4 Neural Architecture Search

Deep Learning systems have achieved tremendous success in lots of areas such as Computer Vision [274,467,481,600], Speech Recognition [204] and Natural Language Processing (NLP) [93,111,565]. Thanks to the rapid growth of availability of big data, computational power, acceleration on hardware and recent algorithmic achievements, deep learning has stepped into a rapid development era. However, the neural architecture designing is a major challenge due to:

- The requirement of neural architecture design is various due to the variety of data types and tasks.

- It is difficult to design one global efficient architecture that can works on various hardware platforms.

Generally speaking, the neural architecture can be formalized as a Directed Acyclic Graph (DAG) [162] where different nodes are connected by operators such as convolution, polling, activation, etc. The different connection topology output different model architectures, so that the key concept of neural architecture designing is to determine the nodes' quantity and how to connect them. Based on this representation, DL models can contain numerous layers and billions of parameters. Models either handcrafted by repetitive experimentation, or modified from existing models, are continuously growing in size and complexity. All of this makes handcrafting model architecture a complex problem that requires deep expertise. To this end, the technology to automatically design efficient architecture named "Neural Architecture Search (NAS)" has draw a lot of attention.

NAS has achieved a lot of success by handcrafting SOTA models in Image Classification [211] and Object Detection [154]. However, these models usually contain millions of parameters and require millions of floating-point operations. This caused huge computational cost and prevent the application in resource-constrained environments. Besides, such models might require specific hardware (e.g. GPUs, TPUs, etc.) to support the computation.

Since the inception of the first NAS algorithm based on reinforcement learning [635], tremendous work has been proposed to study efficient NAS. Specifically, integrating hardware awareness into the loop of architecture search has attracted many attentions and opend a new research direction named Hardware-Aware Neural Architecture Search (HW-NAS). Some HW-NAS efforts balance the trade-off between accuracy and hardware efficiency, some even claim the SOTA performance.

4.1.4.1 Search Space of HW-NAS

In HW-NAS, two different search space have been adapted: *Architecture Search Space* for the architectural topology searching and *Hardware Search Space* for the hardware configuration searching.

Architecture Search Space. The architecture search space defines a set of basic network operations and how these operations can be connected. The existing NAS approaches can be roughly classified into three categories:

- **Layer-wise Search Space.** The model has a fixed macro architecture, and the detailed topology is searched in layer-wise manner. For example, FBNet [559] used one layer-wise search space which fixed the number of layers and each layer's dimension. Besides, the first layer and last three layers' structure is predefined. The rest layers of FBNet needs to be optimized.

- **Cell-based Search Space.** The model is repeatedly stacked by a basic architecture module called blocks or cells. Normally the cell is a small architecture that works as a feature extractor. This design is motivated by the observation that many handcrafted SOTA model utilize repetitive components. The larger and deeper architectures are formed by repeatedly stack these basic components. This search space aims to find a representative cell that can ensemble the whole architecture. Cell-based search space is efficient enough seeking for best model in terms of accuracy, but it lacks flexibility to hardware specialization [503, 559].

- **Hierarchical Search Space.** The model generates several basic cells and uses them to form bigger blocks. The whole architecture is constructed by bigger blocks. MNASNet [503] used such a hierarchical search space and shows more flexibility than original cell-based search space. Compared with global search space, hierarchical search space also reduced the size of total search space without losing flexibility.

Hardware Search Space. Some HW-NAS methods utilized an additional *Hardware Search Space* to generate hardware specifications and optimizations for targeted hardware platforms. For FPGAs, the hardware specifications includes: IP reuse strategy, quantization schemes, tiling parameters, etc. Optimizing all the specifications will greatly increased the whole search space time complexity. Therefore, existing approaches only consider a few optimization goals. The Hardware Search Space can be classified as:

- **Parameter-based Space.** This search space formalize the hardware configurations as a set of parameters. FNAS [248] deployed FPGA chip for deeplearning and finds the optimal model by configuring four tiling parameters for the convolutions. Based on FNAS, FNASs [595] added more optimization parameters such as loop unrolling.

- **Template-based Space.** A set of pre-configured templates are defined as template-based search space. NASAIC [583] utilizes Application-Specific Circuits (ASIC) in NAS. Their search space includes many existing successful design templates. NASAIC is designed to find the best model with different possible paralleizations among all the templates.

4.1.4.2 Targeted Hardware Platforms

According to the hardware platform's memory and computation capabilities, the existing HW-NAS approaches can be categorized into three classes based on their targeted hardware platforms:

- **Server Processor.** It can provide abundant computational resources such as CPUs, GPUs, FPGAs and ASICs. This type of hardware can be found in cloud server, data center or supercomputers. Researchers applied this hardware can focus on accuracy without considering the hardware constraints. However, there are still many HW-NAS works aims at speeding up the training process on Server processor and extensive resources needed in the inference phase.

- **Mobile Device.** It has a broad range of users, but it has a very limited memory and computational capabilities. Many HW-NAS works target smartphones as their hardware platform, including FBNet [559] and ProxylessNAS [100]. Smartphones usually contains different types of processors on their chips, so that there are also some work [361] focusing on the heterogeneous system of smartphone.

- **Tiny Device.** It has attracted a lot of research interest thanks to the vast development of micro-controllers and IoT applications. MCUNet [338] proposes an efficient neural architecture search called TinyNAS for tiny device. TinyNAS handles many different constraints such as energy, latency and memory and it aims to search the optimal architecture under low search cost. TinyNAS can achieve more than 70% accuracy on ImageNet with an off-the-shelf commercial micro-controllers.

4.1.4.3 Trend of Current HW-NAS Methods

In the past few years, the number of HW-NAS researches targeted for GPUs and CPUs more or less remains constant, but we notice that there is a growing popularity of FPGAs and ASICs, which is inline with the increasing of edge learning application. [90, 251] are the recent work target multiple hardware platforms. As for the types of network, NAS has been mostly dominated by CNN or the extended CNN, which involves special convolution operations such as depthwise separable convolution or grouped convolutions. However, for recent researches, there is a growing interest on capsule networks [378], transformers [267] and GANs [296].

4.2 OPTIMIZATION OF TRAINING ALGORITHM

The next step after designing high-performance neural networks is to deploy these models at the edge devices, where computing capacities are typically limited and costly. As a result, training methods must be optimized to decrease the time cost of task processing. Data-adaptive regularization and low-precision data representation are two directions that may help attain this goal. There are two main focuses here, *i.e.,* reducing matrix computing overhead and increasing on-device hardware efficiency.

4.2.1 Low Rank Factorization

The calculation of matrix values is a standard part of the computational processes in machine learning applications. Thus, the fundamental notion of low-rank factorization is to represent the original full-rank matrix by multiplying numerous low-rank matrices. The typical *Singular Value Decomposition* (SVD) method [287] is a potential approach for reducing the computing overhead of two-dimensional matrix operations, particularly when applied to a two-dimensional matrix. The rationale of SVD to transform the original matrix $\mathbf{M}$ can be described as:

$$\mathbf{M} = \mathbf{UAV}^*, \tag{4.4}$$

where $\mathbf{U}_{l \times m}$ and $\mathbf{V}_{m \times n}$ are the orthogonal matrices, and $\mathbf{A}_{m \times m}$ is a diagonal $m \times m$ matrix with non-negative real numbers on the diagonal. Note that the $\mathbf{V}^*$ represents the corresponding conjugate transpose matrix. The SVD method can be employed to the compression of CONV layers in the deep neural networks. In addition, the fully connected (FC) layers' compression ratio may be further increased by utilizing the Sufficient Factor Broadcasting (SFB) approach [571,572,604], which is a specific instance of SVD, since most parameter tensors in the FC layers are sparse, *i.e.,* the matrix rank is frequently one or lower than three [572]. The rationale of SFB can be described as:

$$\mathbf{M} = \mathbf{uv}^\top, \tag{4.5}$$

where $\mathbf{u}_{1 \times m}$ and $\mathbf{v}_{m \times 1}^\top$ are simplified as sufficient factors. It is clear that this low rank decomposition algorithm can successfully compress the layers of the neural network, resulting in a considerable reduction in processing overhead.

4.2.2 Data-Adaptive Regularization

Data-adaptive regularization can also satisfy the criteria of on-device learning with limited user data. Adaptive regularization, which takes into account the fact that on-device learning has a limited amount of training data, is being developed to overcome this difficulty. This regularization uses user-specific data to ensure that the optimization function does not overfit the model. If we adjust the original model's loss function and learning objective, for example, by adding $L1$- or $L2$-normalization to the loss function, we could accomplish this goal easily. For the resource-constrained edge environment, this kind of lightweight algorithm optimization offers significant benefits in speeding up on-device learning tasks.

4.2.2.1 Core Formulation

Because neural network loss functions are adjusted to produce a smaller model that performs as well as its predecessor, it is crucial that model generalization is limited to an acceptable range, which minimizes the generalization gap by taking precedence over other considerations. First, we'll go through the fundamentals of regularization in this section of the book. Preventing the overfitting of tiny models is a common way to ensure their generalizability, although this methodology may incur undesirable side effects. The *Stochastic Gradient Descent* (SGD) optimization and its variants [244, 313] and its derivatives can be used to minimize random sample variance. Therefore, the general formulation can described as:

$$\mathcal{L}(w; x; y) = \mathcal{L}_0(w; x; y) + \lambda \cdot R(w), \tag{4.6}$$

where $mathcalL0$ and $mathcalL$ indicate the total training loss and the error in the objective function, respectively. The $R(w)$ regularization function is used to alter the initial loss, which is commonly based on the $L1$- or $L2$-normalization of the loss. In addition, the hyper-parameter *lambda* (also named the *regularization strength* [535]) controls $R(w)$ and is responsible for balancing training loss with the regularization error.

4.2.2.2   On-Device Network Sparsification

Regularization has a solid relationship with neural network sparsification, a strategy for optimizing neural networks. To increase prediction accuracy after regularization, Han et al. [186] suggested the *Dense-Sparse-Dense* (DSD) technique, which uses the original model's sparseness and density to make predictions more accurate. In order to minimize model over-fitting and offer a robust generalization, it is crucial to relax the optimization restrictions of the model by making the search direction more readily to escape, particularly when a network falls into a local minimum. As a result, the regularization function can be optimized using two standard methods, *i.e.*, the $L1$-normalization and $L2$-normalization, respectively.

Regularization is invoked in the $L1$-normalization based technique by making use of the network's element-wise sparseness. The loss function can be improved by adding the following remaining term:

$$R_1(w) = \sum_{i=1}^{|W|} |w_i|, \tag{4.7}$$

where $|W|$ is the total number of model parameters.

Also, as to the $L2$-normalization, the remaining terms are often described as follows:

$$R_2(w) = \sum_{l=1}^{L} \sum_{i=1}^{n} |w_{l,i}|^2, \tag{4.8}$$

where L and n represent the number of layers and per-layer weights, respectively. By considering these two remaining terms simultaneously, we can adjust the loss function as:

$$\mathcal{L}(w; x; y) = \mathcal{L}_0(w; x; y) + \lambda_1 \cdot R_1(w) + \lambda_2 \cdot R_2(w). \tag{4.9}$$

It is important to note that L1-normalization makes the model simpler and limits the model's training capacity by creating a fraction of the parameters into zero, which is the fundamental difference between these two types of regularization. The quality of model training may be harmed by over-fitting models caused by such simplification. Accordingly, the L2-normalization does not need that all parameters to be zero, so as to get a satisfactory training accuracy.

4.2.2.3 Block-Wise Regularization

In model training, increasing regularity helps speed up the calculation, but fine-tuning each parameter might be challenging to apply in reality because of its complexity. Block-wise regularization, which controls a collection of factors rather than a single one, has recently been the attention of several academics. It is necessary to conduct sparsification on a subset of the group elements by setting them to zero.

According to block-wise regularization, the penalty for data loss should be applied to all groups within a layer in accordance with their own viewpoint. As a result, the following describes the fundamental formulation for the group parameters in layer l as w_l^g:

$$\mathcal{L}(w; x; y) = \mathcal{L}_0(w; x; y) + \lambda_r \cdot R_r(w) + \lambda_g \cdot \sum_{l=1}^{L} R_g(w_l^g), \qquad (4.10)$$

where λ_r and λ_g represent the conventional regularity strength and the group-wise strength, respectively. Moreover, the group-wise remainder term can be further defined as:

$$R_g(w_l^g) = \sum_{g=1}^{G} \|w^g\| \qquad (4.11)$$

$$= \sum_{g=1}^{G} \sum_{i=1}^{|w^g|} (w_i^g)^2, w^g \in w^l, \qquad (4.12)$$

where $|w^g|$ represents the element numbers of the parameter group w^g. Here, the *Group Lasso Regularization* [607] following the formulation of $\lambda_g \sum_{l=1}^{L} R_g(w_l^g)$ can be used to aggregate all the magnitudes of the parameters at the group level.

4.2.2.4 Summary

Among the fine-grained sparsity methods, block-wise regularization is one that focuses on the value pattern and matrix form of the parameters in a dataset. According to recent studies, the number of *Convolutional Neural Network* (CNN) kernels, output feature maps, filter sizes and network layers can be used to establish the metrics for group partitioning. Mao et al. [377], for example, designed a coarse-grained pruning based on CNN properties to balance regularity and inference accuracy. Also, Anwar et al. [22] also uses the structure of intra-kernel strides to minimize model complexity, including kernel size and output feature maps. As a result, all of these methods can significantly lower the computational burden of learning, without sacrificing inference accuracy or quality of the final model. Data-adaptive regularization

Table 4.2 System efficiency when using INT8 and FP32-based instructions.

INT8-based Operation	Energy Reduction over FP32	Memory Reduction over FP32	Processing Speedup over FP32
Addition	31.27×	116.21×	3.29×
Multiplication	19.25×	25.03×	7.62×

uses network sparsification to simplify the network topology and minimize inference latency, which is a critical assessment parameter for on-device learning acceleration.

4.2.3 Data Representation and Numerical Quantization

Reducing the number of bits required to represent a number is known as quantization. FP32, or 32-bit floating point, has been the most often used numerical format in recent deep learning research and application. Researchers have turned to lower-precision numerical forms since deep learning models need tremendous I/O bandwidth and computing power. Integer-based representations of weights and activations have been widely tested and indicate no substantial loss of accuracy. An important area of study is the use of reduced bit widths, such as 4 or 2 bits, which have shown remarkable development.

The gist of quantization is to lower the number of bits in a data value, which focuses on representing a number with a relatively low degree of accuracy. The floating-point value with a 32-bit width, known as the FP32 format, is often used in on-device learning systems for arithmetic multiplications and matrix computations. The conventional FP32-based operations, on the other hand, may easily exceed the available computational capacity in the resource-constrained on-device environment, including limited I/O bandwidth and insufficient computational primitives, making them impractical for rapid model training and low-latency inference. Therefore, improving the data representation is essential to decrease the processing cost. Although prior research has demonstrated that neural networks are generally over-parameterized, the model parameters tended to be redundant [360]. This phenomenon reveals that it is not required to represent the data in the complete FP32 precision, and parameters can be handled with reduced accuracy without harming the model quality. The INT8 format is a typical approach to convert the FP32 data type into a fixed-point value with 8 bits of width. Data may be encoded in even lower-bit-width formats, including [564], ternary [346], XOR and XNOR [444].

The weights, activations and gradients may be quantized simultaneously for greater system efficiency, which includes lowering per-iteration time, decreasing memory footprint and conserving energy cost, considering the repetitive pattern of model training. As given in Table 4.2, a more exact comparison illustrates that in terms of efficiency, INT8-based quantization may reduce resource costs by adopting FP32-based quantization. Consequently, quantization is a prominent technique to accelerate on-device learning tasks. There are several critical components to quantization that we will cover in the following sections. In order to handle on-device inference, we need

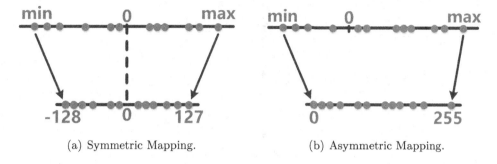

(a) Symmetric Mapping.   (b) Asymmetric Mapping.

Figure 4.3 Common value mapping schemes used in data quantization.

to have a basic understanding of quantization methods, as well as the post-training quantization and quantization-ware training.

4.2.3.1 Elements of Quantization

Value mapping, zero point, linear scaling, range clipping and integer rounding are five fundamental ideas utilized in quantization algorithms that we shall discuss to grasp the rationale of quantization better.

Value Mapping. Data values are reduced in precision from the original fully-precision FP32 format, which is the essence of quantization (*e.g.*, INT8). The following explanation is based on an INT8-based quantization for simplicity. An 8-bit-wide fixed-point value may be mapped to a floating-point number in the macro perspective of quantization, which can be regarded as a mapping function. The most basic transformation of quantization can be expressed as follow:

$$q = \frac{r}{s} + z, \tag{4.13}$$

where q and r represent the quantized value and the original number, respectively. On top of this basic tranformation, the scale s is an essential part of the mapping function, since it determines the final quantized range. There is also an extra parameter, z (sometimes known as the quantization bias), for adjusting the quantized domain with an offset to relocate the base point of the number axis. This means the quantized value in one layer may need to be restored to its original range before moving to the next layer in a sequential manner. The dequantization is the term given to this operation, which can be formulated as:

$$r = (q - z) \cdot s. \tag{4.14}$$

Zero Point. Two types of value mapping algorithms can be distinguished by their usage of zero points, *i.e.*, the symmetric and the asymmetric scheme in Figure 4.3(a) and Figure 4.3(b), respectively. If the absolute value between the maximum and lowest is more than zero, then the symmetric approach may be used to map the original range. Since the zero point is not required, it is a straightforward implementation. The asymmetric approach, on the other hand, uses the quantization bit width to find the zero point depending on the scale range.

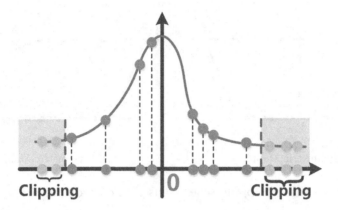

Figure 4.4   Range clipping removes the outliers according to the data distribution.

Linear Scaling. According to the scale s, the basis of quantization is the scalar division operation. An appropriate scale is thus required, since using the original value and multiplying by a constant scale would result in data distribution, which is inconsistent with the initial FP32-INT8 exponential interval. Due to the fact that parameters tend to be distributed across a broad and sharp domain, it is crucial to extend the range of the quantized data to include the whole original data set as well. For example, the gap between maximum and minimum can be calculated by taking a restricted bit range into account. Consequently, we summarize the rationale of scale s as follows:

$$s = \texttt{scale}(a, b; n) = \frac{b - a}{2^n - 1}, a < b, \tag{4.15}$$

where a and b represent the starting and end point of the quantized range, respectively. Besides, n is the limited bit width, *e.g.*, $n = 8$ for INT8 asymmetric quantization.

Range Clipping. When FP32 values are so vast, it may not be feasible to cover the whole range with a restricted bit width. We need to eliminate outliers in the data distribution in this situation. Figure 4.4 illustrates a process known as range clipping, which may be summarized as follows:

$$\texttt{clip}(r; a, b) = \min\{\max\{r, a\}, b\}. \tag{4.16}$$

Integer Rounding. After performing the division, the results need to be rounded to match the INT8 quantization integer type. One of the most prominent approaches is to use the *Stochastic Rounding* method [179], which is defined as:

$$\texttt{round}(r) = \begin{cases} \lfloor x \rfloor, & w.p. \quad 1 - \dfrac{x - \lfloor x \rfloor}{\delta} \\ \lfloor x \rfloor + \delta, & w.p. \quad \dfrac{x - \lfloor x \rfloor}{\delta} \end{cases}, \tag{4.17}$$

where δ represents the smallest interval of the fixed-point numbers with the given bit width. Combining the integer rounding, the common formulation of quantization can be finally described as:

$$q = \text{round}\left(\frac{\texttt{clip}(r; a, b)}{\texttt{scale}(a, b; n)} + z\right). \tag{4.18}$$

Based on the above discussion, there are two primary application scenarios for on-device learning quantization algorithms: (1) *Post-training Quantization* (PTQ) for inference and (2) *Quantization-aware Training* (QAT) for online learning.

4.2.3.2 Post-Training Quantization

The network models can be immediately quantified in inference without the need for additional re-training. The *Post-training Qunatiztion* (PTQ) [180] is a term for these kinds of techniques. In order to dynamically change the quantized domain and confine the tensor values to integer data types, PTQ often works in conjunction with fine-tuning systems that use the scale parameter as a fundamental element. It is necessary to record the maximum and lowest values in each layer, since the scale parameter is dependent on each tensor weight in each layer. As the data distributions vary widely across multiple layers and channels, the single scale parameter needs to be generated in the layer or channel-wise granularity to reflect the value range features.

Weights and biases may be readily managed by quantizing them after being updated at the end of training. In addition, the activations can be quantized following the data distribution of the original FP32 tensors for higher model quality. Before deploying a model, it is practical to gather all of the activation information, *i.e.,* using the *offline* mechanism. Performing a few trial calibrations on the initial FP32-based model is required to provide this critical information to the on-device learning framework. Thus, the relevant scale parameter can be adjusted without additional modification. Although the offline approach cannot anticipate all possible data distributions, the outside values should be clipped before the inference, resulting in lower prediction accuracy. Since the maximum and lowest runtime values for each of the tensors can be measured online, we can bypass the range clipping constraint. In addition, it is essential to mention that this dynamic inspection will need additional computations, which will increase the burden of the learning process.

Recent studies have revealed that PTQ-based approaches cannot well preserve model quality when using INT8 data [239,271]. More seriously, models like MobileNet [212] and ShuffleNet [613] models are not able t adapt since the limited representation capacity in the INT8 model may not be able to capture all of the learning information that was initially included in their design.

4.2.3.3 Quantization-Aware Training

The burst of data flow on computing primitives (such as CPU and GPU) often leads to the bottleneck for the whole system in a real-world setting because of the restricted I/O bandwidth of machines. Additionally, current neural network models typically include a significant number of parameters, such as megabytes in ResNet-like models [198,576]. The quantity of network traffic generated by transmitting these parameters necessitates a prolonged flow completion time. The ML framework time consumption is dominated by communication of data flow inside and among machines, which will reduce system performance. Since extreme accuracy is required in digital calculations, machines often represent real numbers in the form of 32-bit or 64-bit float-point values (FPV) [460]. However, this will put a heavy burden on the computer's processing power, memory footprint and bandwidth consumption. As a result of the rich redundancy of the statistics in neural networks, a certain amount of representation mistakes or data noise will not yield significant impact on the outcome output [360]. The resource bottleneck may be alleviated in part by reducing the amount of data that is represented in the neural network. A typical example of this reduction is the activation function, as well as weights, biases and gradients. An essential factor in the quantization process is to prevent the introduction of substantial cumulative error, while still representing the data in a low precision manner.

Currently, methods used in the industry include 16-bit float [179] and 8-bit fixed-point [79] representations. NVIDIA Pascal GPUs can natively represent, compute and store intermediate results in 16 bits due to the processing units using the 16-bit float-point format [24]. Additionally, the NumPy toolbox also contains a programming framework that allows researchers to work with 16-bit numbers without sacrificing accuracy [419]. Even more impressive fact is that ML applications, such as DL inference on mobile phones [539] and edge devices [132], can benefit greatly from the 8-bit fixed-point format. The *Binarized Neural Network* (BNN) [344] have been extensively investigated for their potential to speed up model training, by using data quantization based on binary [564], ternary [346], XNOR [444] and variable-length [628] representation. For forward propagation, BNNs use just two types of weights: -1 and $+1$, which dramatically decreases the computational cost and improves training performance over their float-point format based counterparts [97].

When converting an FP32-based model to INT8 without retraining, the model quality and prediction accuracy could be degraded, making it challenging to fulfill the criteria of on-device learning. Therefore, *Quantization-aware Training* (QAT) [620] is developed to overcome the aforementioned problems. Quantization of both forward and backward propagation phases is included in the whole training process of QAT algorithms, which differ from fixed PTQ-based systems and use a low bit width to simplify the weight, activation and gradient data representation. The system-level performance barrier caused by restricted I/O bandwidth, small memory capacity and scarce computing primitives may be effectively eased by using QAT. Therefore, the processing speed of on-device learning tasks can be significantly improved. Figure 4.5 illustrate the QAT pipeline in a specific layer, with the FP and BP phases of the training process.

FP Stage. Weights and activations are quantized in the forward propagation (FP) [625]. Data and weights are quantized into INT8 format before being used in the matrix calculations, such as FC layer dot product and CONV layer convolution multiplication, to make sure they are compatible with each other. Then, the activation function's output is quantized with the optional batch normalization, which calibrates the distribution of intermediate values [387]. In addition, range clipping is required for quantized activations to better fit the data distribution [89]. Before being utilized as an input to another layer, the encoded data must first be dequantized to

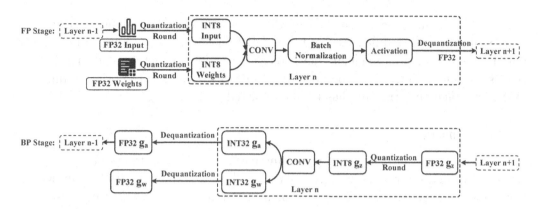

Figure 4.5 The workflow of QAT of FP and BP stages.

FP32 format by scaling the magnification used in quantization. A new independent scale factor determined by the next layer's value distribution is applied to the FP32 input in the next layer, which results in a re-quantization of the data. There are diverse scale factors for each layer in FP phase. Hence, the layers will employ different quantization and dequantization techniques, sequentially applying them in the whole network.

BP Stage. For backward propagation (BP) quantization, the partial differential used to calculate gradients will be applied in a chain-based manner, from the last to the first layer [435]. Prior to the differential operation, the gradients of the final layer will be quantized in the INT8 format, which includes both activation and weights. As a result, the INT8 data format is used to determine the activation gradients and weights of the current layer. This layer needs to be dequantized into FP32 format and the model parameters are updated in complete precision for higher optimization accuracy, when calculating the total gradients [631]. As a result, so as to update the model in the FP32 data type, a duplication of the primary weights and activations with complete accuracy is required.

Gradient Sketch. Distributed on-device learning can minimize communication traffic between workers by reducing the requirement to communicate data at the gradient level [238,245,455]. Various sketch approaches use discrete values as an approximation of the multivariate tensor functions. The frequency [96] and quantile [165] sketches are the two most often used techniques for quantizing gradients and speeding up flow transmitting. The significant distinction between the two is that the former relies on element occurrence frequency while the latter depends on the assessment of the tensor's value distribution. Due to the substantial estimation bias of the partial derivative operations, it is difficult to reach the optimum using standard gradient-based approaches when the quantized parameters map from a continuous distribution to integer-based discrete variables [360]. Furthermore, finite-difference estimators and continuous relaxation estimators can be used to solve this issue [19].

Before performing the inner multiplication between tensors, the weights and gradients are both compressed. INT8 is used primarily for arithmetic operations, which results in a significant decrease in processing time. In order to compensate for the rounding procedure, the weight and gradient tensors will be dequantized when the inner multiplication is finished. The FP and BP phases will be quantized repeatedly until the model is converged [620]. Low-precision weights and activations quantified in the last training iteration will be utilized for inference, which is the primary function of the FP stage once training has been completed.

4.2.3.4 Summary

In practice, data quantization is a promising method to address the performance bottleneck. The major target is to overcome the challenges of the limited I/O bandwidth, low memory capacity, scarce computational primitives and network transmission latency of on-device learning, which can be achieved by representing the data value relatively lowly precision while not compromising the final quality of model training. The PTQ quantization approach seeks to reduce the model size after complete training, which is often used in offline inference settings and does not need a massive quantity of data to be employed in offline inference scenarios. In contrast to fine-tuning and transfer learning, the QAT approach trains a quantized model from the start and has a better level of precision. It is clear that data quantization can be used in combination with other optimization strategies, such as network pruning and knowledge distillation, to minimize computational cost and speed up on-device learning further.

4.3 CHAPTER SUMMARY

As stated in this section, current strategies for optimizing neural network models are being explored. These techniques provide the potential for significant cost savings in terms of computing and communication overhead. These approaches make machine learning methods economical on small devices and enable AI applications to be used in everyday human activities, such as shopping and driving.

CHAPTER 5

Hardware-Level Design: Neural Engines and Tensor Accelerators

Implementing current machine learning (ML) applications requires not only neural network model design and algorithm level training optimization but also hardware support for deploying on-device learning tasks and increasing their processing speed in order to alleviate resource constraints. In this chapter, the on-device learning hardware implementation will be discussed in three primary elements to help readers accomplish this goal: (1) On-chip resource scheduling, (2) domain-specific hardware acceleration and (3) cross-device energy efficiency. To optimize the hardware implementation of on-device learning applications, it is important to consider these four optimization aspects to increase processing speed and enhance execution performance.

5.1 ON-CHIP RESOURCE SCHEDULING

5.1.1 Embedded Memory Controlling

One of the most important difficulties for on-device learning deployment is resolving the constraint of limited memory, since commodity learning applications generally depend on sophisticated neural networks that need a large memory footprint. Memory is often required during the runtime of on-device learning to store intermediate data and model parameters. The cost of in-memory connectivity is high for on-device applications since the data access speed in memory is substantially slower than in the CPU cache or registers. Furthermore, the RAM available on most edge devices is insufficient to run contemporary machine learning algorithms. For example, the storing of network and parameters for the relatively shallow ResNet18 model [198] generates gigabytes of memory footprint when dealing with image classification tasks.

As a result, a large amount of resource will be wasted if the on-device learning frameworks cannot well manage the memory ahead [132]. The SCALEDEEP system created by Venkataramani *et al.,* [530] uses the communication and computational aspects of model training to better optimize the memory allocation and interconnection across multiple machines. Prior knowledge of floating-point operation per second (FLOP) and the corresponding FLOP ratio in various layers of the neural network is used by SCALEDEEP, so as to improve memory management in a hierarchical design and reduce the cost of parameter synchronization. Data movement and fine-grained pipelining [406, 604], which overlap computation and communication, are used to improve embedded memory management efficiency for further [227, 435].

5.1.2 Underlying Computational Primitives

An important approach for on-device learning acceleration is to cope with the high computing overhead of the matrix operation, which demands optimization of computational capacity. In terms of decreasing computing load and speeding up processing, software-level optimizations can only provide incremental improvements. A popular research path is to build specialized computational primitives and the associated domain-specific instructions to control the hardware on the device.

To speed up distributed processing, specialized hardware has been explored extensively. DaDianNao [83], a multi-chip based system, was developed by Chen *et al* to speed up common machine learning applications. When it comes to large-scale neural network training, this approach takes into account of both the computational aspects of neural networks, as well as the communication patterns of internal connections using the Fat-Tree topology [10]. The principle of leveraging specialized hardware to simplify software calculations and speed up learning can be applied to on-device learning situations while these ML systems derived in the cloud.

As a result, the most important thing is to create a series of edge-specific computing primitives. For neural network processing speed, Jouppi *et al.*, developed an ASIC called *Tensor Processing Unit* (TPU) [254] and implemented these devices in Google's data center. The TPU-based machine may deliver up to 15 times and 30 times speedup over the commodity GPU and CPU, respectively, according to the assessment of typical ML workloads, including RNNs and LSTMs.

The neural engine in Apple CPUs [127] created for Animoji [21] and augmented reality applications on the iPhone is a relevant industrial case in point. Huawei's NPU in Kirin CPUs [418], on the other hand, aids with intelligent image rendering for portraits and night settings. As to the Xilinx neural network engines, Settle *et al.*, [468] presented a protocol for low-precision data representation, which implements quantization methods for 16 bits of floating point and 8 bits of fixed point data on a FPGA platform. Therefore, dedicated neural network chips, as opposed to commodity GPU-based devices, can also significantly speed up the training process.

5.1.3 Low-Level Arithmetical Instructions

Additional low-level instructions are needed for edge devices in order to properly use the hardware capacity. Domain-specific hardware refers to both the instructions and primitives used in such scenarios [280].

This has been a hot research topic with various works in the past decade. Phoenix [560], a quantization-aware processor, was developed by Wu et al. to solve the issues of poor hardware efficiency and accuracy loss while quantizing floating-point integers. Designing a floating-point multiplier with a width of 8 bits is the key instruction for reducing memory and computational overhead. The INT8 quantization is outperformed by these instructions, which are built into FPGA-based computers. A hardware acceleration system developed by McDanel et al. [381] attempts to improve the inference speed of learning applications by implementing the whole stack optimization methodologies on FPGA-based chips, including neural network models and computational paradigms and chip architecture. There is a decent balance between model accuracy and hardware efficiency in this system. Even more importantly, multiplication and division may be replaced with low-level left/right shifting instructions, which can be implemented on commodity CPUs and greatly reduce the computational cost. As a result, using specialized hardware and the underlying instructions to speed up on-device learning applications is an exciting research direction.

5.1.4 MIMO-Based Communication

The on-device learning scenario can be extended by using mobile communication to conduct the operation in a decentralized way. The system's efficiency will be hindered by the communication overhead in this scenario. As a result of advances in *Multiple-input Multiple-output* (MIMO) technology, on-device learning may now be conducted at a far lower cost. Typically, a MIMO-enabled equipment has a large number of antennas. The *over-the-air computation* computing makes use of the superposition feature in radio signals to allow a number of devices to broadcast their model updates at the same time, and the server immediately restores the cumulative of these changes. On-device training is greatly simplified thanks to the related encoding and decoding methods, which enhance the overall capabilities of wireless infrastructures.

Various mobile applications can benefit from MIMO-based solutions. The cell-free MIMO transmission was enhanced for federated learning across mobile devices by Vu et al. [534], which can be recognized as a distributed variant of on-device learning. The efficiency of energy conservation and processing speed can also be increased simultaneously by capturing the intrinsic interactions and transmission characteristics of training participants, which are two key variables for on-device learning.

Additionally, Huang et al. [225] devised the *Physical-Layer Arithmetic* (PhyArith) to take use of the physical layer's feature of coding approaches. The natural superposition of radio frequency (RF) signals on mobile devices helps encode gradients and interchange them with other partners when a learning job requires decentralized participation, taking account the demands of on-device learning. This physical-layer hardware compatibility may be used with the algorithm-level compression approaches (*e.g.*, data quantization) stated in this chapter to achieve the best possible results.

As a whole, over-the-air MIMO communication is well adapted to the edge device configuration and can significantly speed up the learning progress.

5.2 DOMAIN-SPECIFIC HARDWARE ACCELERATION

The coordination of the underlying hardware, which is essential to the deployment of all distributed ML architectures, is a crucial aspect of the theoretical study and algorithm optimization of ML applications. There are four areas of hardware implementation that we need to cover in this chapter: (1) Multiple Processing Primitives Scheduling, (2) I/O Connection Optimization, (3) Cache Management and (4) Topology Construction.

5.2.1 Multiple Processing Primitives Scheduling

In the industrial environment, approaches based on multiple compute primitives (e.g., GPU and CPU) are often used to manage large-scale ML applications [593]. ML workloads are often deployed in parallel on the GPU cluster due to the high computational resource requirements of model training [146]. One of the most critical aspects of system design in this situation is cluster management, which takes into account four factors: To begin, we must figure out how to reduce the average completion time of an ML project, assign tasks to the most qualified workers, efficiently distribute computational and bandwidth resources between them, and last, make this schedule available online. Effective cluster management is challenging in reality since the total knowledge of jobs and user choice task information is commonly unknown in advance. This challenge makes us to develop a scheduling method that can work with no complete knowledge [434].

Some intelligent and adaptive cluster managers have been developed to meet this requirement. Xiao et al. [568] developed the Gandiva, an introspective GPU cluster scheduling system, to take use of deep learning workloads and domain-specific expertise, in order to minimize job latency and increase model training efficiency. By using the intrinsic feature of the mini-batch based model training technique, Gandiva can forecast job characteristics in time. This enables Gandiva better manage the task processing scheme and adapt the computational operation to the numerous GPUs, so that the training efficiency in the cluster can be completely improved with this information. Tiresias [166], a GPU cluster manager without the need for previous knowledge, was proposed by Gu et al., by considering the constraints of time-sharing work scheduling and error job consolidation on Gandiva. Tiresias uses an age-based scheduler to dynamically reduce the average time to completion of tasks and assign them a class priority. Tiresias can effectively assign assignments to suitable workers without extra information from user-level requests by using the profile-based management paradigm.

5.2.2 I/O Connection Optimization

In many distributed ML systems, large-scale model training frequently requires the coordination of numerous GPUs and CPUs, which involves careful design of inter-primitive communication. Integrating these compute primitives is an impediment to task processing performance. Consequently, the workload scheduling and hardware connection topology must be taken into account by cluster administrators such that the limited computing capacity could well be assigned to appropriate workloads and make the cluster resources fully utilized.

For example, Kindratenko *et al.* [262] created a separate GPU framework that wraps CUDA to modify the APIs for device management and task scheduling. These APIs take into account the placement of the GPUs in the network architecture in order to reduce the amount of bandwidth required for communication. On the other hand, Faraji *et al.* [134] has designed a topology-aware GPU manager to improve the collective communication library and lower the execution time of MPI operations on distributed P2P GPUs [525]. Recent systems have focused on topology optimization by mapping link connections into dependency graphs, which are designed to produce GPU scheduling algorithms using graph embedding methods. Real-world GPU clusters are mainly composed of NVLink [141] and PCI-e [619] connections, where Amaral *et al.* [12] captured the advantages of these attributes to enhance the topology-aware inter-GPU communication.

5.2.3 Cache Management

When using deep neural networks (DNNs), the computing needs and cross-machine connections are commonly enormous. An effective cache management method is the key to building high-performance machine learning frameworks, since all of these criteria present a severe barrier to the coordination of distributed clusters. The attributes of processing tiles and compute chips, particularly in the cross-modality scenarios [196, 232, 244], must be considered while designing cache management. In addition, the distributed cache interconnection architecture among the devices also needs to fit the matrix computation and intermediate data permanence [428].

5.2.4 Topology Construction

Intermediate data sharing will lead to frequent I/O access and generate a large number of synchronized parameters in current machine learning systems, which are often implemented in decentralized collaborative schemes. When building models, the communication between computing primitives (such as a GPU and a CPU) takes up the majority of the per-iteration time, holding complicated flow characteristics. Conventional flow-aware scheduling and link connections become useless when the cluster is big. Considering this phenomenon, it is necessary to create a collective communication mechanism and capture its properties to govern the underlying network structure better.

When scheduling jobs in a high-performance distributed machine learning (ML) system, topology issues should be considered. The main goal of optimization is to reduce the average training time for ML while maintaining hardware and resource efficiency at a high level. For this reason, it is possible to develop task schedulers that consider network topology when scheduling tasks over several GPUs, such as the NVIDIA Collective Communications Library (NCCL) [134]. The Message Passing Interface (MPI) can also be used to manage the communication programming, providing adjustable parameter synchronization across the cluster nodes.

With the emergence of large-scale graph computing, topology-aware scheduling can be optimized by abstracting communication patterns and network connections into dependency graphs. Learning-based technologies, such as deep reinforcement learning and graph embedding neural networks [525], can be used to enhance inter-GPU communication systems.

5.3 CROSS-DEVICE ENERGY EFFICIENCY

Mobile technologies, such as wireless sensors, cell phones and Internet of Things (IoT) devices [243, 438], are increasingly used to handle large-scale distributed processing applications in green cities [144, 630]. Resource-constrained environments need consideration of aspects such as decreasing heat dissipation and conserving energy [606]. Energy internet (EI) [368, 523, 542] is a potential technology for generating and storing electricity in a "green" way as an essential foundation for implementing an energy management system. It is still a challenge to properly manage computation-intensive tasks (e.g., training neural networks [441]) through mobile devices for green cities despite the availability of specialised hardware (e.g., energy router [493]).

5.3.1 Multi-Client Collaboration

Many studies have been undertaken to minimize the energy cost of green city applications from energy management. Ashraf et al. [27] introduced multi-level queues to deal with data rates and decrease the communication time for IoT sensor devices. When it came to managing energy, Keerthisinghe et al. [260] developed an approximation offline approach that relied on machine learning to improve the efficiency of photovoltaic storage systems. Deshmukh et al. [110] developed an adaptive method to enhance the energy efficiency of specialized micro-grid networks by abstracting virtual energy production. In the work of Lu et al. [362], the performance of hybrid storage systems is increased by reducing energy consumption and expanding data storage capacity. Using an intelligent agent, Manbachi et al. [374] devised a new technique for energy management that enhanced the performance of customized microgrid networks. Nizami et al. [417] devised a decentralized energy management system for residential regions to optimize the power grid's offloading and consumption. Through collaborative edge computing, Ruan et al. [457] presented a priority-based strategy for reducing resource delay and improving processing efficiency.

5.3.2 Efficiency Analysis

On the other hand, existing techniques are mainly based on the optimization of energy scheduling. They require a comprehensive knowledge of resource information during task runtime, which is difficult to collect in advance, particularly in the cutting-edge scenario of distributed model training applications. There is also a lack of understanding of application-level features such as work completion deadlines and computational resource needs in these techniques, which concentrate on energy. Consequently, current methods cannot minimize energy costs while maintaining dispersed processing performance. With the constraints of prior research in mind, we may mutually

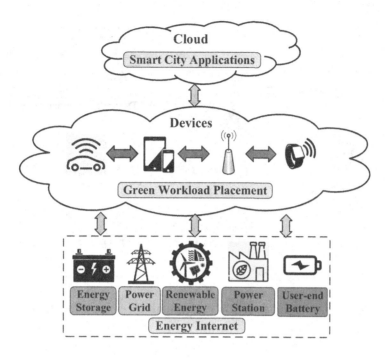

Figure 5.1 The energy internet in green cities.

discuss ways to save energy while still speeding up production. As an issue of task distribution, this aim is transferable.

There are several smart city applications in the cloud, each with its own set of device requirements, model complexity, data quantity and resource requirements. Figure 5.1 shows the context of the energy internet for green cities. A range of mobile devices (*e.g.,* smart cars, smartphones, personal hotspots and wearables) work together to handle these tasks, where the system must ensure that these applications are correctly prioritized. Because of the variety of hardware configurations, network conditions and application requirements, it is vital to plan the task scheduling approach thoroughly. In addition, the realistic training model is quite large, typically surpassing the computing power and memory storage of a single device. As a result, model parallelism (*i.e.,* the division of the model into many pieces) is required [228]. The models are then allocated to separate devices, so that each device may do a local computation with its restricted resources. After each cycle, the cloud side will blend the interim findings from various devices into the global model. The following iteration begins with all the devices re-entering the new data. This iterative method is kept in progress to complete the model convergence. Various energy sources such as chemical energy storage, power grids, renewable energies, conventional power station and user-end batteries provide power to the device cluster throughout the energy internet. When the neurons and functions are assigned, varying devices have different energy and computation requirements. Therefore, aiming at minimizing energy consumption and work completion time, the key for effectively handling the job

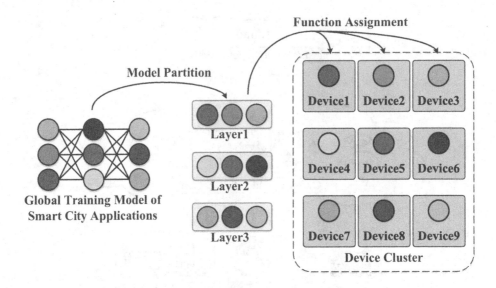

Figure 5.2 Model partition and function assignment for large-scale distributed training jobs in smart cities.

operation is to partition the training model into manageable subsets and assign the relevant neurons to the appropriate devices.

With the targets mentioned above, it's possible to formulate a workload allocation issue that considers the dynamic runtime aspects and non-linear limitations of the resources. This issue can be solved using multi-action deep reinforcement learning (DRL) since standard optimization approaches cannot solve it directly [121, 203, 498]. Introducing DRL-based strategies to increase energy internet performance is not new, there are some existing works focusing on this combination. Glavic et al. [159] examined current technologies that use DRL-based optimization to regulate the energy internet systems. An essential step for green city applications is to establish a green workload method that minimizes both cumulative energy costs and average task completion time. A multi-action DRL agent can be created by using the *proximal policy optimization* (PPO) [347, 465, 549] method, which is based on the *actor-critic* [4, 514] network, so as to achieve the above-mentioned goals simultaneously.

5.3.3 Problem Formulation for Energy Saving

The model training procedures in green cities are often complex due to the limited resources. Hence, large-scale deep learning (DL) tasks are often split among several devices to use the limited resources better. We can split the model into several devices based on the sequence of the layers, which is illustrated in Figure 5.2. For the most part, a neuron corresponds to a distinct function on the graph highlighted in various colors. The time and energy required to complete a task vary depending on which device a neuron is assigned. There is a high correlation between total time spent on task calculation and communication across the network in an energy internet scenario. Since we want to minimize work completion time and save energy costs, we

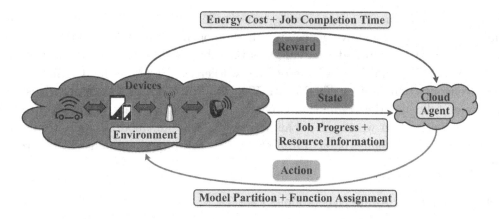

Figure 5.3 The workflow of the DRL-based green workload placement approach.

must carefully consider partitioning the model amongst devices. The method used to achieve this goal's optimization is referred to as *green workload allocation*.

5.3.4 Algorithm Design and Pipeline Overview

When using the learning-based method to tackle the challenge outlined in *Sec.* 5.3.3, it is essential to dynamically divide the global training model and allocate the compute functions to various devices, so as to reduce energy consumption and task completion time. As shown in Figure 5.3, it is promising to use DRL method to achieve this goal, where the agent's action must be considered, depending on the environmental state and reward feedback. We can use the *proximal policy optimization* (PPO) [347, 465, 549] approach with the *actor-critic* [4, 514] network and build the green workload allocation algorithm, considering the live environment of large-scale distributed processing in smart cities. The DRL agent is placed on the parameter server in the cloud, which contains the critic and actor model. At the beginning of each iteration, the agent gathers the execution state of all mobile devices and adjusts the strategy for model partition and function assignment among the cluster. PPO neural networks (actor and critic) are optimized based on real-time input on task completion time and energy cost from the agent. The PPO agent can eventually learn how to do the near-optimal action to achieve green workload allocation via the iterative method of action, state, and reward. The Markov Decision Process (MDP) [289, 335] governs this learning process since the agent's actions are solely dependent on the present state of the system . As a result, the suggested algorithm can generate a proper allocation strategy according to the most recent action of the DRL agent.

5.4 DISTRIBUTED ON-DEVICE LEARNING

A practical methodology to implement distributed Deep Learning (DL) applications [311, 312] is to adopt the parameter server (PS) architecture [5, 77, 88, 98, 206, 213, 230, 244, 578]. Co-designing hardware utility, communication overhead and the training convergence time are essential to an effective PS system's performance [5, 213, 230, 247, 311]. As real-world clusters are usually heterogeneous in terms of network circumstances and processing capacity [69, 397, 488], PS systems take more time to reach training convergence over the homogeneous environments [244]. There have been past attempts at resolving this issue by emphasizing quick workers' contributions and minimizing the role of slow workers, *i.e.,* training models in a nearly homogeneous configuration [69, 73, 244, 504]. One problem of this approach is that it cannot fully use the computing capacity of sluggish workers, while the other is that it may lead to workload imbalances while building models. As a result, the *Community-aware Synchronous Parallel* (CASP) technique can be used to overcome these restrictions.

5.4.1   Community-Aware Synchronous Parallel

Abstraction of Community. The term *community* refers to a group of devices working together. PS cluster workers will be divided into numerous communities for better synchronization and communication in order to eliminate any impact from the diverse environment. The following are the primary factors to describe this abstraction. Iteration significance and computation capacity are three features of intra-cluster similarity that each worker has in high-cohesion communities. In other words, there should be little inter-cluster resemblance across communities with low coupling. Division standards need to adapt to a wide range of environments, with varying levels of model complexity.

Community-aware Parameter Server. The server-worker architecture is often used in parameter server systems. DL task training can be decomposed into numerous epochs, each with a large number of iterations. There are four steps in an iteration: (1) *Pulling*, (2) *computation*, (3) *pushing* and (4) *updating*. Once the latest parameters have been fetched from servers, workers will train models locally before pushing updated parameters back to servers. When all of the local models have been merged, the server changes the global parameters for the training in subsequent iterations.

Instead of managing the cluster in fine-grained granularity for each worker, we manage the cluster as a community, which serves as a scheduling unit for the whole cluster. Synchronizing gradients can be regarded as the cooperation between these communities once workers have been separated into groups. This operation can be handled by the Community-aware Synchronous Parallel (CASP). The PS cluster is restructured as a server-community structure, inside which workers with similar interests are clustered together. A master-worker and a number of slave worker are the major components of each community.

With the help of slave workers, the master-worker serves as an aggregator of the gradients calculated by these workers and creates the community model. As to the synchronous mode, gathering and scattering techniques are used to interact between the master-worker and the slave workers. The logical central server maintains the global model and organizes all communities. Local models are uploaded to the server, and the most recent global models are downloaded by each community. Asynchronous transmission and receiving methods are also used by the communities to connect with the server. We introduce the SSP scheme to control the inter-community synchronization, where the hyperparameters (such as staleness threshold and learning rate) are defined at the community leve. In general, CASP follows BSP for intra-community synchronization and SSP is used to manage the inter-community synchronization.

5.4.2 Infrastructure Design

The server-community topology can be used to construct CASP. The community manager, weight learner and distributed training controller are the three essential server-side components. All of the slave workers in each community are under the direct management of one or more master workers. It is possible to put the dataset on a global file system, where each worker searches for the data they need for training by looking up the data hash index. There will be a detailed discussion of these modules in the following section.

5.4.3 Community Manager

Unsupervised clustering concepts can be applied to dividing the workforce into separate communities. As a result, the following measures may help us manage communities. The initial step in clustering a community is to identify representative features which can be used to describe each worker. To calculate the distance between workers, it is necessary to use a distance metric that accurately represents the importance of each feature value. Attribute vector weights are critical to distance measurement. Following the weights of each feature have been determined, we must adopt an effective clustering approach to divide communities correctly.

We have two options when it comes to dynamically adjusting the community configuration during dispersed training jobs for greater convergence efficiency, since it is hard to know the ideal community number priorly. First, the clustering algorithm may automatically regulate the amount of communities by using *Distance Metric Learning* (DisML) [579] to determine appropriate weights. Second, there are two ways for identifying the number of communities and their weights using Reinforcement Learning (RL). *Density-Based Spatial Clustering of Applications with Noise* (DBSCAN) [128] (DBSCAN) and *Asynchronous Advantage Actor-Critic* (A3C) [389] can be used to accomplish the first option (A3C). Using DBSCAN, we found that the worst-case computational complexity was $O(n^2)$, where n is the number of workers. Because of this, we will cover the A3C-based method used in CASP rather than the DisML-based DBSCAN. In addition, the convergence perfromance of CASP will be measured against DisML in order to provide a suitable baseline comparison.

5.4.4 Weight Learner

With the right weights, it is possible to separate communities into distinct communities. DisML and A3C are the two approaches we will use to achieve this target.

5.4.4.1 Distance Metric Learning

Using a static configuration, DisML generates the weight of each characteristic for use in image classification on Alexnet [273] using CIFAR-10 [272] dataset. Keep in mind that the relative importance of each characteristic is normalized to a float value between zero (the least important) and one (the most important). For each attribute, the default Weight is one, indicating all characteristics are equally important. Capacity at the computing level is plainly critical, whereas network condition is only of minor importance. Due to the fact that network configurations used to create instances are often near-homogeneous, cloud instances do not have a lot of heterogeneity in terms of their network conditions. Worker-server bandwidth ranged from 5 to 10 Gbps in preliminary tests. It is possible that a different network setting has little impact on training time. To make weight learning more effective, we choose to remove this property in A3C. Furthermore, since DisML generates weights in advance and cannot alter them as training progresses, it cannot capture the significance of task-level importance. The performance of DisML is hampered by the agnostic to task-level attributes. Since the A3C-based technique takes advantage of this feature and dynamically changes the weights, the full potential of CASP can be completely realized.

5.4.4.2 Asynchronous Advantage Actor-Critic

By adopting A3C, the correct weights for community clustering can be determined in the learner module for weights. Because there is a large configuration space for community partition, we utilize A3C to learn the attribute weights and then use the weights for community clustering, instead of making A3C determine the community configuration directly. For instance, the configuration space for a 15-worker cluster is over 1.3 billion, which exceeds the device computational capacity using typical optimization approaches.

For each learner in A3C, it uses a hyper-thread in a repeated mechanism. At each step, the A3C agent performs an action based on its current state, and learns from this feedback reward in order to optimize the corresponding neural networks (the actor and critic). The optimized models are eventually be learned by the actor-critic agent through a succession of actions, states and rewards, so that they can finally output the near-optimal parameters and an appropriate community number based on the current state. Agents use the *Markov Decision Process* (MDP) to learn by simply acting on the current state. This reduces training convergence time by updating action depending on attribute weights and community numbers. As a result, it is possible to build a community configuration using these weights and clustering results.

A3C learning is commlonly implemented on a server with a multi-core CPU, and multiprocessing is introduced to further speed up the learning rate. Each hyper-thread of a core in the CPU may independently perform actor-critic network learning, and one of these hyper-threads accumulates all of the learning outcomes from the other hyper-threads. In the same amount of time, CASP is able to get substantially more information thanks to this method. This means that A3C may automatically adapt the action based on the job progress and produce near-optimal attribute weights, as well as the community number. Keep in mind that if we utilize DBSCAN based on DisML for community clustering, the computational complexity would be significant, increasing the server-side overhead. The lightweight *prototype-based clustering* approach may be used to segment communities since A3C determines the community number. For example, the K-means clustering [372], which has a lower computational cost, is a practical option.

5.4.4.3 Agent Learning Methodology

With the above modules to establish the distance measurement metrics, we can formulate the A3C agent based on the *surrogate objective* [465]. The gist of our methodology is that the policy $\pi(a_k|s_k; \boldsymbol{\theta}_k)$ after updating will be more advisable to maximize the long-term reward, over the previous policy. We can formulate the expected gain $E_{\pi(\boldsymbol{\theta})}[\mathcal{G}]$ of the policy $\pi(\boldsymbol{\theta})$ as:

$$E_{\pi(\boldsymbol{\theta})}[\mathcal{G}] = E_{\pi(\boldsymbol{\theta}_k)}[\mathcal{G}] + E_{\pi(\boldsymbol{\theta})}\left[\sum_{t=0}^{+\infty} \gamma_t a_{\pi(\boldsymbol{\theta})}(\mathcal{S}_t, \mathcal{A}_t)\right], \tag{5.1}$$

where γ_t is the discount factor of the step t. Also, $a_{\pi(\boldsymbol{\theta})}$ is the action according to the polity $\pi(\boldsymbol{\theta})$, under the restriction of the state space $\mathcal{S}_t$ and action space $\mathcal{A}_t$. Our target is to maximize the expected return $E_{\pi(\boldsymbol{\theta})}[\mathcal{G}]$, which can be achieved by maximizing $E_{\pi(\boldsymbol{\theta})}\left[\sum_{t=0}^{+\infty} \gamma_t a_{\pi(\boldsymbol{\theta})}(\mathcal{S}_t, \mathcal{A}_t)\right]$. Here, we can replace the expectation of $\mathcal{A}_t \sim \pi(\boldsymbol{\theta})$ via the expectation of $\mathcal{A}_t \sim \pi(\boldsymbol{\theta}_k)$. This transformation can be described as:

$$E_{\mathcal{S}_t\sim\pi(\boldsymbol{\theta}),\mathcal{A}_t\sim\pi(\boldsymbol{\theta})}[a_{\pi_k}(\mathcal{S}_t, \mathcal{A}_t)] =$$
$$E_{\mathcal{S}_t\sim\pi(\boldsymbol{\theta}),\mathcal{A}_t\sim\pi(\boldsymbol{\theta}_k)}\left[\frac{\pi(\mathcal{A}_t|\mathcal{S}_t; \boldsymbol{\theta})}{\pi(\mathcal{A}_t|\mathcal{S}_t; \boldsymbol{\theta}_k)} a_{\pi(\boldsymbol{\theta}_k)}(\mathcal{S}_t, \mathcal{A}_t)\right], \tag{5.2}$$

where a_{π_k} represents the action based on the updated policy of step k. Due to the hardness of calculating the expectation of $\mathcal{S}_t \sim \pi(\boldsymbol{\theta})$ directly, we can use the approximate expectation of $\mathcal{S}_t \sim \pi(\boldsymbol{\theta}_k)$ and rewrite Eq. (5.2) as:

$$E_{\mathcal{S}_t\sim\pi(\boldsymbol{\theta}),\mathcal{A}_t\sim\pi(\boldsymbol{\theta})}[a_{\pi_k}(\mathcal{S}_t, \mathcal{A}_t)] \approx$$
$$E_{\mathcal{S}_t\sim\pi(\boldsymbol{\theta}_k),\mathcal{A}_t\sim\pi(\boldsymbol{\theta}_k)}\left[\frac{\pi(\mathcal{A}_t|\mathcal{S}_t; \boldsymbol{\theta})}{\pi(\mathcal{A}_t|\mathcal{S}_t; \boldsymbol{\theta}_k)} a_{\pi(\boldsymbol{\theta}_k)}(\mathcal{S}_t, \mathcal{A}_t)\right]. \tag{5.3}$$

Moreover, we can get the approximate expression $\hat{\mathcal{G}}(\boldsymbol{\theta})$ of $E_{\pi(\boldsymbol{\theta})}[\mathcal{G}]$ as follows:

$$\hat{\mathcal{G}}(\boldsymbol{\theta}) = E_{\pi(\boldsymbol{\theta}_k)}[\mathcal{G}] +$$
$$E_{\mathcal{S}_t\sim\pi(\boldsymbol{\theta}_k),\mathcal{A}_t\sim\pi(\boldsymbol{\theta}_k)}\left[\sum_{t=0}^{+\infty} \gamma_t \frac{\pi(\mathcal{A}_t|\mathcal{S}_t; \boldsymbol{\theta})}{\pi(\mathcal{A}_t|\mathcal{S}_t; \boldsymbol{\theta}_k)} a_{\pi(\boldsymbol{\theta}_k)}(\mathcal{S}_t, \mathcal{A}_t)\right], \tag{5.4}$$

where $\hat{\mathcal{G}}(\boldsymbol{\theta})$ and $E_{\pi(\boldsymbol{\theta})}[\mathcal{G}]$ own the same value of $E_{\pi(\boldsymbol{\theta}_k)}[\mathcal{G}]$ and gradient at the point of $\boldsymbol{\theta} = \boldsymbol{\theta}_k$. Therefore, we can increase the expected gain and update the policy parameters by following the gradient direction. The optimization rule can be formulated as:

$$E_{\mathcal{S}_t\sim\pi(\boldsymbol{\theta}_k),\mathcal{A}_t\sim\pi(\boldsymbol{\theta}_k)}\left[\sum_{t=0}^{+\infty} \gamma_t \frac{\pi(\mathcal{A}_t|\mathcal{S}_t; \boldsymbol{\theta})}{\pi(\mathcal{A}_t|\mathcal{S}_t; \boldsymbol{\theta}_k)} a_{\pi(\boldsymbol{\theta}_k)}(\mathcal{S}_t, \mathcal{A}_t)\right]. \tag{5.5}$$

Combining the updating property of the PPO agent, we can finally rewrite the optimization objective as:

$$E_{\pi(\boldsymbol{\theta}_k)}\left[\min\left(\frac{\pi(\mathcal{A}_t|\mathcal{S}_t;\boldsymbol{\theta})}{\pi(\mathcal{A}_t|\mathcal{S}_t;\boldsymbol{\theta}_k)}a_{\pi(\boldsymbol{\theta}_k)}\left(\mathcal{S}_t,\mathcal{A}_t\right)+\xi\right)\right], \tag{5.6}$$

where $\xi = \varepsilon|a_{\pi(\boldsymbol{\theta}_k)}\left(\mathcal{S}_t,\mathcal{A}_t\right)|$ and the hyper-parameter ε satisfies $\varepsilon \in (0,1)$. With this equation, we can optimize the synchronization efficiency in long term and eliminate huge fluctuations between two steps.

5.4.5 Distributed Training Controller

CASP Infrastructure uses a specific module, the distributed training controller, to conduct distributed training based on the clustering manager and weight learner settings. Note that the inter- and intra-community synchronization schemes are both under its control. In each round, the former uses communication with an imposed synchronization, whereas the latter uses asynchronous communication with a delay bound.

5.4.5.1 Intra-Community Synchronization

The imposed synchronization may be used for intra-community synchronization due to the obvious premise that all members of a community have comparable computational power. When all workers are required to update parameters with strong consistency, BSP is a good contender since it provides an explicit barrier at the completion of every iteration.

A community has two types of workers: A master worker and a group of slave workers. Slave workers begin an iteration by requesting the most recent model parameter from the master worker. Once the calculation is complete, each slave worker calculates the gradient using the model parameters. Local gradients will be pushed to the master-worker as soon as all slave workers have finished their tasks. Finally, the master workers integrate these gradients and adjust the intra-community model parameters for subsequent processing.

5.4.5.2 Inter-Community Synchronization

As long as the distance between the fastest and slowest communities does not exceed the staleness criterion, communities may undertake parameter synchronization asynchronously. The server may monitor all communities by coordinating with all the master workers in the community. Community members exchange parameters with the aggregate server in A3C's workflow process.

Generally, the server gathers all of the parameters from each master worker, calculates the global parameters, and responds to pull requests from the communities. The asynchronous peer-to-peer transmission technique used here differs from the broadcasting strategy used for intra-community communication. The master-workers can support iteration development inside their own communities without being restricted by slower communities, in order to keep the staleness threshold at a reasonable level.

5.4.5.3 *Communication Traffic Aggregation*

The gradients determined by each slave worker might be aggregated on the master-worker in order to decrease the communication traffic between the slave workers. Consequently, for each community, the master-worker is deployed with a parameter cache to aggregate gradients.

To minimize the loss function, real-world distributed training tasks employ textitStochastic Gradient Descent (SGD) [326], which is based on concurrent data processing. Element-wise addition may be used to merge the gradient matrices of several slave workers into a single tensor. By using the parameter cache, this tensor will be buffered and serialized for network transmission. The server does not get the updated settings from these slave workers. The intra-community updates will be gathered by two master workers, who will serialize them into packages. A serialized tensor, for example, is created by combining the gradients of two slave workers. Keep in mind that these operations will be repeated by other master workers.

As a result, the server is finally able to receive gradients from all workers, lowering significant network demand on the server and decreasing communication traffic between master workers.

5.5 CHAPTER SUMMARY

Model compression is a potential strategy for reducing computing overhead and increasing processing speed in ML systems, which are generally constrained by limited computational resources. Research into how to perform machine learning tasks on mobile and edge devices has been a hot topic in recent years. In order to maximize training acceleration, model compression methods can be integrated into the design of specialized hardware. New-generation mobile phones and computational primitives might leverage FPGA chips that allow 8-bit or fewer float-point operations to implement the data quantization approach (e.g., NVIDIA Ampere architecture or Apple CoreML framework).

It is also necessary to have the appropriate hardware to use neural network architecture and training algorithm optimization properly. We inspect this problem from multiple aspects to demonstrate the relationship between real-world on-device learning requirements and hardware implementation. Researchers might use this conversation to develop learning frameworks. The introduction of model compression into specialized hardware design is thus still an open issue that requires more investigation.

CHAPTER 6

Infrastructure-Level Design: Serverless and Decentralized Machine Learning

Nowadays, cloud computing has become a promising technology that holds its importance in the Internet of Things (IoT) and smart cities/homes [302,303]. Traditionally, the cloud applications with Infrastructure-as-a-Service (IaaS) deployment, especially in enterprise application architectures, are instantiated, operated and managed in cloud servers by network service providers, and their demanded resources (computing resource, storage resource, memory, etc.) are reserved exclusively for a long term in clouds [325, 340, 370]. Nevertheless, it will inevitably lead to a low level of resource utilization and management, because of the inefficient resource allocation and retainment in cloud servers [306,308,310,469].

Therefore, it has attracted enormous attention from worldwide researchers in academic and industrial fields to develop an elastic and flexible service platform with an on-demand manner to achieve a higher resource utilization [75,307]. To this end, many global IT giants, such as Google, Facebook and Amazon are contributing to the emergence of serverless computing to provide elastic network services and avoid keeping a large amount of resources continuously engaged, rather than the traditional cloud computing services [33,304,309].

6.1 SERVERLESS COMPUTING

6.1.1 Definition of Serverless Computing

According to the existing literature, the authors in [253] delivered a Berkeley View for the concept of serverless computing in 2019, which is commonly acknowledged. The detailed definition of the serverless computing in Berkeley View is given as follows.

DOI: 10.1201/9781003340225-6

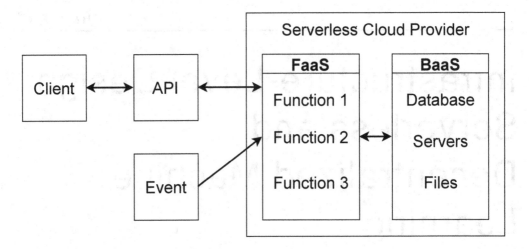

Figure 6.1 An example of a serverless computing platform.

- The serverless computing concept is comprised of Function-as-a-Service (FaaS) and Backend-as-a-Service (BaaS). The cloud applications are packed to provision cloud services with isolation and invocation in the light of FaaS. Meanwhile, the cloud services are provided with Backend support, e.g., database management, cloud storage and Application Programming Interfaces (APIs), in terms of BaaS.

- The FaaS model follows a pay-as-you-go manner, where the network service users only need to pay for the function when it is used. To this end, a service (application) is decomposed into a series of functions or microservices at the function level.

- The BaaS model enables the developers to focus on the frontend without the hassle of thinking about the backend. Then the developers incline to adopt event-driven and high-level programming to simplify the utilization of the cloud resources.

Figure 6.1 illustrates an example of a serverless computing platform.

In general, serverless computing emerges as a new trend to bring about resource-efficient computing based on cloud computing, through packing services as isolated functions running in ephemeral containers to facilitate deployment and management of services. Serverless computing then caters to the prevailing event-driven service execution, which is essential in the paradigm of Internet of Things (IoT), in order to improve resource efficiency, and mitigate latency and hosting cost. The authors in [9] claimed that it reduces the hosting costs by 66% to 95% through executing a cloud application under a serverless computing architecture. Moreover, the edge computing technique further accelerates the processing of IoT services on a serverless computing platform [67].

Figure 6.2 illustrates an example of a serverless application. It can be seen that the client deploys function **F1** to send a data retrieving request to the database. After

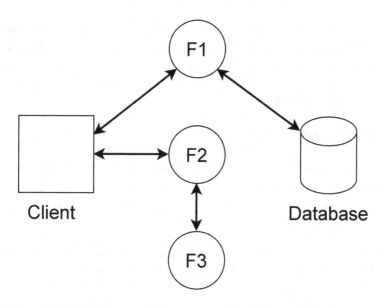

Figure 6.2 An example of a serverless application.

function **F1** receives the data from the database, the data will then be sent to the client. In another case, the client first deploys function **F2**. Then function **F2** will invokes another function **F3**, which will be executed to obtain a result. Finally, the result will be sent to the client by function **F2**.

In the following, we identify the main features and characteristics of serverless computing:

- **Auto-scaling.** Derived from the FaaS model, a serverless system endows functions the inherency to automatically scales horizontally or vertically in the case of experiencing workload dynamics. For example, if there exists no active function running in a serverless platform, then the serverless platform automatically become idle, i.e., scaling to zero, to refrain from wasting resources. However, when a function starts from scratch (scaling from zero), the function has to face the cold startup procedure, i.e., environment initialization and loading, etc. Therefore, such a cold startup procedure heavily influences the Quality of Services (QoS).

- **Flexible scheduling.** The serverless platform leverages the multi-region collaboration to offer robust and agile services. In other words, the serverless platform determines an efficient scheduling to make utilization of multiple available servers in a cluster to make sure workload balancing among servers while fulfilling the QoS requirements of users. The flexible scheduling of the serverless platform distributes the workload to dodge unpredictable server crashes and guarantee service resiliency and continuity.

- **Event-driven.** Over a serverless computing platform, the applications are triggered by their specific events, e.g., information queries, message updates and data storage. It can be seen that such a binding between applications and events contributes to the service encapsulation and the efficient coordination among a series of events. According to the CloudEvents specifications from Cloud-Native Computing Foundation (CNCF), the common event metadata are elaborated to enhance interoperability.

- **Transparent development.** Hiding the backend by the serverless platform, the users are agnostic about the execution environment, and needless to understand how to manipulate the underlying host resources. On the other hand, the cloud service vendors are supposed to isolate sandboxes and construct a reliable execution environment, which provides transparent deployment instructions and parameterized information to users.

- **Pay-as-you-go.** Now it comes to the billing model of serverless computing, which relates to capital expenses, rather than operating expenses. In this way, the users are no longer necessary to rent or buy dedicated servers. Through uniting resources (e.g., CPU, storage resource and memory resource) of cooperative cloud servers, users will be only charged for the needed resources of the demanded services, rather than being required to pay for a specific amount of resource which may or may not be fully used [301].

The aim of the serverless computing paradigm is categorized by researchers as follows.

- Relieve the service users from figuring out how to manipulate the cloud platforms or infrastructures.

- Adopt the pay-as-you-go model, instead of the traditional billing model for cloud services; and

- Automatically scale the services to cater to the dynamic demands of each service user.

6.1.2 Architecture of Serverless Computing

In this section, we analyze the architecture of serverless computing, which is decoupled into four layers: Virtualization layer, encapsulation layer, system orchestration layer and system coordination layer.

6.1.2.1 Virtualization Layer

The virtualization layer isolates each service function in a sandbox with high security. The cloud vendors usually utilize containers or virtual machines to create such sandboxes for isolation, which provide codes for applications, system environment, function dependencies and running libraries. Then the virtualization layer refrains users from accessing different resources in a general cloud platform.

6.1.2.2 Encapsulation Layer

The encapsulation layer consists of a series of dedicated middlewares, and generates customized triggers for event executions, gathering information for efficient communication. These middlewares distinguish the various features and the underlying logic of services, while coupling the diverse functions and the cloud platform.

The encapsulation layer also adopts a prewarm pool to accelerate the startup procedures of functions. There are the following strategies. The prewarm pool is built by analyzing the patterns and using a prediction mechanism, then the serverless system can be prewarmed by a one-to-one or one-for-all approach. Such a prewarm pool can be built with the following methods:

- **One-to-one prewarm pool with a fixed size.** In this method, a prewarm pool is generated with a fixed size for each service function. Then whenever a new user request arrives, the corresponding codes are loaded and invoked. In order to protect privacy, the one-to-one prewarm pool makes each user privacy inaccessible, through constructing analyzers that are user-level, and only the analyzers are able to approach the privacy of users. In other words, the one-to-one prewarm pool prevents the leakage of the service function portraits, and the encapsulation obstructs the malicious users or devices.

  Through constructing one-to-one prewarm pools with fixed sizes, the serverless computing platform guarantees the reliability and stability of provided function services.

- **One-to-one prewarm pool with predictive warm-up.** Since the one-to-one prewarm pool is supposed to prewarm each service function, it is essential to determine how to predict the time of warm-up. Otherwise, it will cause a cold startup to reduce system efficiency, while function instances are left idle in the backside and the resources in the cloud platform are not manageable.

  To determine the warm-up time, the researchers devised efficient prewarm strategies with predictions and heuristics. Xu *et al.* [581] adopted the LSTM (Long Short-Term Memory) network to detect the potential dependencies from historical inform, and proposed an adaptive warm-up method through predicting the startup time of each service function to warm-up service functions in advance referring to the ACPS (Adaptive Container Pool Scaling) strategy. Shahrad *et al.* [470] investigated how to manage different resources efficiently to prewarm startup in a one-to one manner. They studied the dynamic features of Function-as-a-Service (FaaS), and adjusted the lifetime of the service functions for recycling, with devising a novel prediction mechanism following the time series.

- **One-for-all prewarm pool by caching-aware.**

  The one-for-all prewarm pool is proposed with a similar logic of the **Template** approach. This means that the template first receives the notification from the socket, then the template imports the potentially needed bins or libraries in advance. When a service function is invoked for a user, the serverless computing platform only needs to initialize/specialize the service function from the preset templates.

For example, Du *et al.* [119] addressed the problem about how to accelerate the recovery procedure of the RCPs (Retrenched Critical Paths) through improving the performance of the restore procedure for C/R. They also devised a gadget, a sandbox fork, in order to manipulate the deployed sandboxes, which have loaded the request service functions for resuing states. Mohan *et al.* [392] then preloaded the virtual network interfaces and adopted the lazy binding method, thereby devising a self-evolving pause container pool to ease the startup latency and avoid the cold startup.

- **One-to-one and one-for-all prewarm pool.** It can be seen that both the one-to-one and one-for-all prewarm pools are beneficial to ameliorate the cold startup with the encapsulation layer. Specifically, the one-to-one prewarm pool trades more memory resource to shorten the latency for initialization. However, it is difficult to predict the exact time for warm-up while pre-allocating a reasonable amount of memory resources. In addition, when the historical trace is scarce, it is hard to design an accurate prediction mechanism. Moreover, the prediction mechanism will inevitably introduce high computing resources (e.g., CPU resources) overhead with a large number of service functions.

  Meanwhile, the one-for-all prewarm pool adopts the aforementioned template mechanism to mitigate the expensive overhead for the cod startups of service functions from scratch. Then it consumes less extra resources to manage and maintain a global prewarm pool than the one-to-one prewarm pool method. However, the one-for-all prewarm pool method suffers from some drawbacks. For example, the templates own high image sizes, the pre-loaded bins and libraries is highly likely to have conflicts, and the privacy of users may disclose. The one-for-all prewarm pool method will inevitably demonstrate the portrait in which the service functions adhering to some common characteristics and portraits.

  Then we are able to stride to pursue the optimal remedy for old startups in diverse scenarios. For example, we prefer the one-for-all prewarm pool, when the historical trace is insufficient to develop an accurate prediction mechanism, like there exists no invocation of the service function before. On the other hand, the one-to-one prewarm pool is favored for service functions with general patterns and characteristics, and vice versa.

6.1.2.3 *System Orchestration Layer*

The system orchestration layer endeavours to provide massive service functions elastically in serverless computing. Even though there are different serverless orchestrators, they face the similar dilemmas. For example, how to devise an efficient scheduling of a variety of service functions with intricate and inextricable dependencies in each server, and how to manage the massive service functions with granular permissions.

Then the system orchestration layer focuses on the performance security, i.e., how to provision as less resources as possible while guaranteeing the system performance. The researchers aim to predict the exact amounts of computing resources, together with an resource-efficient service scheduling. In particularly, The load balancer, as well as the resource monitor, is introduced to the serverless controller. The load balancer component is designed to coordinate the usages of different resources, and refrain from resource overloading. At the same time, the resource monitor component concerns the on-demand resource provisioning of each server node, while sending the updates to the load balancer component.

With the assistance of the resource monitor component and load balancer component, the proposed serverless controller inclines to deliver an efficient scheduling strategy in the following three levels: Resource level, instance level and application level.

- **Resource level.** In serverless computing, an orchestrator configures the different resources (e.g., CPUs, storage resource and memory resource) for encapsulation and stability, while it restricts the access to the resources. The serverless controller then will isolate the execution environment of the service function in case of a cold startup, while deploying a new function instance on demand. Therefore, the serverless controller is supposed to automatically allocate the just-right amount of different resources to deal with the assigned workloads, catering to the dynamic resource demands and the imprecise specifications of resources in the system.

- **Instance level.** Besides the ability of dynamic adjusting resource allocation, a serverless controller should have an eye on the instance-level scheduling. Intuitively, the cloud service vendors desire to improve the profit, throughput and resource utilization, while the users favor the services with cheaper costs and lower service latency. To achieve the finest trade-off, the serverless controller should carefully schedule the function instances for user service demands over the server cluster. To this end, the load balancer is leveraged to schedule service functions and balance the workloads among server nodes.

  Specifically, the instance-level strategies are summarized as hash-based and multi-objective-based methods.

  The serverless controller can adopt the hash-based method through designing hash functions to assign the executor node of each function for routing by default. If the default assigned executor node is not available or have sufficient resources for the function, then the serverless controller will recursively figure out an alternative executor node for the function, until such an assignment is feasible.

  On the other hand, the multi-objective-based method is adopted by the serverless controller to optimize multiple objectives, such as profit, throughput, and workload balancing.

- **Application level.** The serverless controller also cares about the application-level scheduling, comprised of the spread scheduling strategy and the bin-pack scheduling strategy.

  The spread scheduling strategy aims to allocate the function instances of each application across the server nodes, and has an edge on achieving workload balancing and mitigating resource contention. However, the spread scheduling strategy will introduce a higher overhead for data transmission, and the data locality diminishes.

  The bin-pack scheduling strategy is proposed for data-dependent functions, which are placed in the same server node.

6.1.2.4 *System Coordination Layer*

The system Coordination layer of serverless computing is composed of Backend-as-a-Service (BaaS) elements and integrate a series of Application Programming Interfaces (APIs) and Software Development Kits (SDKs) into encapsulated functions. Then the users can leverage such BaaS elements, instead of traditional middleboxes, to develop diverse services, such as computing and storage services.

6.1.3 Benefits of Serverless Computing

- **Cost-effective.** Based on the server infrastructure, serverless computing develops serverless applications to provision cost-based services which relate to the resource usage. For instance, even though the applications may keep running for a long term, and the cloud vendors only need to pay for the used resources that are provided to users.

- **Scalability.** Serverless computing has the nature of scalability to resolve the key challenge for cloud service provisioning. Then the applications are able to automatically scale with the dynamic changing of user demands, and the developers on the serverless computing platform do not need to care about how to scale the applications.

- **Management in server-side.** Similarly, the serverless service providers are responsible for managing the hardware and software for service applications on clouds. That is to say, the serverless service providers will address the administration operations, while the developers on the serverless computing platform only focus on the allocation and utilization of different resources, such as CPU resources, memory resource, and storage resource.

- **Easy to deploy.** Clearly, the applications in serverless computing can be deployed and managed by users easily. For example, the serverless service providers will manage the serverless infrastructures for service provisioning, and the developers on the serverless computing platform only need to concern themselves with managing their requested functions.

- **Reduce latency.** The requested serverless application of a user is not deployed on a fixed server node, i.e., the service of the serverless application can be provided from any server node. For example, a cloud vendor can deploy the serverless service of a user on a server that is in proximity of the server, thereby reducing the experienced service delay.

6.1.4 Challenges of Serverless Computing

6.1.4.1 Programming and Modeling

Since serverless computing is in its infant stage, the development tools and models of serverless computing are incomplete and prone to errors. Then the software developers face the challenge for programming, and the imperfect modelling paradigms will complicate and affect the synergy across multiple developers [469].

6.1.4.2 Pricing and Cost Prediction

In recent days, many technology institutes and enterprises have been providing serverless computing services in diverse specifications to users with different prices over the world. At the same time, it inclines to be difficult to standardize the pricing of serverless computing services among all technology institutes and enterprises.

There are many factors contributing to the pricing of serverless computing services, such as the energy costs (decided by the execution regions or the time slots) and the revenue strategies of enterprises. Also, the workload level of the service provider imposes an impact on the service pricing. For example, the pricing of a service provider under a peak demand is considerable and much higher than that under a low demand. As a result, the research community is endeavouring to design an efficient pricing modelling for serverless service providers, which will contribute to building a competitive serverless service marketplace. On the other hand, the customers can select the available serverless services in an online manner, and the prices of serverless services of providers usually change dynamically. Then an induced inextricable challenge is how to optimize the costs of users, through requesting serverless services from different service providers dynamically while guaranteeing the quality of experienced serverless services.

6.1.4.3 Scheduling

When customers apply for serverless service applications, the service provider will then receive invocation requests, and the requested applications usually have predefined service deadlines. Then it is critical to provide delay-sensitive services for service providers, through efficient scheduling strategies. That is to say, the service provider is supposed to schedule when and where to deploy and execute the requested functions within their deadlines, while considering the constraints, such as the energy budget constraint and the resource consumption constraint.

In what follows, we categorize the existing scheduling in serverless computing strategies into energy-aware scheduling, resource-aware scheduling and workflow-aware scheduling.

- **Energy-aware scheduling.** The energy-aware scheduling usually changes the idle containers into a hibernate mode to save energy consumption. However, the changing from a hibernate mode to an active mode will cause inevitable delays of the invoked service functions, which may violate the service deadlines. Then it is challenging to minimize the energy consumption of serverless services while meeting the service deadlines.

- **Resource-aware scheduling.** The applications in serverless computing are diverse, so are the resources demand patterns of the applications. For instance, a scientific-computing service application usually consumes more CPU resourecs, while an analytic service application usually consumes more memory resources. Therefore, placing multiple CPU-intensive service functions in a single server node will cause resource contention and extra service delay. This is true for any other resource, such as bandwidth resource, disk resource and memory resource. Then a resource-aware scheduling strategy is needed for a serverless service provider to place multiple service functions on multiple server nodes to meet the resource demands of customers.

- **Workflow-aware scheduling.** The deployment of a serverless service application usually consists of the executions of a series of service functions, which are orchestrated as a service function chain (i.e., a serverless workflow). With the knowledge of the service function chain invocations, the service provider can allocate containers for executing the next service functions in advance.

- **Dataflow-aware scheduling.** In the current serverless computing setting, the service functions may need some external data sources for processing. For example, the dependencies of the machine learning service applications are high. Therefore, the service provider also has to consider the delay of external data sources and the data availability.

- **Package-aware scheduling.** After receiving a service request, the serverless computing platform usually install some service libraries, bins and dependent packages need by the service functions.

- **Hybrid scheduling.** In recent days, the serverless scheduling and virtual machine scheduling are jointly taken into consideration for a central scheduler to allocate a service request to either a serverless computing service provider or a private virtual machine.

6.1.4.4 Intra-Communications of Functions

A serverless service instance usually compromises a series of service functions as a chain to offer integrated functionality. Then the service functions are supposed to communicate together to share data efficiently. In the traditional cloud service platform, such data sharing is accomplished via network addressing.

For instance, in the traditional cloud computing, a Virtual Machine (VM) can send the data to another VM through specific network addresses. Therefore, it is challenging to facilitate the intra-communication of functions in serverless computing. Then the patterns and characteristics of functions should be taken into consideration to deliver some addressing schemes to enable intra-communication of functions as follows.

First, because serverless computing has the characteristic to automatically scales functions, then the functions can be invoked with function names or locations.

Second, the lifespans of the serverless functions are usually short. Then the addressing schemes should be deployed as soon as possible to track the dynamic changes of functions.

Finally, with the development of serverless computing, the number of serverless functions has increased drastically. Then the addressing scheme should be scalable to deal with a numerous number of serverless functions.

6.1.4.5 Data Caching

In serverless computing, data caching is commonly leveraged by network service providers to obviate the need for persistent storage and reduce costs, which is similar to traditional cloud computing. However, how to make full utilization of different levels of data caching in serverless computing meets a daunting challenge.

For example, imagine a service function intends to retrieve data from the database, then the serverless computing platform inclines to cache the data for further data retrieving requests, thereby mitigating the induced costs for database accesses. However, in a serverless computing architecture, the functions are independent on the specific infrastructures, while the further function are likely to be executed in another server node and the data caching then becomes futile. Hence, an efficient caching scheme is essential for serverless computing to reduce costs and service latency.

6.1.4.6 Security and Privacy

One of the common concern of serverless computing is about the security and privacy issues. This is because the service functions are executed on a serverless computing platform, which is shared across a large number of users. In what follows, we then investigate different aspects of security and privacy issues in serverless computing.

- **Authentication and authorization.** First of all, it is challenging to determine how to authenticate user applications and authorize them the access to the available functions in the serverless computing platform. Then a freeloader is able to make use of the available resources of the platform without any authentication. The common remedies are to adopt security protocols and authentication tokens within the requests headers.

- **Resource exhaustion attacks.** An attacker may overuse the resources of the serverless computing platform to disrupt existing services and impose excessive costs and workloads. A potential remedy is to adopt monitoring approaches to block these attacks.

- **Privacy issues.** In current Internet of Things (IoT), there exist many privacy-sensitive service applications, and an attacker may attempt to steal the users' privacy. Therefore, the serverless computing architecture introduces comprehensive anonymity and disguise methods to avoid the leakage of the privacy of service users.

6.2 SERVERLESS MACHINE LEARNING

6.2.1 Introduction

It is widely acknowledged by researchers that Machine Learning (ML) is playing an imperative role in a diversity of fields, such as Natural Language Processing (NLP) and Computer Vision (CV). However, ML is facing daunting challenges, which substantially hinder the efficiency of ML [62].

First of all, ML developers are supposed to manually adjust a large number of system-level parameters, such as the topologies, number of allocated parameter/-worker servers, and number of allocated CPUs [305, 322]. In addition, ML developers are required to configure numerous ML-specific parameters, such as the number of epochs, learning rate, adopted neural networks and learning algorithms, which are coordinated with the system-level parameters. Also, the workflows of ML consists of a series of processing stages, such as pre-processing, training and hyperparameter search. Then the ML developers usually need to consider the computational demands of each processing stage. Therefore, it always leads to a case of resource overprovisioning, and the current general ML frameworks do not have the flexibility to handle such workloads.

The serverless computing paradigm emerges as a new method to deal with the resource management problem in clouds (data centers). Serverless computing is based on stateless lambda functions, and the resources in cloud infrastructures are automatically managed, maintained and scheduled. Hence, serverless computing obviates the need for the long-term configuration, management and maintenance of the compute units, such as virtual machines [246].

6.2.2 Machine Learning and Data Management

Currently, the advanced analytics technologies (e.g., machine learning (ML) and data mining) are contributing to the construction of data management systems. For example, a large number of databases support the ML model training and inference tasks. Then the ML functions within a data management system assist in mitigating data transmission to leverage the build-in database to perform functions, such as controlling access or checking integrity. Then the database is forcing the development of distributed ML.

6.2.3 Training Large Models in Serverless Computing

In this section, we focus on the training task of large Machine Learning (ML) models in serverless computing. In particular, a large ML model is referred to as the one,

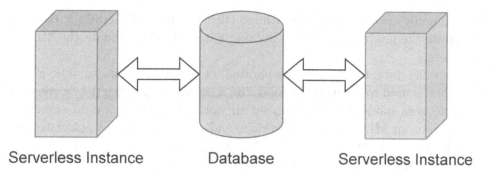

Serverless Instance   Database   Serverless Instance

Figure 6.3 The data transfer between serverless instances.

the training of which needs the assistance of multiple serverless instances, because of execution constraints, such as running time, computing resource and memory constraints [138].

6.2.3.1 Data Transfer and Parallelism in Serverless Computing

The serverless instances are different from the traditional distributed computing instances. The main difference is that the serverless instances are stateless and have time limitations, distinguished from the parallel threads adopted in Deep Neuron Networks (DNNs).

Today, the serverless computing platform does not support the data exchange between any two serverless instances, and it is not available to endow a serverless instance with the affinity with another serverless instance to share data for processing. As a result, the serverless computing platform adopts intermediate storage (e.g., a database) to save the states, which are shared between any serverless instances in subsequence. The data transfer between serverless instances is illustrated in Figure 6.3.

Because any two serverless instances are not allowed to communicate directly in a serverless computing platform, then the parallelized data or models will lead to extra delays as follows:

- Data transfer delay from the source serverless instance to the intermediate database;

- Data transfer delay from the intermediate database to the destination serverless instance; and

- Warm-up delay for loading data.

6.2.3.2 Data Parallelism for Model Training in Serverless Computing

With a given dataset, the model training based on the dataset is to configure the Machine Learning (ML)-specific parameters, such as learning rate and edge weights. Then the inference results of the trained ML model match the data in the dataset.

The commonly used training algorithms, such as Stochastic gradient descent, are to compute the gradients with the training data, and then update the ML-specific parameters.

To parallel data, the dataset is separated into a series of data subsets. Each data subset then is used to train an ML model on a serverless instance (i.e., worker). Then an ML network model is shared among all works. Especially, a data subset is first used to train an ML model by a worker, and the gradients are calculated by the work with the data subset. Then all calculated gradints from all works are collected and aggregated by a parameter server to update the ML-specific parameters. Different from traditional ML, all the machines for training are serverless instances in serverless computing.

6.2.3.3 Optimizing Parallelism Structure in Serverless Training

Manifestly, it exists multiple data transfers among worker servers and the parameter server to achieve data parallelism. Then there are two types of data transfers as follows:

- The parameter server transfers data to worker servers.

- The worker server transfers data to the parameter server.

In particular, the data transfer delay from the parameter server to a worker server is a constant, because the sent data is fixed due to the fixed given ML network model. Then all worker servers are capable of receiving and obtaining the same ML-specific parameters in parallel.

Now it comes to the data transfer from the worker server to the parameter server. Given n worker servers, the parameter server has to aggregate n gradients from n worker servers, and such data transfer delay depends on how the parameter server aggregates n gradients. For example, if the parameter server aggregates the gradients one by one, then the total data transfer delay is the summation of each data transfer delay from each worker server to the parameter server. Also, the parameter server can aggregate the gradients in some intermediate nodes from workers to shorten the data transfer delay. Different structures for aggregating data of the parameter server are illustrated in Figure 6.4.

6.2.4 Cost-Efficiency in Serverless Computing

The key advantage of serverless computing services over traditional cloud computing services is cost-efficiency.

In the traditional cloud computing, Machine Learning (ML) training jobs are executed in the Infrastructure-as-a-Service (IaaS) architecture and IaaS delivers an abstraction of Virtual Machines (VMs) through multiplexing VMs on the physical machines. Different from this, serverless computing delivers a convenient abstraction of service functions which are stateless, based on the running time of the programming languages. Therefore, in serverless computing, a developer deploys his service application through submitting a request of the application to a serverless computing

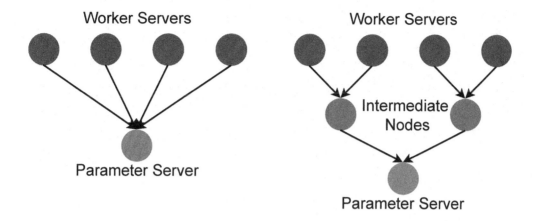

Figure 6.4 Different structures for aggregating data of the parameter server.

platform. Then the serverless computing platform will adopt the input data to invoke the requested service application, which is stateless. In serverless computing, the pricing structure relies on the number of running service functions and the execution time.

6.3 CHAPTER SUMMARY

This chapter presents the research topics in serverless machine learning. The model training procedure of Machine Learning (ML) usually consumes large amounts of time and cost, and need to be improved. Following the footsteps of conventional ML architecture, the emerging serverless computing paradigm brings new opportunities for ML to mitigate running time and operational overheads. Moreover, the ML developers then only need to define and manage the stateless functions, rather than the dedicated servers or middleboxes. Hence, serverless machine learning is envisioned by global researchers as a promising trend of ML techniques and applications.

CHAPTER 7

System-Level Design: From Standalone to Clusters

Big data and machine learning are enabling technologies for smart decision making, automation and resource optimization. These technologies collectively promote intelligent services from concepts to practical applications. Traditionally, big data are collected and stored in a centralized machine, i.e., a cloud data center, for further analysis and processing to develop intelligent service and applications. Due to the powerful capabilities of the cloud, it has made great achievements in learning from the big data, specially for applications that allow long response delay and all data aggregated to the cloud, e.g., e-commerce services and recommendation systems. However, the limited computing power of a single machine and the non-centralized big training data itself pose many challenges to traditional centralized learning frameworks, such as significant communication overhead, service latency, as well as security and privacy issues. Therefore, it is urgent to shift learning framework from centralized to distributed. From this aspect, ML can be developing in a distributed scenario, which can be also called distributed machine learning (DML). In DML, multiple workers cooperate with each other with communication and train the model on parallel. In this section, we will discuss how to design efficient distributed learning framework from the following six parts: (1) Staleness-aware pipeline, (2) introduction to federated learning, (3) training with Non-IID data, (4) large-scale collaborative learning, (5) personalized learning and (6) practice on FL implementation.

7.1 STALENESS-AWARE PIPELINING

With the growth of model complexity and computational overhead, modern ML applications are usually handled by the distributed systems, where the training procedure is conducted in parallel. In order to design a high-performance distributed ML system, we need to determine how to divide the primary large task into several small subtasks. The consideration factors contains the dataset, neural network model and available hardware resource. In this section, we will discuss how to handle the training parallelism mainly in two categories: (1) *Model parallelism* [147, 194, 297], in which the model is partitioned to different workers; and (2) *data parallelism*

DOI: 10.1201/9781003340225-7

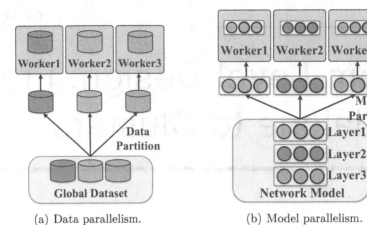

(a) Data parallelism.　　　　　　(b) Model parallelism.

Figure 7.1　Illustration of the training parallelism.

[73, 244, 311, 530, 568, 604], in which the dataset is partitioned to different workers. The following sections will present the details of these two schemes. Moreover, considering some latest researches that handle distributed training via multiple primitives, we also discuss the extension of training parallelism at the end of this section.

7.1.1　Data Parallelism

In commodity clusters built in the datacenter networks, the machine may not be able to share their memory via the remote procedure calling because these nodes are often organized in the geo-distributed manner [214]. Besides, with the rise of edge intelligence, plenty of ML applications are deployed in the edge-to-cloud environment [99, 475], where the machine's processing speed is bound by the scarce on-device memory, especially for the mobile and Iot devices [133, 152, 380]. In this condition, loading the network model or the whole data to a single machine is not feasible in practice. We need to partition the workload into several subtasks and handle the job via distributed processing, so as to alleviate the huge computation pressure and resource demands. It is a natural way to handle the parallel processing based on data division scheme, which is often called the data parallelism.

We use Figure. 7.1(a) to illustrate the rationale of data parallelism, where the entire dataset is partitioned into several pieces and each machine is allocated with a part of these data. With its own dataset, each machine can conduct the model training and update the local model independently. According to partition dimension of the training data, there are two branches in data parallelism: (1) Sample-level partition [107, 383] and (2) feature-level partition [240].

7.1.2　Model Parallelism

In the edge intelligence or mobile learning applications, the devices are usually in a resource-constraint environment, where the available on-device memory is quire scarce. In this condition, we need to resolve the large model into several small parts to alleviate the memory pressure. Each worker only handles a sub-model and update the parameters contained inside. According to the model structures, we mainly discuss two branches, i.e., the linear models [210, 409] and non-linear neural networks [198, 576].

7.1.2.1 Linear Models

As the parameter amount in linear models is strongly dependent on the number of data dimensions, it is natural to uniformly partition the entire model and each worker is allocated with a part of the global model. In this condition, the *Coordinate Descent* [408] approach is a promising way to handle the searching of the optimized parameters. Also, considering the linear separability of the optimization objective, it is possible to update each dimension of the parameters by calculating the data of the objective function in the corresponding dimension, while the data in other dimension will not yield interference. As a result, we can merge the training results of all the workers from the perspective of dimension-level data aggregation, rather than exchanging the entire model.

7.1.2.2 Non-Linear Neural Networks

Modern neural networks are usually designed in a non-linear structure, where each layer's weights and activations are dependent in sequence. Therefore, dividing the global model requires to consider the factors of network structures, neuron amounts and block functions. Basically, we can resolve this problem in three directions.

- The first is the horizontal layer-wise partition [406], which stands in the perspective of layer depth. Each worker conducts the matrix calculations according to the layers assigned to it. All the workers collaborate in a sequential order, from the shallow layer to the deeper layer.

- Other common direction is the vertical cross-layer partition [146], which is often used in the wide-layer models. The key difference from the horizontal layer-wise partition is that the neurons of a layer can be allocated to different machines, i.e., following the neuron-level partition. Therefore, the workers can update the parameter to a single neuron. However, as the neurons often hold the computation dependency according to the network structure, intermediate data need to be exchanged during model training. As a result, huge communication traffic will be generated. This is the key challenge limiting the effectiveness of vertical cross-layer partition.

- Moreover, considering the parameter redundancy of neural networks, it is possible to use a simpler small model to mimic the function of the complex large model. A promising manner is to use the model random partition methods [187, 494], which aims at extract a "backbone" structure of the original model by assembling the training results from different workers. This procedure can be designed from both horizontal and vertical directions. Therefore, random partition has become a hot topic in model parallelism, with a promising improvement space.

7.1.3 Hybrid Parallelism

Hybrid parallelism refers to combine the model parallelism with model parallelism when the model size exceeds the local storage memory of a worker. Specifically, the original neural network model is divided into several sub-models and the parameter of each sub-model is assigned and updated in one worker [422, 486]. HetPipe is a typical system applying hybrid parallelism [430]. In HetPipe system, each virtual worker uses pipelining to process concurrently N_m minibatches that depend on memory requirements. Let local staleness be the maximum tolerable missing of updates from the most recent updates, and the local staleness threshold, $S_{local} = N_m - 1$. The weight of the minibatch p used for training is w_p. For a given initial weights w_0, the first N_m minibatches are executed with $w_0 = w_1 = \ldots = w_{N_m}$. When the executing of minibatch p completes, the local weights are updated with $w_{local} = w_{local} + u_p$, where u_p is the computed gradients of processing minibatch p. The processing of minibatch p will use the latest w_{local}, which is updated by minibatch $(p - S_{local} - 1)$.

The data parallelism of HetPipe can be illustrated as follows. HetPipe uses a parameter server to maintain the global weight, that is, the gradient results calculated by each virtual worker are uploaded to update the global weight. At this time, heterogeneous virtual workers will lead to the inefficiency of synchronous data parallelism mode across virtual workers. Therefore, in HetPipe, a method similar to SSP is used to improve the efficiency, that is, each virtual worker does not have to wait for the gradient calculation results of all virtual workers every time. Each virtual worker maintains a local clock c_{local}, and the global clock c_{global} is saved by parameter server. The two clocks are 0, initially. A wave means a sequential minibatches that are simultaneously executed in the virtual worker. When a virtual worker completes all the minibatches in a wave c, the updates from minibatch $c * (s_{local} + 1) + 1$ to minibatch $(c+1) * (s_{local} + 1)$ are aggregated by the virtual worker. Then, the virtual worker pushes the updates to the parameter server. Let D represents the distance between the fastest and slowest of c_{local}. When $D = 0$, the global weights across virtual workers are synchronized, because each virtual worker must ensure the processing of minibatch in the same order wave.

7.1.4 Extension of Training Parallelism

Apart from the data and model parallelism, recent researches also have focused on the distributed training by using multiple primitives, which is closely linked to the computational resource sharing. By such means, all workers share a same area of the memory, where the training data and model parameters are stored. Similar to multi-thread on a single machine, datasets and model do not need to be partitioned among workers. As all the workers can access the shared memory and global dataset, each worker can independently conduct the optimization algorithm in parallel to accelerate the distributed DL training.

Besides, as to the stochastic optimization algorithm used in this scheme, two assumptions are usually hold when generating the training data: (1) Online data generation [126] and (2) offline data generation [70]. The online generation assumes that the real-time training data accessed by any workers can be generated based on the real distribution. In contrast, the offline generation uses the real distribution to yield an offline dataset and each worker employs the bootstrapping (i.e., random sampling with replacement [278]) on this dataset to form the corresponding training data, following the uniform distribution. Generally, the online generation is useful to the theoretical analysis of computation-parallel algorithms while the offline generation is widely used in real-world training scenarios.

7.1.5 Summary

Overall, training parallelism is a key part for the implementation of high-performance distributed ML systems. In practice, data parallelism and model parallelism have been widely used in many scenarios, from the perspective of data scale and model complexity. In addition, the extension of parallelism based on multiple computation primitives is also a promising may to handle the distributed training. Basically, the research of training parallelism is still a hot topic because we need more efficient training paradigm for the emerging edge intelligence and the TinyML application on micro IoT devices.

7.2 INTRODUCTION TO FEDERATED LEARNING

Recently, the rapid development and widespread applications of artificial intelligence technologies has prompted growing concerns about data privacy. A simple example is that the collection of user data must be open and transparent between organizations and companies, and data belonging to one use or organization cannot be exchanged with others without the user authorisation. It brings new challenges to traditional machine learning technologies: if the data between organizations cannot be shared and communicated, and the amount of data in an organization is limited, the large amount of data are only monopolized by a small number of giant companies. In this case, it is difficult for small companies to obtain enough data, forming large and small "data islands". In this case, how to training a joint model where there is no authority to obtain enough user data?

Federated learning (FL) was proposed to tackle above dilemmas by enabling multiple distributed workers to collaboratively train a shared global model without exposing their raw data. FL is essentially a kind of distributed learning. But it still has several differences when compared with distributed learning. In Table 7.1, we compare the characteristics of FL and traditional distributed learning. First, in traditional distributed learning, we usually assume that the centralized server has full control of the data and worker nodes. However, as shown in Figure 7.2, the worker nodes in FL are usually unstable, and the data are controlled by owners. Furthermore, the local datasets are heterogeneous since the data is independently generated by the worker nodes. The server and participants in federated learning can not only be the edge devices, but also be the data-center or isolated organizations. Beyond

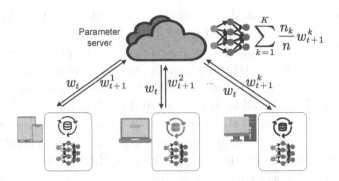

Figure 7.2 An illustration of federated learning.

that, FL concerns more about the privacy and security. In FL, the training process works round by round. First, the global model is initialized in the server. Then, at the beginning of each communication round, the server randomly selects a subset of the clients to participant the local training, and then distributes the latest global model to the selected clients. These selected clients update the model on their private dataset by using stochastic gradient descent (SGD) algorithm for several epochs. When finishing the local updates on the selected clients, the server aggregates the local model parameters from these clients to obtain a new global model (Algorithm 3).

Table 7.1 Comparison of federated learning with traditional distributed learning.

Characteristics	Distributed Learning	Federated Learning
The server has full control over the data and worker nodes	√	×
The worker nodes are stable	√	×
The local datasets are homogeneous	√	×
Concerns about the privacy and security	×	√

Fig 7.2 showcases a typical architecture and detailed workflow of an FL system. In general, two main entities are included in an FL system, i.e., the data owners (also called clients/participants) and the model owner (also called federated server). Considering a multi-classification learning task, we denote $\mathcal{M} = \{1, 2, \cdots, K\}$ as the set of clients, and each of which has a private dataset $\mathcal{D}_k := \{(x_i^k, y_i)\}_{i=1}^{N_k}$, where x_i^k is the i-th sample of client $k \in \mathcal{M}$, y_i is the corresponding label of x_i^k. N_k denotes the number of training data samples in dataset $\mathcal{D}_k$, and $N = \sum_{k=1}^{K} N_k$.

During the FL training process, each client k will first download a global model w from the server and independently train a local model w_k based on its own dataset $\mathcal{D}_k$. Then, updated local model parameters instead raw data will be uploaded to the server for aggregation, and a new global model will be generated for the next round of training. The training objective of an FL system can be formulated as minimizing the total loss on all data samples, i.e., $D = \cup_{k \in \mathcal{M}} \mathcal{D}_k$:

$$\min_{w} \quad F(w) = \frac{1}{N} \sum_{k=1}^{K} N_k F_k(w), k \in \{1, 2, \cdots, K\}, \tag{7.1}$$

Algorithm 3 FederatedAveraging. The K clients are indexed by k; B is the local minibatch size, E is the number of local epochs, and η is the learning rate

---

Input: Set of clients $\mathcal{M}$, minibatch size B, local epochs E, learning rate η.
Output: Updated model parameters w_T.

1: **procedure** SERVER EXECUTES:
2:     initial w_0
3:     **for** each round $t = 1, 2, ...$ **do**
4:         $S_t \leftarrow$ randomly select max $(C \cdot K, 1)$ clients
5:         **for** each client $k \in S_t$ **in parallel do**
6:             $w_{t+1}^k \leftarrow$ CLIENTUPDATE(k, w_t)
7:         **end for**
8:         $w_{t+1} \leftarrow \sum_{k=1}^{K} \frac{n_k}{n} w_{t+1}^k$
9:     **end for**
10: **end procedure**
11: **procedure** CLIENTUPDATE(k, w) :   ▷ Run on client k
12:     **for** each local epoch $i = 1, 2, ..., E$ **do**
13:         **for** batch $b \in \mathcal{D}_k$ **do**
14:             $w \leftarrow w - \eta \nabla \ell(w; b)$
15:         **end for**
16:     **end for**
17: **return** w to server
18: **end procedure**

---

where $F_k(w) = \frac{1}{N_k} \sum_{i \in \mathcal{D}_k} \ell(w; x_i^k, y_i)$, and $\ell(\cdot)$ is the loss function, which can be squared-error, likelihood or cross-entropy, etc. More specifically, the FL training process can be summarized into three steps: initialization, local model updates, and global aggregation. It should be noticed that the global model refers to the model aggregated by FL server, and local model refers to the model trained locally at each participating client.

Step 1: Initialize. After deciding the training task, the FL server initializes the parameters of the global model randomly. Then, the server selects a random set of clients and distributes the initialized parameters w_0 of the global model to the selected clients.

Step 2: Local model updates: The selected clients download the latest global model w_t from the server, where t denotes the current round index. Then, each selected client updates the local model parameters based on their local data by using stochastic gradient descent algorithm. The update rule in each client can be represented as follows:

$$w_{t+1}^k = w_t^k - \eta \nabla \ell(w_t^k) \tag{7.2}$$

Where $\nabla \ell(w_t^k)$ represents the gradient of loss function, η is the learning rate. After that, the updated local model parameters will be sent to FL server.

Step 3: Global Aggregation: In this step, the server receives the local updated parameters from the selected clients and updates the global model by averaging these model parameters, which can be formulated as:

$$w_{t+1} = \sum_{k=1}^{K} \frac{N_k}{N} w_t^k, k \in 1, 2, ..., K \qquad (7.3)$$

Then, the updated global model w_{t+1} is sent back to the data owners for the next round of training.

The above steps are repeated until the global model reaches convergence. As compared to traditional machine learning model training approaches, the FL training framework has the following advantages:

- *Lower latency:* With FL, each client can consistently train and update a local ML model. The updated model can be used to make predictions on the user's device. In this case, the response delay is much lower than that of making decisions at the centralized server.

- *Privacy Preservation:* As the users' raw data do not need to be sent to the server, the data privacy can be guaranteed well. Actually, more users will be willing to participant the collaborative model training process under guaranteed privacy, and thus better inference model can be obtained.

- *Highly efficient use of network resources:* In FL training process, only the updates instead of raw data are required to uploaded to the FL server, which reduces the total communication overhead. Moreover, the computation resource can be highly used in multiple local updates. As a result, both the computation and communication resources can be efficient use in FL.

In FL, the data are generated and stored in end users' own devices such as mobile phones and personal computers, which causes data heterogeneity. In the next part, data heterogeneity and related training frameworks will be introduced.

7.3   TRAINING WITH NON-IID DATA

A common assumption in most of machine learning algorithms is that the training data is is independently and identically distributed (IID), such as regression, decision tree, random forest etc. However, this assumption may not be guaranteed in many real-world applications where data are usually shown strong correlation between both attributes and labels.

In federated learning, due to the decentralized architecture, the data are independently generated by the multiple node devices. The data from different devices have different distribution characteristics, namely, the training data is Non-IID on each device, which degrades the efficiency of the training process as it heavily relies on stochastic gradient descent (SGD) [106, 153, 263]. Without the strong assumption that the local data are IID, it is hard to provide an guarantee to the convergence rate. Therefore, it is great important to improving the learning efficiency on Non-IID data for federated learning.

7.3.1 The Definition of Non-IID Data

In general, independent means there is no correlation among different items. In other words, each item can be regarded as an independent event. Identically distributed means the distribution is stable and all items can be sampled from a same probability distribution. The concept of IID can be formally described as follows.

- We can always obtain $x_i \sim \mathcal{Q}$ (Identically Distributed)

- For any two different items x_i and x_j, the following equation is always satisfied: $\forall i \neq j, p(x_i, x_j) = P(x_i)P(x_j)$ (Independently Distributed)

To guarantee that the stochastic gradients are unbiased estimates of the full gradient, it is important to make IID sampling over the training data. That is, owning IID data on the client-side means that each minibatch of data used for local updates is statistically identical to a sample (with replacement) drawn uniformly from the whole training datasets (i.e., the union of all local datasets on the client-side). However, it is unrealistic to assume that the local data on each device is always IID in practical scenarios. More specifically, the data in real-life applications usually has following characteristics:

- **Non-Independence**: The data may be processed in an insufficiently-random order due to the effect of different participate order on each client. Furthermore, the clients that located in same region may have highly correlations among the training data.

- **Non-Identicalness**: Since the data on each client are generated locally, the geographical characteristics may lead to differences on label distributions. Moreover, the number of training data are likely different among different clients.

Thus, Non-IID data can be also technical defined as

- Data on each client i is generated via a distinct distribution $x_i \sim \mathcal{P}_i$

- There may be a big different between the number of data samples on each client

- The relationship among different clients and their local distributions, could also be explained by an underlying structure.

As shown in Figure 7.3, in FL, a statistical model involves two levels of sampling: the first one is to sample a client from multiple available participants, i.e., $i \sim \mathcal{D}$; the second one is to sample data point from the local distribution of client i, i.e., $(x, y) \sim \mathcal{P}_i$, where x denotes the features and y means the corresponding label. Non-IID data in FL can be represented as the differences between $\mathcal{P}_i$ and $\mathcal{P}_j$ for different clients i and j. Many researchers focus on finding effective solutions to alleviate the impact of Non-IID data on the performance of FL training.

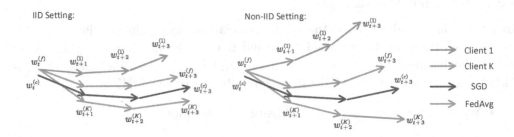

Figure 7.3 Illustration of the weight divergence for federated learning with IID and non-IID data.

7.3.2 Enabling Technologies for Non-IID Data

Due to the Non-IID data in federated learning, many of the methods have been designed to improve the performance of federated learning from different research perspectives. existing solutions can be categorized into three types: data sharing, robust aggregation methods, and other optimized methods.

7.3.2.1 Data Sharing

The most straightforward idea to solve Non-IID data is to share a small IID dataset that contains a uniform distribution over classes from the server to the clients. For example, Zhao et al. [617] design a *distance* metric to measure the skewness of the data distributions. That is, by calculating the divergence between the local model parameters and global model parameters, the distance between the local data distribution and global distribution can be approximately described and interpreted as follows.

$$divergence = \frac{\left\| \boldsymbol{w}^f - \boldsymbol{w}^c \right\|}{\left\| \boldsymbol{w}^c \right\|} \qquad (7.4)$$

More specifically, they assume there are K clients in a federated learning system. Let w_t^c denote the model parameters after t-th round of training in a centralized setting (i.e., collecting all the data to the server), and w_t^f denote the model parameters calculated after the t-th round of aggregation in a federated setting. As shown in Fig. 7.3, if data among the clients is IID, the divergence between w_t^k and w_t^c may be small for each client. The increase of training rounds would not influence the divergence between w_t^f and w_t^c. While for Non-IID settings, the divergence between w_t^k and w_t^c may be larger due to the skewness of the local data distributions. Worse still, the negative impact of divergence on model training would be accumulated and increased fast. In this case, the distance between w_T^f and w_T^c becomes much larger.

Furthermore, the authors declare that the skewness of the local data distributions can also be measured by the earth mover's distance (EMD) among distributions. It is obvious that sharing IID data from the server to clients can reduce EMD, which leads to the performance improvement.

Therefore, they propose a IID data-sharing mechanism to mitigate the impact of Non-IID data on FL training performance, which is shown in Figure 7.4. More specifically, an IID shared dataset is stored in the FL server and a random percentage of the shared data are distributed to all the clients, i.e., α. Then, the clients can performs local training process over the augmented dataset (i.e., the union of the shared data and local private data).

Although this method can help create more accurate models, it still faces several limitations, the most critical one is that we usually cannot ensure the availability of such a public dataset. Even if exists a public dataset, sending shared public dataset would increase the communication overhead, which imposes burdens on network bandwidth. Besides, the addition of the public data to the private data may cause overfitting problem, especially for the number of private data samples is small. Based on the above reasons, we argue that sharing IID data from the FL server to clients is insufficient to solve the fundamental problems of federated learning algorithms on Non-IID data [462].

Jeong et al. [242] combine the generative model with federated learning to construct IID dataset. In their proposed federated augmentation (FAug) framework, multiple clients need to collectively train a generative adversarial network (GAN) model, and synthesize the data samples of all clients in local. In this case, the trained GAN augments its local data towards yielding an IID dataset. Instead of direct data sample exchanges, which may increase the communication overhead. FAug first trains a generative model in server by uploading some seed samples of the labels being lacking in each device. Then, the server oversamples the data from the updated seed samples to train a conditional GAN [386]. After that, each client downloads the generator of the trained GAN to supplement the missing data samples until the local training data distribution becomes IID. By such means, the additional communication overhead can be significantly reduced, especially for large-scale FL system where the number of clients is huge. However, sending local data or related information (missing labels) to server may bring potential privacy concern, i.e., leak information about the user data profile.

7.3.2.2 Robust Aggregation Methods

Due to the existing of Non-IID data, there maybe huge differences between the models on different clients after the process of local update. There are several works focus on estimate the contribution of each update according to the data distribution or local model performance on clients [14, 366, 415].

Only the relevant updates and valuable clients are selected in each aggregation phase. Gaia [215] propose to quantify the contribution of each update on the training performance. Specifically, by computing the magnitude (i.e., Euclidean norm $\frac{\|local\_update\|}{\|model\|}$) of a update, the significance of each client on model training can be described and used to client selection. For example, for a given threshold ϵ, any update satisfies $\frac{\|local\_update\|}{\|model\|} < \epsilon$ is considered insignificant and will be excluded in the aggregation phase. Wang et al. [366] argue that model-parameter-based magnitude

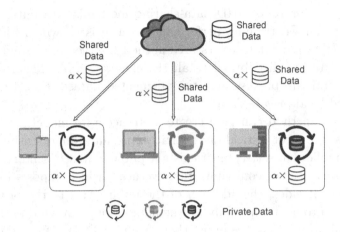

Figure 7.4 Illustration of the data-sharing strategy.

cannot effectively indicate the importance of each client. Instead, the model updates from other clients also need to be considered.

Moreover, the updates' magnitude will decreases exponentially when the training approaches convergence. It is hard to tune the value of threshold that used in identifying updates' significance. To address these limitations, Wang et al propose a novel measurement to estimate the helpless of the local update. More specifically, they focus on compare the differences between local update and global update by calculating the number of parameters with the same sign in both updates. Then, the result is normalized by the total number of parameters. Finally, the proportion of same-sign parameters are used to quantify the significance of the update. The relevance of a local update can be expressed by:

$$e(\mathbf{w}, \overline{\mathbf{w}}) = \frac{1}{d} \sum_{i=1}^{d} I(sgn(w_i) = sgn(\overline{w})) \qquad (7.5)$$

where $\mathbf{w} = < w_1, w_2, ..., w_d >$ denotes a local update parameters with dimension of d. $\overline{\mathbf{w}}$ represents the aggregated global update. $I(sgn(w_n) = sgn(\overline{w}_i)) = 1$ if and only if w_i and $\overline{w}_i$ are of same sign, and 0 otherwise. This method can not only eliminate the impact of Non-IID data, but also reduce the communication overhead.

Another method considers to design robust averaging mechanism. Yeganeh et al. [587] consider to perform a weighted aggregation in the server. More specifically, the weighting coefficient of each client is adaptively determined by the difference between local model parameters and global model parameters. The goal is to optimize the aggregation phase over Non-IID data so as to obtain a more robust global model at the server side. The averaging process can be expressed as follows,

$$w_t^{Avg} = \sum_{k=1}^{K} \alpha_k \cdot w_{t-1}^k \qquad (7.6)$$

where α_k is the weighting coefficient for client k, w_t^g and w_{t-1}^k are global model parameters in t-th round and local model parameters of client k, respectively. In [587], the authors denote Inverse Distance Aggregation (IDA) to calculate the coefficient α_k, which is based on the statistical properties of each local model parameters to the average global model, i.e.,

$$\alpha = \frac{1}{Z} \left\| w_{t-1}^{Avg} - w_{t-1}^k \right\|^{-1} \tag{7.7}$$

where $Z = \sum_{k=1}^{K} \| w_{t-1}^{Avg} - w_{t-1}^k \|^{-1}$ denotes the normalized distance. Note that $\alpha_k = 1$ if and only if client k's parameters is equal to the average model parameters, and $\alpha_k = n_k$ can be regarded as equivalent to the *FedAvg*.

7.3.2.3 Other Optimized Methods

In addition, some solutions make a small modification on the *FedAvg* method to help deal with Non-IID data. The objective function in *FedAvg* is

$$\min_w f(w) = \sum_{k=1}^{K} p_k F_k(w) \tag{7.8}$$

Another line of work focus on optimizing the local update on each client so as to reduce the variance between different clients. For example, FedProx [318] considers to add a regularization term into original objective function with the goal of minimizing the distance between the local and global models. A key insight behind in developing FedProx is that an interplay exists between systems and data heterogeneity in federated learning. Indeed, both dropping stragglers (as in *FedAvg*) or naively incorporating partial information from stragglers (as in FedProx with the proximal term set to 0) implicitly increases data heterogeneity and can adversely impact convergence behavior. The added proximal term to the objective can help to increase the stability of the method. While tolerating nonuniform amounts of local updates to be performed across devices can help alleviate negative impacts of systems heterogeneity, too many local updates may still cause the methods to diverge due to the underlying heterogeneous data. So they propose to add a proximal term to the local sub-problem to effectively limit the impact of variable local updates, e.g.,

$$\min_w h_k(w; w_t) = F_k(w) + \frac{\mu}{2} \left\| w - w_t \right\|^2 \tag{7.9}$$

$F_k(w)$ is the original local loss function, and w_t is the global model parameters in t-th round. The proximal term is beneficial in two aspects: (1) It addresses the issue of data heterogeneity by restricting the local updates to be closer to the initial (global) model without any need to manually set the number of local epochs. (2) It allows for safely incorporating variable amounts of local work resulting from systems heterogeneity. It should be noticed that μ is an important parameters in this method, which affects the convergence speed in training process. The setting of the μ has a big infuence on the whole model training. Similarly, Shnham et al. [477] add a penalty term to the loss function in multi-task federated learning framework.

Huang et al. [224] consider to further optimize the local models with a high cross-entropy loss before model averaging on the server. Since they focus on health dataset that the data labels are either 0 (survival) or 1 (expired), binary cross-entropy loss is adopted as the error measure of model-fitting, such as

$$-\sum_{i=1}^{N} [y_i \log f(x_i) + (1 - y_i) \log (1 - f(x_i))] \tag{7.10}$$

where N denotes the number of samples. x_i is the input features, and y is the binary label. $f(\cdot)$ represents the machine learning model in the FL system. The goal of the learning task on each client is to minimize Equation 7.10. The proposed method utilizes the median cross-entropy loss L_{t-1}^{median} of clients which participated in the training in round $t - 1$ as the threshold to measure whether current client need boost or not. Based on this idea, each client can update local models for several epochs based on the local loss. Furthermore, Sattler et al. [461] focus on clustering the clients into several groups and design a clustering loss to solve the Non-IID problem.

When modeling Non-IID data, fairness may also be an important issue that has effect on the training performance of FL. Simply minimizing the average loss of each local model may cause potential advantage or disadvantage on some of the clients, i.e., the huge differences on the number of data samples between different clients, or similar preferences properties on different group of clients may cause bias among the clients. Other more principled approaches to address these issues is Agnostic Federated Learning [394], which aims at optimizing any local model instead of the average of the whole local loss. Another similar work that is proposed by Li et al. [319] is to design a weighted average loss function q-FFL to adaptively adjust the weight of each local model on training performance. The modified objective can be represented by

$$\min_{w} f_q(w) = \sum_{k=1}^{K} \frac{p_k}{q+1} F_k^{q+1}(w) \tag{7.11}$$

where $F_k^{q+1}(\cdot)$ denotes $F_k(\cdot)$ to the power of $(q + 1)$. Hyperparameter q indicates the level of fairness used in model training. Equation 7.11 with $q = 0$ can be regarded as the equivalent of classic federated learning framework, e.g., the objective on *FedAVg* (Equation 7.8). Setting a larger value of q means higher importance for whole training process. By such means, the fairness among different clients is guaranteed.

7.4 LARGE-SCALE COLLABORATIVE LEARNING

In this section, we will discuss two major system architectures for large-scale collaborative model training: the Parameter Server (PS) [311] and decentralized P2P scheme. Employing these architectures in the real-world scenarios requires the careful consideration of application-level job characteristics, communication-level flow patterns, algorithm-level optimization theory and topology-level network construction.

7.4.1 Parameter Server

The Parameter Server (PS) [311] architecture is one of the most widely-used distributed training paradigms, which follows a server-worker structure. The servers and workers directly connect to each other. This scheme decouples the data processing and model update on the workers and servers, respectively. As each worker owns a copy or a part of the global model, the workers can train their local models based on local datasets. The latest model parameters will be fetched from the servers at the beginning of the training. With these parameters, the workers can yield the predicted labels and figure out current loss. The gradients are calculated by each worker to minimize the loss function. The workers will send their local gradient to the server for global model update. Meanwhile, the servers collect all the local gradients and merge them into the global gradients, which are usually calculated by the average operation. With this global gradient, the servers can update the global model parameters under the control of the hyper-parameter called learning rate. The number of servers used in the PS cluster can be adjusted to match the transmission requirements. It is worth noting that workers do not communicate to each other. All the data are exchanged between servers and workers.

As the training procedure is compromised by a serious of iteration, we intend to discuss the distributed processing details within an iteration. Generally, each worker will be initialized by using the latest model parameter fetched from the server side at the beginning of each round. This parameter fetching is usually handled by the pull interface. After the model parameters is set, all the workers will conduct their local training by using the local datasets. Then, each worker will calculate the gradients to optimize the values of loss function. These gradients will be sent to the servers via the push interface. The server will aggregate all the local updates and update the global model parameters. Finally, the current iteration is ended and the next iteration will start.

As to the implementation of distributed parameter synchronization, the *Bulk Synchronous Parallel* (BSP) [373, 546, 604] scheme is the most straightforward choice for many systems, where all the workers are synchronized by a barrier at the end of each iteration. Under this strongly consistent control, the synchronization error will be bound and the system can holds a sub-linear convergence rate.

7.4.2 Decentralized P2P Scheme

In spite of the implementation convenience of PS architecture, the frequent data exchange between workers and servers will yield huge amount of network traffic, especially in a large-scale cluster [562, 596]. This communication pattern will become the performance bottleneck of the distributed ML systems because the data transmission time will dominate the time consumption in each iteration.

Consequently, it is natural to study how to handle the distributed ML training in a decentralized scheme. Existing decentralized training approaches often achieve this target by employing the P2P communication techniques [473, 474]. The rationale of decentralized training is to make each worker communicate with its adjacent neighbours. Therefore, all the workers collaborate together in a P2P mode and the centralized servers can be removed.

Among existing decentralized algorithms, the Gossip collaboration scheme [327, 505] is widely used in many researches due to its ease-of-use. In the Gossip scheme, each worker calculates its own local gradients based on the local data and just exchange these gradients to other workers who are directly linked to it. As the data volume for gradient exchange is significantly reduced, the Gossip scheme can fundamentally alleviate the communication pressure and bring the training speedup over the PS paradigm. Additionally, all the workers are equally treated in the Gossip scheme without the control of the servers. The bandwidth bottleneck of large-scale clusters can be well addressed. Therefore, the training cluster based on Gossip scheme holds a highly elastic scalability and can provide robust fault tolerance of link connections. Moreover, the corresponding optimization algorithms need to be carefully designed to match the Gossip scheme. A promising way to handle the P2P parameter synchronization is to use the *decentralized parallel stochastic gradient descent* (D-PSGD) algorithms [395]. Related researches on this topic have shown that the D-PSGD requires less gradient aggregation and yields less network traffic. Basically, the decentralized P2P scheme can provide a better training convergence efficiency while not degrading the final model quality.

7.4.3 Collective Communication-Based AllReduce

The Message Passing Interface (MPI) [423] is a widely used collective communication framework in distributed process, which can also be adopted to ML training. Different the centralized PS architecture, the AllReduce programming interface is a highly efficient method to handle decentralized parameter and gradient exchange among the workers. e.g., the Baidu Ring-AllReduce [509] and Uber Horovod [466]. The AllReduce method can be used to synchronize any kinds of information via the distributed operation, including calculating the average, minimum, maximum and sum. As the model aggregation in distributed ML applications is mainly calculating the sum of the local gradients and the corresponding average, the AllReduce method is feasible for the processing logic of these operations. The Allreduce method is an abstract programming interface, which can be implemented via different kinds of algorithm and supports various network topologies, including the Fat-Tree [10] and BCube [170] networks. Note that the communication overhead of the AllReduce method depends on the topology of underlying network topology.

7.4.4 Data Flow-Based Graph

Another method to deploy distributed ML procedure is to deploy the functions to different workers. The data flow of a ML task can be described as a *Directed Acyclic Graph* (DAG), where each vertex is a worker or an operation, and the edge between two vertices represents the data flow (the logic dependency) of different stages. Also, if two functions are deployed on two workers, these two workers need to communicate to each other for information exchange. Figure. 7.5 shows the dataflow of training MNIST [105] via Keras [512]. We can observe that there are two kinds of flows between

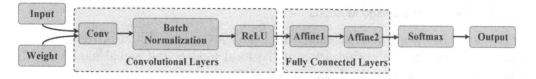

Figure 7.5   The dataflow of training MNIST via Keras.

the vertices (rectangles), the operation logic flow and the intermediate result flow. The operation logic flows control the execution logic of the entire program and the intermediate result flows transfer the computational information between different stages. Actually, the data flow-based graph can also be employed to the previous mentioned three scenarios. A pertinent case in industry is the Google TensorFlow [5] framework.

7.5   PERSONALIZED LEARNING

FL [382] has emerged as an efficient paradigm that collaboratively trains a shared machine learning model among multiple clients without exposing their local raw data. One of the biggest challenges for FL is the issue of data heterogeneity, that is, the data is non-IID across different clients [256, 318]. In such settings, learning a single global model for all clients (e.g., by minimizing average loss) can result in significant bias and poor performance [216,618]. To deal with such statistical diversity, personalized federated learning (pFL) mechanisms are proposed to allow each client to train a personalized model to adapt to their own data distribution [130,189,229,317]. Various approaches have been proposed to realize pFL, which can be classified into *data-based* and *model-based* categories. Data-based methods aims at reducing the statistical heterogeneity among clients' datasets to improve model convergence, while model-based approaches emphasize on producing customized model structures or parameters for different clients.

7.5.1   Data-Based Approaches

Data-based pFL methods focus on smooth the divergence of statistical heterogeneity among different clients. The most straightforward way is to share a small amount of IID data from the server to all clients [618]. Jeong et al. [120, 242] focus on data augmentation methods by generating the missing data to augment its local data so as to conduct an IID dataset. However, these methods usually require the FL server to know the statistical information of the clients' local data distributions (e.g., class sizes, mean and standard deviation), which may potentially violate privacy policy. Another type of work considers to design efficient client selection strategies to enable sampling from a more homogeneous data distribution [369,537,584].

7.5.2   Model-Based Approaches

Model-based pFL methods can also be divided into two types: *single-model, multiple model* approaches.

7.5.2.1 Single Model-Based Methods

Single-model based methods extended from the conventional FL algorithms like Fe-dAvg [382] combine the optimization of the local models and global model, which consist of five different kinds of approaches:

- Local fine-tuning [25, 464, 540], which focuses on build a personalized model for each client by customizing a well-trained global model, i.e., using the private data of each client to produce a personalized model.

- Regularization [189, 190, 501], which is a common practice to prevent overfitting and improve model convergence. Specifically, regularization techniques can be applied by adding a regularized term in the original objective function. This ensures the generalization and the convergence stability of the global model. What's more, it can also be used to train better personalized models.

- Mixture of global model and local models [109, 375], which is proposed to balance generalization with personalization. A penalty parameter λ on global model is added to each client's local loss function to control the similarity between the local model and global model.

- Meta learning [130, 250]. The main concept is to train a meta model by using meta-learning algorithms, such as Model-Agnostic Meta-Learning (MAML) [139]. Then, the personalized model can be obtained with few steps of gradient descent method on the meta model.

- Parameter decomposition [?, 25, 55, 92], which refers to decompose the entire model into several parts, e.g., feature extractor and classifier. FedRep [?] considers to only aggregate local feature extractors from different clients at the server side, while the classifiers are updated locally.

7.5.2.2 Multiple Model-Based Methods

Considering the diversity and inherent relationship of local data, a multi-model based approach where multiple global model is trained for heterogeneous clients is more suitable. Some researchers [155, 229, 375] propose to train multiple global models at the server, where similar clients are clustered into several groups and different models are trained for each group. Another strategy is to collaboratively train a personalized model for each individual client, e.g., FedAMP [229], FedFomo [610], MOCHA [483].

Apart from above methods, another way of personalization is to use Knowledge Distillation (KD) in heterogeneous FL systems ([64, 72, 168, 195, 237, 242, 492, 627]). The principle is to aggregate local soft-predictions instead of local model parameters in the server, whereby each client can update the local model to approach the averaged global predictions. As KD is independent with model structure, some literature [300, 341] are proposed to take advantage of such independence to implement personalized FL with heterogeneous models at client sides. For example, Li et al. [300] propose FedMD to perform ensemble distillation for each client to learn well-personalized models. Different from FedMD that exchanging soft-predictions between the clients and the server, FedDF [341] first aggregates local model parameters for model averaging at the server side. Then, the averaged global models can be updated by performing knowledge transfer from all received (heterogeneous) client models.

7.6 PRACTICE ON FL IMPLEMENTATION

In this section, we conduct a practice on how to implement a FL system, which contains the following three steps: (1) Data distribution; (2) Local model training; (3) Global model aggregation.

7.6.1 Prerequisites

Firstly, we need import some necessary packages:

```
1 import copy
2 import torch
3 import torch.nn as nn
4 import torchvision
5 import torchvision.transforms as transforms
6 import torch.nn.functional as F
7 import numpy as np
8 from torch.utils.data import Dataset, DataLoader
9 import ssl
10 ssl._create_default_https_context = ssl._create_unverified_context
```

Then, we define a ML model (i.e., LeNet).

```
1 class LeNet(nn.Module):
2     def __init__(self, number_classes):
3         super(LeNet, self).__init__()
4
5         self.conv1 = nn.Conv2d(3, 6, kernel_size=5)
6         self.conv2 = nn.Conv2d(6, 12, kernel_size=3, stride=1, padding=1,
        bias=False)
7         self.conv3 = nn.Conv2d(12, 16, kernel_size=5)
8         self.conv4 = nn.Conv2d(16, 20, kernel_size=3, stride=1, padding
        =1, bias=False)
9         self.fc1 = nn.Linear(20 * 5 * 5, 120)
10        self.fc2 = nn.Linear(120, 84)
11        self.fc3 = nn.Linear(84, number_classes)
12
13     def forward(self, x):
14         x = F.relu(self.conv1(x))
15         x = F.relu(self.conv2(x))
16         x = F.max_pool2d(x, 2)
17         x = F.relu(self.conv3(x))
18         x = F.relu(self.conv4(x))
19         x = F.max_pool2d(x, 2)
20         x = x.view(x.size(0), -1)
21         x = F.relu(self.fc1(x))
22         x = F.relu(self.fc2(x))
23         x = self.fc3(x)
24         return x
```

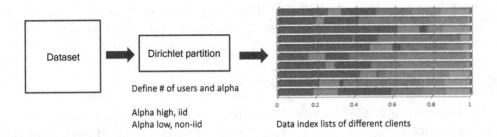

Figure 7.6 The workflow of splitting datatset via Dirichlet distribution.

Taking Cifar10 as an example, we also need to load the corresponding dataset:

```
1 train_dataset = torchvision.datasets.CIFAR10(root='./data/', train=True,
      transform=transforms.ToTensor(), download=True)
2
3 test_dataset = torchvision.datasets.CIFAR10(root='./data',train=False,
      transform=transforms.ToTensor(),download=True)
```

7.6.2 Data Distribution

As shown Figure 7.6, we use Dirichlet distribution [217] to simulate the non-IID data in FL. The Dirichlet distribution function can be defined as

```
1 def dirichlet_partition(training_data, testing_data, alpha, user_num):
2     idxs_train = np.arange(len(training_data))
3     idxs_valid = np.arange(len(testing_data))
4
5     if hasattr(training_data, 'targets'):
6         labels_train = training_data.targets
7         labels_valid = testing_data.targets
8     elif hasattr(training_data, 'img_label'):
9         labels_train = training_data.img_label
10         labels_valid = testing_data.img_label
11
12     idxs_labels_train = np.vstack((idxs_train, labels_train))
13     idxs_labels_train = idxs_labels_train[:,idxs_labels_train[1,:].
      argsort()]
14     idxs_labels_valid = np.vstack((idxs_valid, labels_valid))
15     idxs_labels_valid = idxs_labels_valid[:, idxs_labels_valid[1,:].
      argsort()]
16
17     labels = np.unique(labels_train, axis=0)
18
19     data_train_dict = data_organize(idxs_labels_train, labels)
20     data_valid_dict = data_organize(idxs_labels_valid, labels)
21
22     data_partition_profile_train = {}
23     data_partition_profile_valid = {}
24
25     for i in range(user_num):
26         data_partition_profile_train[i] = []
27         data_partition_profile_valid[i] = []
```

```
28
29       ## Distribute rest data
30       for label in data_train_dict:
31           proportions = np.random.dirichlet(np.repeat(alpha, user_num))
32           proportions_train = len(data_train_dict[label])*proportions
33           proportions_valid = len(data_valid_dict[label]) * proportions
34
35           for user in data_partition_profile_train:
36               data_partition_profile_train[user] = set.union(set(np.random.
         choice(data_train_dict[label], int(proportions_train[user]) , replace
         = False)), data_partition_profile_train[user])
37               data_train_dict[label] = list(set(data_train_dict[label])-
         data_partition_profile_train[user])
38
39               data_partition_profile_valid[user] = set.union(set(
40                   np.random.choice(data_valid_dict[label], int(
         proportions_valid[user]),
41                                   replace=False)),
         data_partition_profile_valid[user])
42               data_valid_dict[label] = list(set(data_valid_dict[label]) -
         data_partition_profile_valid[user])
43
44           while len(data_train_dict[label]) != 0:
45               rest_data = data_train_dict[label][0]
46               user = np.random.randint(0, user_num)
47               data_partition_profile_train[user].add(rest_data)
48               data_train_dict[label].remove(rest_data)
49
50           while len(data_valid_dict[label]) != 0:
51               rest_data = data_valid_dict[label][0]
52               user = np.random.randint(0, user_num)
53               data_partition_profile_valid[user].add(rest_data)
54               data_valid_dict[label].remove(rest_data)
55
56       for user in data_partition_profile_train:
57           data_partition_profile_train[user] = list(
         data_partition_profile_train[user])
58           data_partition_profile_valid[user] = list(
         data_partition_profile_valid[user])
59           np.random.shuffle(data_partition_profile_train[user])
60           np.random.shuffle(data_partition_profile_valid[user])
61
62       return data_partition_profile_train, data_partition_profile_valid
63
64 def data_organize(idxs_labels, labels):
65     data_dict = {}
66
67     labels = np.unique(labels, axis=0)
68     for one in labels:
69         data_dict[one] = []
70
71     for i in range(len(idxs_labels[1, :])):
72         data_dict[idxs_labels[1, i]].append(idxs_labels[0, i])
73     return data_dict
```

After defining the Dirichlet distribution function, the original dataset can be splitted accordingly, i.e., set the number of users as 10, data heterogeneity level (α) as 0.1.

```
1 class DatasetSplit(Dataset):
2     """ An abstract Dataset class wrapped around Pytorch Dataset class
3     """
4
5     def __init__(self, dataset, idxs):
6         self.dataset = dataset
7         self.idxs = [int(i) for i in idxs]
8
9     def __len__(self):
10        return len(self.idxs)
11
12    def __getitem__(self, item):
13        image, label = self.dataset[self.idxs[item]]
14        return torch.tensor(image), torch.tensor(label)
15
16 train_data_list = []
17 user_num = 10
18 alpha = 0.1
19 train_index, test_index = dirichlet_partition(train_dataset, test_dataset
       , alpha=alpha, user_num=user_num)
20 for user_index in range(user_num):
21     data_temp = DatasetSplit(train_dataset, train_index[user_index])
22     train_data_list.append(data_temp)
```

7.6.3 Local Model Training

When successfully splitting the Cifar10 Dataset, the process of local training on each client in FL system should be carefully designed. To this end, we use SGD algorithm to update the local model on each client.

```
1 def local_trainer(dataset, model, global_round, device, local_epoch,
       batchsize):
2
3     dataloader = DataLoader(dataset, batch_size=batchsize, shuffle=True)
4     criterion = nn.CrossEntropyLoss().to(device)
5     model.train()
6     epoch_loss = []
7     optimizer = torch.optim.Adam(model.parameters(), lr=0.001)
8     for iter in range(local_epoch):
9         batch_loss = []
10        for batch_idx, (images, labels) in enumerate(dataloader):
11            images, labels = images.to(device), labels.to(device)
12            model.zero_grad()
13            logits = model(images)
14            loss = criterion(logits, labels)
15            loss.backward()
16            optimizer.step()
17
18            if batch_idx % 10 == 0:
19                print('| Global Round : {} | Local Epoch : {} | [{}/{}
       ({:.0f}%)]\tLoss: {:.6f}'.format(
20                    global_round, iter, batch_idx * len(images),
```

```
21                  len(dataloader.dataset),
22                  100. * batch_idx / len(dataloader), loss.item()))
23          batch_loss.append(loss.item())
24      epoch_loss.append(sum(batch_loss)/len(batch_loss))
25  return model.state_dict(), sum(epoch_loss) / len(epoch_loss)
```

Moreover, we define the inference function as follows,

```
1 def inference(model, testloader):
2      """ Returns the inference accuracy and loss.
3      """
4      model.eval()
5      criterion = nn.CrossEntropyLoss().to(device)
6      loss, total, correct = 0.0, 0.0, 0.0
7      for batch_idx, (images, labels) in enumerate(testloader):
8          images, labels = images.to(device), labels.to(device)
9
10         # Inference
11         outputs = model(images)
12         batch_loss = criterion(outputs, labels)
13         loss += batch_loss.item()
14
15         # Prediction
16         _, pred_labels = torch.max(outputs, 1)
17         pred_labels = pred_labels.view(-1)
18         correct += torch.sum(torch.eq(pred_labels, labels)).item()
19         total += len(labels)
20     loss /= batch_idx
21     accuracy = correct/total
22     return accuracy, loss
```

7.6.4 Global Model Aggregation

At the end of each communication round, the clients will upload their updated models to the server for aggregation.

```
1 def average_weights(w):
2      """
3      Returns the average of the weights.
4      """
5      w_avg = copy.deepcopy(w[0])
6      for key in w_avg.keys():
7          for i in range(1, len(w)):
8              w_avg[key] += w[i][key]
9          w_avg[key] = torch.div(w_avg[key].float(), len(w))
10     return w_avg
```

7.6.5 A Simple Example

Using above functions, we can achieve a simple FL training framework:

```
1 global_rounds = 100
2 local_epochs = 5
3 for round_idx in range(global_rounds):
4     local_weights = []
```

```
5    local_losses = []
6    global_acc = []
7
8    for user_index in range(user_num):
9        model_weights, loss = local_trainer(train_data_list[user_index],
     copy.deepcopy(global_model), round_idx, device, local_epochs,
     batch_size)
10       local_weights.append(copy.deepcopy(model_weights))
11       local_losses.append(loss)
12
13   global_weight = average_weights(local_weights)
14   global_model.load_state_dict(global_weight)
15   test_acc, test_loss = inference(global_model, test_loader)
16   print('Global Round :{}, the global accuracy is {:.3}%, and the
     global loss is {:.3}.'.format(round_idx, 100 * test_acc, test_loss))
```

7.7   CHAPTER SUMMARY

In the scenario of big data analytics, operating large-scale machine learning applications often resort to distributed processing and parallel computing, where handling the collaboration between edge nodes, especially in the heterogeneous environment has become a promising research direction for both algorithm design and system implementation. We intend to elaborate an efficient and scalable Tiny ML platform, which is well compatible with the heterogeneous environment and fully exploits the capacity of edge devices when conducting machine learning applications. To achieve this goal, one critical question is how to build a high-performance architecture for large-scale edge learning systems.

In this chapter, we first summarize the existing parallelism mechanisms for Tiny ML system. Then, we introduce an emerging distributed training framework — Federated Learning (FL), whose key idea is to collaboratively train multiple ML models among different participants without sharing their raw data during the whole training process. We comprehensively explore the Non-IID data, which is the most important challenge in FL. Some enabling technologies are also investigated to improve the performance of FL. Besides, we extent the Non-IID data problem into the personalization of FL, state-of-the-art methods are explained to achieve high-performance of personalized models. Finally, we conduct a practice on FL implementation. Following the steps in this practice, the readers can easily construct a FL training platform, which would be helpful to understand the concept of FL.

CHAPTER 8

Application: Image-Based Visual Perception

8.1 IMAGE CLASSIFICATION

The task of image classification is to classify an image to its corresponding category(s). In practice, the image classification is one of the most fundamental tasks in computer vision, and it is also the task with the most rich benchmark models and datasets. From the relatively simple 10-class handwritten digit recognition task MNIST [105] at the beginning, to the larger 10-class cifar10 [1] and 100-class cifar100 tasks, to the later ImageNet [2] task. Image classification models gradually become more accurate as the dataset grows. Now, in a dataset of more than 10 million images and more than 20,000 categories such as ImageNet, the level of image classification by computers has surpassed that of humans.

The main process of image classification includes image pre-processing, feature extraction and classifier design. Image pre-processing includes image filtering, such as median filtering, mean filtering, Gaussian filtering, and image normalization. Its main function is to filter some irrelevant information in the image, to maximize the retention of useful information on the premise of simplifying the data, and to enhance the reliability of feature extraction. Feature extraction is the most critical part of image classification tasks. It transforms the input image according to certain rules to generate another feature representation with certain features. The new features often have low dimensionality, low redundancy, low noise and other advantages, thereby reducing the requirements for the complexity of the classifier and improving the performance of the model. Finally, the extracted features are classified by training the classifier.

8.1.1 Traditional Image Classification Methods

In the research of traditional image classification, most of them are classification based on image features, that is, according to the differences of categories in images, image processing algorithms are used to extract the corresponding features, and statistical analysis is performed on these features. In terms of feature extraction, it mainly includes low-level visual features such as texture, color, shape, scale-invariant feature

DOI: 10.1201/9781003340225-8

transformation, local binary pattern, directional gradient histogram and other local features. These manual features lack good generalization performance and rely on the designer's prior knowledge and cognitive understanding of the classification task. At present, massive and high-dimensional data also makes it exponentially more difficult to manually design features.

In terms of traditional classifiers, it mainly includes k-nearest neighbor (KNN) [163, 171, 611], decision tree [236, 314], support vector machine(SVM) [172, 221, 298], artificial neural network (ANN) [91, 479], etc. These classifiers greatly improve the performance of image classification, but their classification accuracy cannot meet the actual needs for dealing with a huge amount of data and serious image interference, so traditional classifiers are not suitable for complex image classification.

8.1.2 Deep Learning-Based Image Classification Methods

Image classification tasks have experienced decades of development from traditional methods to deep learning-based methods.

The earliest model based on convolutional neural network (CNN) is LeNet [292]. In the late 1990s and early 2000s, SVM and kNN methods were mostly used. The method represented by SVM can reduce the MNIST classification error rate to 0.56%, which is still higher than the method represented by the neural network, namely the LeNet. The LeNet network was born in 1994, and after many iterations, the LeNet5 [292] in 1998 was the widely known version.

This is a classic CNN that contains some important properties that are still at the core of today's CNN networks.

1. Each layer of CNN consists of convolution, pooling, and nonlinear activation functions. From 1998 to the present, after 20 years of development, CNN still follows this design. Among them, convolution has several variants, pooling has gradually been completely replaced by convolution with stride, and nonlinear activation functions also have many variants.

2. Sparse connection, also known as local connection, is the biggest prerequisite for the development of technologies represented by CNNs. Using the local similarity of images, which is different from the traditional full connection, promotes the development of the entire neural network.

Although the error rate of LeNet5 was still at the level of 0.7% at the time, not as good as the SVM method, with the development of the network structure, the neural network method soon surpassed all other methods, and the error rate was also reduced to 0.23% , and even some methods have reached the level of error rate close to 0.

This was accompanied by the release of the ImageNet dataset [2] in 2009, and the ImageNet Large-Scale Visual Recognition Challenge, ILSVRC, held annually since 2010. Traditional machine learning models are beginning to struggle with such large-scale datasets, and neural networks have begun to enter the view of researchers again. However, due to the limitation of the hardware, the training and optimization of neural networks are still very difficult. Until the emergence of AlexNet [273] in 2012.

AlexNet [273] is the first deep network. Compared with the 5 layers of LeNet-5 [292], its number of layers has increased to 8 layers, the number of parameters of the network has also been greatly increased, and the input has also changed from 28 to 224. At the same time, the use of GPU has also brought deep learning into a new era.

The innovation of AlexNet [273] mainly exists in the following points:

1. The ReLU activation function is used to accelerate the convergence and solve the gradient dispersion problem of Sigmoid when the network is deep.

2. Using operations such as crop and flip enhances the generalization ability of the model.

3. Dropout layer is added to prevent overfitting.

In 2014, the VGG network (VGGNet) [481] was the runner-up of the ILSVRC. VGGNet [481] includes two versions, 16-layer and 19-layer, with a total of about 550M parameters. The network structure uses a 3×3 convolution kernel and a 2×2 max-pooling kernel, which simplifies the structure of the convolutional neural network. VGGNet [481] nicely shows how the performance of the network can be improved by simply increasing the number and depth of the network based on the previous network architecture. Although simple, it is extremely effective. Today, VGGNet [481] is still selected as the benchmark model for many tasks.

The core of GoogleNet [500] is the Inception Module, which uses the parallel mechanism. A classic inception structure consists of four components: 1×1 convolution, 3×3 convolution, 5×5 convolution, 3×3 max pooling, and finally concatenate the four component operation results. This is the core idea of the Inception Module. The information of different scales of the image is extracted by multiple convolution kernels and then fused to obtain a better representation of the image. Compared with VGGNet [481], the GoogLeNet [500] model architecture has a deeper and smaller model under the well-designed Inception structure, and is more computationally efficient. Since then, the classification accuracy of deep learning models has reached the human level.

The proposal of Deep Residual Network (ResNet) [200] is a milestone event in the history of CNN images. In the 2015 ILSVRC, ResNet [200] won first place in one fell swoop. ResNet [200] solves the problem that deep CNN models are difficult to train. Compared with VGGNet [481] in 2014, which has only 19 layers, ResNet [200] in 2015 has 152 layers, so many researchers think that ResNet [200] wins by depth. However, ResNet [200] is able to have such a deep network because of the trick in the architecture. This trick is residual learning.

The depth of the network is critical to the performance of the model. When the number of network layers increases, the network can extract more complex feature patterns, so theoretically better results can be achieved when the model is deeper. However, when the network depth increases, the network accuracy declines, which is called the degradation problem of deep networks. The degradation problem of deep networks at least shows that deep networks are not easy to train, and residual learning is used to solve the degradation problem.

For a stacked-layer structure (several layers stacked), when the input is x, the learned features are denoted as $H(x)$. Now we hope that it can learn the residual $F(x) = H(x) - x$, so that the original learned feature is actually $H(x)$. The reason for this is that residual learning is easier than direct learning from raw features. When the residual is 0, the accumulation layer only does the identity mapping at this time, at least the network performance will not be degraded, in fact, the residual will not be 0, which will also enable the accumulation layer to learn new features based on the input features, resulting in better performance.

ResNeXt [575], which was born in 2016, won the runner-up of the ILSVRC that year. ResNeXt [575] is a combination of ResNet [200] and Inception, but ResNeXt [575] does not need to manually design a complex Inception structure, and each branch adopts the same topology. Among them, Inception is a very obvious "split-transform-merge" structure. The author of ResNeXt [575] believes that the different topological structures of different branches of Inception mean the carving of features, and often adjusting the internal structure of Inception corresponds to a large number of hyper-parameters. These Hyper-parameters are very difficult to fine-tune. So they let each Inception structure use the same topology and combined the residual network to get the final output.

2017 was the last year of ILSVRC, and SENet [219], the champion of the last competition, aroused researchers' enthusiasm for channel-wise attention. The idea of SENet [219] is very simple, and it is easy to expand in the existing network structure. For CNN, the core is the convolution calculation, that is, the new feature map is learned from the input feature map through the convolution kernel. Essentially, convolution is a feature fusion of a local area. This fusion can be channel-wise or spatial-wise. For convolution, recent work is to improve the receptive field, that is, to spatially fuse more feature fusions, or to extract multi-scale spatial information. The innovation of SENet [219] is to focus on the relationship between channels, hoping that the model can automatically learn the importance of different channel features. Therefore, SENet [219] proposes the Squeeze-and-Excitation (SE) module. The SE module first performs the Squeeze on the feature map obtained by convolution to obtain the channel-level global features, then performs the Excitation on the global features, learns the relationship between each channel, and also obtains the weights of different channels, and finally multiplies the original feature map to get the final feature. In essence, the SE module performs the attention operation on the channel dimension. This attention mechanism allows the model to pay more attention to the channel features with the largest amount of information while suppressing those unimportant channel features. Another point is that the SE module is generic, which means it can be embedded into existing network architectures such as VGGNet [481] and ResNet [200].

In recent years, we are also motivated to enable machines to generalize learned knowledge to the unknown domain by mimicking the ability of human being. Previous study has proven that humans can recognize over 30,000 object classes with many more sub-classes [41], such as breeds of birds and combinations of attributes and objects. Besides, humans are quite skilled at recognizing classes of objects without seeing real examples of them in advance. For example, if a learner who has never seen a panda is told that the panda is a bear-like animal with black and white fur, he or she can easily recognize a panda when seeing a real example. In machine learning, this scenario is defined as the problem of zero-shot learning (ZSL) [53, 66, 142, 173–176, 268, 284, 285, 357, 476, 506, 550, 616, 634]. The ZSL can be considered as an extreme case of transfer learning: the model is trained to mimic the ability of humans to recognize examples of unseen classes that were not shown during the training phase. ZSL is usually achieved by extracting some *common knowledge* from the labeled seen class examples, where these knowledge can be shared and transferred between seen and unseen classes. This common knowledge is per-class, semantic and high-level features for both the seen and unseen classes [284], which enables easy and fast implementation and inference to ZSL. Among them, semantic attributes and semantic word vectors have become the most popular common knowledge in recent years. The semantic attributes are meaningful high-level information about examples, such as shape, color, component, and texture. In contrast, semantic word vectors are vector representations of words learned from a large external corpus, of which two word vectors are expected to have a small distance if two words more frequently appear in context than others. As such, similar classes should have similar patterns in the semantic feature space, and this particular pattern is defined as the prototype. Each class is embedded in the semantic feature space and endowed with a prototype, so the ZSL can be easily extended to much broader classes by collecting class-level prototypes instead of example-level collecting and labeling, which are expensive and time consuming. In conventional supervised learning (CSL), the training and testing examples belong to the same class-set, which means that the learned model has already seen some examples of all the classes it encounters during testing. In contrast, the ZSL only trains the model on seen class examples, and the learned model is expected to infer novel/unseen class examples. Thus, the essential difference between the ZSL and CSL is that the training and testing class sets of ZSL are disjoint from each other. As a result, the ZSL can be regarded as a complement to the CSL and can handle some scenarios where labeled data are scarce or difficult to obtain for some classes.

8.1.3 Conclusion

Before deep learning, neural networks did not perform well compared to traditional machine learning models such as SVM. But as the number of data increases, traditional machine learning models reach a computational bottleneck. The advent of GPU-accelerated computing, along with the holding of ILSVRC, has greatly facilitated the advancement of image classification tasks. These advances are starting to benefit other computer vision tasks as well.

8.2 IMAGE RESTORATION AND SUPER-RESOLUTION

8.2.1 Overview

Image restoration is a broad research topic in image-based visual perception. It aims at restoring degraded images into their clean and original version. In reality, such

(a) Image de-raining [605] (b) Image de-hazing [57]

(c) Image coloring [85]

Figure 8.1 Some examples of image restoration: (a) image de-raining that removes the rain-lines in images, (b) image de-hazing that removes the haze in images, and (c) image coloring that transforms gray images into colored version (better viewed in color and zoom-in mode).

degradation can be any type of operation(s) that can generate imperfect and defective images in our real-world applications, such as adding noisy and blur, lossy compression, watermarks, resolution drawing, and so on. For example, one can restore an image that captured with a camera in the rainy day or foggy day, where mussy rain-lines or blurry haze may result in visually unpleasant photographs and affect the its utilization. Worse still, such blur version of images may also degrade the performance of several further applications based on them, such as the visual-based automatic driving, security monitoring (e.g., CCTVs), etc. In image processing, we call such a restoration as De-raining [605] as demonstrated in Figure 8.1(a) and De-hazing [57] as demonstrated in Figure 8.1(b), respectively. Recently, some other research also focusing on restoring gray images into colored ones and thus can remake several artistic works such black and white drama and old picture renovates. Such a restoration is Coloring [85] as demonstrated in Figure 8.1(c).

In another scenario, one can also observe that the images or videos that captured in the past decades may have very low-resolutions. For examples, the first digital

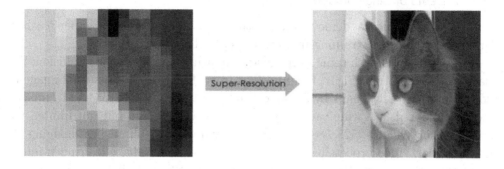

Figure 8.2 Image super-resolution based on the architecture in [49].

camera designed by Kodak [1] can only capture 0.01 megapixel images in 1975 and only for professional use, while nowadays, even the consumer-level digital cameras can easily produce and store hundreds megapixel images and greatly improved the visual quality of photographs in various applications. In image processing, we can also restore a low-resolution image into a high-resolution version that facilitates the utilization of previous images and videos. As demonstrated in Figure 8.2, such a restoration is the so-called image super-resolution that can be utilized in various applications [114, 158, 177, 192, 334, 614], such as improving the recognition performance, image contents understanding, pedestrian re-identification in monitoring, computer game remaking, and so on.

8.2.2 A Unified Framework for Image Restoration and Super-Resolution

Deep learning is the current main-stream technique for image restoration and super-resolution. In summary, a corrupt image and its clean/original counterpart are formed as a training pair. Such corrupt image can be any form of low-quality representations such as low-resolution, blurriness, watermark embedded, grey-scaled, hazed, and so on. For the training pair, the corrupt image is first fed into the deep neural network. Then, the clean counterpart is used as the supervision for the training, i.e., the network is forced to output an estimated clean version of the inputted corrupt image such that the difference between the estimated clean version and the ground-truth clean counterpart can be minimized. The training process can be conceptually described as:

$$\min_{\Theta} \|Net(I_{Cor}, \Theta) - I_{Ori}\|_2 \tag{8.1}$$

where I_{Cor} and I_{Ori} are the corrupt image and its original clean counterpart, respectively. $Net(cot, cot)$ denotes the deep neural network and Θ is the trainable parameter set. Such a supervision is an unified framework for any image restoration and super-resolution tasks that can be easily implemented in various kinds of deep models.

---

[1] https://www.kodak.com

8.2.3 A Demo of Single Image Super-Resolution

Hereby, we introduce a demo work for the task of single image super-resolution. Consistently, the basic training framework is also based on Eq. 8.1.

As a popular research topic in the field of multimedia and computer vision, Single Image super-resolution (SISR) focus on Recovery of high-resolution (HR) image from a low-resolution (LR) image by SR algorithms [114, 158, 177, 192, 334, 614]. Image SR is widely adopted in a wide variety of applications, including but not limited to security and surveillance [528, 588], satellite image analysis [40], medical imaging [420], high-definition video processing [226], etc. Since LR images have lost much information compared to their HR counterparts, the image SR is an ill-posed problem that has multiple solutions for LR inputs [31, 345]. Recently, with the rapid development of deep learning techniques, deep learning based SR algorithms achieve superior performance compared with traditional SR algorithms in terms of not only quantitative metrics including peak signal-to-noise ratio (PSNR) and structural similarity index (SSIM), but also qualitative measures with more visually pleasing HR images. The deep learning based SR algorithms can be categorized into two main-streams. One is based on the generative adversarial networks (GANs) involving two neural networks that contest with each other in a zero-sum game framework. This technique helps to generate images that look at least superficially authentic to human observers. Some representative methods include SRGAN [293], EnhanceNet [459] and CinC-GAN [597]. The other is built upon deep convolutional neural networks (DCNNs), which adopts a deep network architecture to learn a mapping from LR images to their HR counterparts with L1 or L2 loss in pixel space. Some representative methods include SRCNN [114], FSRCNN [115], VDSR [261], LapSRN [283], EDSR [334], RDN [615], DBPN [192], RCAN [614], etc. Generally speaking, the GANs based SR algorithms can obtain more visually pleasing images, contributing to the improvement of qualitative performance. However, they do not perform very well in quantitative performance, i.e., PSNR and SSIM. Furthermore, the training of GANs is more difficult and costly, which relies on more training data and tough convergence.

In contrast, DCNNs based SR algorithms are much easier to train and can achieve better quantitative performance in PSNR and SSIM. Meanwhile, they perform satisfactorily in qualitative performance in practical applications. In recent years, The DCNNs based image SR algorithms can far outperform traditional image SR algorithms by achieving significant improvements and obtaining successive state-of-the-art performances. However, most of them do not pay enough attention to the limited high-frequency information from LR images. This motivates us to consider that highlighting high-frequency components from LR inputs and treating LR features unequally are also crucial for recovering higher quality HR images. In this demo, we present the Dual-view Attention Networks to alleviate these problems for SISR (termed as DAN-SISR). Specifically, we propose both local-aware (LA) and global-aware (GA) attention approaches to adaptively handle LR features with unequal manners. On the one hand, the attention of LA unequally highlights the high-frequency components inside each LR feature map in the local view. On the other hand, in the global view, each feature map is unequally re-weighted by the GA attention after the LR

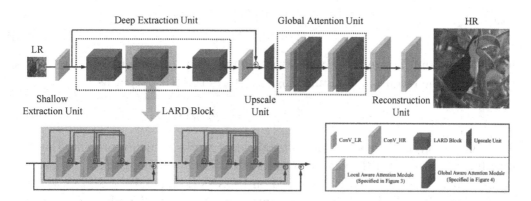

Figure 8.3 Framework of the demo.

inputs have passed through the upscale unit into the HR feature space. In addition, to achieve a deeper yet easily trainable architecture, we also propose the local attentive residual-dense (LARD) block, which combines LA attention with multiple residual and dense connections in the LR feature space.

8.2.3.1 Networks Architecture

As shown in Figure 8.3, the DAN-SISR mainly consists of five parts: (1) Shallow extraction unit, which is exactly a convolution layer (ConV). (2) Deep extraction unit, which contains several local attentive residual-dense (LARD) blocks in series. It can extract rich deep features with sufficient high-frequency information by combining the LA attention with multiple residual and dense connections. (3) Upscale unit, which resizes the low-resolution (LR) input to high-resolution (HR) scale. (4) Global attention unit, which unequally re-weights each feature map in the HR feature space. (5) Reconstruction unit, which restores the HR output. Considering an input LR image I_{LR}, we denote its HR counterpart as I_{SR}. In our DAN-SISR, we first input I_{LR} to the shallow feature extraction unit and obtain its shallow feature as:

$$F_S = E_S\left(I_{LR}\right), \tag{8.2}$$

where $E_S\left(\cdot\right)$ and F_S is defined as the shallow feature extraction unit and the shallow feature, respectively. Then F_S is inputted into the deep feature extraction unit for the next step as:

$$F_D = E_D\left(F_S\right), \tag{8.3}$$

where F_D denotes the deep feature and $E_D\left(\cdot\right)$ denotes the deep feature extraction unit with k LARD blocks. This unit help us to construct a very deep and trainable network architecture. Next, the obtained deep feature F_D continues passing through the upscale unit $E_U\left(\cdot\right)$ and resizing to the HR feature maps, i.e.,

$$F_U = E_U\left(F_D\right). \tag{8.4}$$

Since the upscaled F_U is still in a deep and general stage [590], the global attention unit can be applied to discriminate and re-weight each feature map in the HR feature space as:

$$F_G = E_G\left(F_U\right), \qquad (8.5)$$

where $E_G\left(\cdot\right)$ and F_G are the global attention unit and the obtained feature, respectively. Last, the reconstruction unit $E_R\left(\cdot\right)$ restores the HR output as:

$$I_{SR} = E_R\left(F_G\right) = \Phi_{DAN-SISR}\left(I_{LR}\right), \qquad (8.6)$$

where $\Phi_{DAN-SISR}\left(\cdot\right)$ denotes the will-trained networks, which represents the mapping function from an LR image I_{LR} to its HR counterpart image I_{SR}.

Similar to most SR algorithms based on DCNNs [114, 115, 192, 261, 283, 334, 615], we also introduce L_1 loss into the optimization of our DAN-SISR. Given a set of training data $\mathcal{D}_{Tr} = \{I_{LR}^i, I_{SR}^i\}_{i=1}^n$, which contains n LR input images and their corresponding HR counterparts. The loss function is defined as:

$$\mathcal{L}\left(\theta\right) = \frac{1}{n}\sum_{i=1}^n \left\|\Phi_{DAN-SISR}\left(I_{LR}\right) - I_{SR}\right\|_1, \qquad (8.7)$$

where $\|\cdot\|_1$ denotes the L_1 norm and θ denotes the parameter set of our model. The loss function can be optimized through stochastic gradient descent with a decreasing learning rate.

8.2.3.2 *Local Aware Attention*

The local-aware (LA) attention module is a key building block in our model, while the previous DCNNs based SR algorithms typically process each feature from LR inputs equally in their network layers. However, according to our observation, the LR image has lost much high-frequency information compared with its HR counterpart, e.g., sharp contrast edges, textures, etc. The LR inputs only contain limited high-frequency components which make the restored HR images visually uncomfortable. Worse still, with low-frequency information redundancy, the SR algorithms tends to generate excessively smooth images to cater for higher quantitative results such as PSNR and SSIM metrics. Therefore, the limited high-frequency information from LR inputs is very significant in image recovery, which requires more attention.

Based on above analyses, we propose to process each LR feature with an unequal manners. First, we process LR inputs in the LR feature space. The LA attention module focus on highlighting the high-frequency components in the local view, which is the interior of each LR feature map in the LR feature space. As shown in Figure 8.4, we illustrate more details about the structure of LA attention module. Consider a layer in the deep feature extraction unit, we have a tensor T_D with size $H \times W \times C$, which denotes that there are C feature maps in C channels, and each feature map has the height H and the width W. We first apply the average pooling on T_D, i.e.,

$$T_{DA} = AvgPool(T_D, ks, s), \qquad (8.8)$$

where ks and s are the pooling kernel size and stride, respectively. In this step, we set $s = ks$, so that the obtained tensor T_{DA} have a size of $\frac{H}{ks} \times \frac{W}{ks} \times C$, and each value

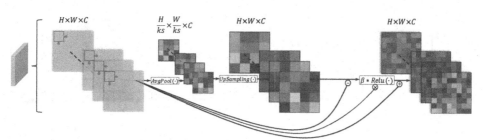

Figure 8.4 Local aware attention.

in T_{DA} represents the average intensity of a specific sub-region in the corresponding feature map of T_D. Next, by using up-sampling with a scale parameter equal to ks, an $H \times W \times C$ tensor T_{DU} can be obtained with the same size as T_D:

$$T_{DU} = UpSampling(T_{DA}, ks). \qquad (8.9)$$

The obtained T_U can be regarded as an expression of the average smoothness information of the sub-regions in the original T_D. Essentially, each element in the feature map represents the embedded feature and signal intensity of a specific region in the feature map of the previous layer. Thus, to highlight the high-frequency information in the local view, i.e., the sub-regions of each feature map, we design an alternative strategy to highlight the elements in each feature map of the next layer. To achieve our purpose, we subtract T_{DU} from T_D in element-wise and activate the remainings, i.e.,

$$T_{DR} = Relu\left(T_D - T_{DU}\right), \qquad (8.10)$$

where $Relu\left(\cdot\right)$ is the rectified linear unit which takes the positive part of its argument, and T_{DR} is the regional average residual. Each value in T_{DR} denotes whether its corresponding sub-region in the feature map of the previous layer is beyond the average sub-smoothness or not. Finally, two shortcuts from T_D to T_{DR} (element-wise multiplication), and to the very end (element-wise sum) are constructed as:

$$\hat{T}_D = T_D + \beta T_{DR} \otimes T_D, \qquad (8.11)$$

where β is a tiny hyper-parameter, which controls the highlighting degree and $\otimes$ denotes the element-wise multiplication. The updated $\hat{T}_D$ is further inputted to the next layer of the deep feature extraction unit.

8.2.3.3 Global Aware Attention

In contrast to the LA attention, the global aware (GA) attention is designed to process the global view of the LR inputs, i.e., unequally discriminating and re-weighting each feature map after passing through the upscale unit in the HR feature space, which is illustrated in Figure 8.5. Conventional DCNNs based SR algorithms treat each feature map equally in their networks. However, when performing convolution operations, different filters generate different types of features. These features will form different feature maps to represent an input data in multi-level aspects. In other words, the

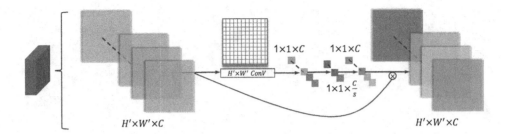

Figure 8.5 Global aware attention.

representation ability of each feature map varies from each other. Therefore, it is necessary to pay more attention to discriminate these feature maps in our model.

Based on these analyses, we propose the global aware attention unit as shown in Figure 8.5. We consider an $H' \times W' \times C$ tensor T_G with the same height H' and width W' as HR images. First, we perform a convolution operation with kernel size $H' \times W'$ to T_G as:

$$V_G = ConV(T_G, [H', W']). \quad (8.12)$$

The $H' \times W'$ filter generates a $1 \times 1 \times C$ tensor V_G for T_G. Each element in V_G denotes some statistics information of each feature map of T_G. Different from existing attention models that use global average pooling operation, we adopt a trainable $H' \times W'$ filter to obtain this statistics information, which makes the model more robust and expressive. Then by utilizing two convolution operations for the obtained V_G, we can have:

$$V_G' = \sigma(ConV_2(Relu(ConV_1(V_G, C, C')), C', C)), \quad (8.13)$$

where $ConV_1$ is the first convolution operation that shrinks V_G from C to C' channels ($C' < C$), and the second one $ConV_2$, upscales it back. $Relu(\cdot)$ and $\sigma(\cdot)$ are the rectified linear unit and sigmoid gateway, respectively. The updated V_G' can represent a more general global statistics for each feature map in the HR feature space. Finally, a shortcut from T_G to the updated V_G' is constructed, and the original T_G is re-weighted as:

$$\hat{T}_G = V_G' \cdot T_G. \quad (8.14)$$

With the well-designed GA attention, our DAN-SISR can adaptively pay unequal attention to different feature maps in the global view.

8.2.3.4 LARD Block

It has been illustrated that the network depth has crucial importance to image SR task [261]. In our DAN-SISR, the deep extraction unit contains several local attentive residual-dense (LARD) blocks in series, as shown in Figure 8.6. This architecture allows us to easily construct a deep yet easy to train networks by repeatedly stacking the LARD block.

It is investigated in ResNet [200], as the depth increases, the residual learning framework can dramatically alleviate the problem of vanishing gradients and better

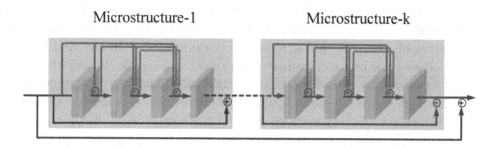

Figure 8.6 LARD block.

guarantee the model's representation ability by adopting skip connections from one layer to latter layers. The DenseNet [223] further extends the skip connections to each single layer and constructs the dense connections in the network architecture. Consequently, one layer receives the feature maps of all preceding layers, resulting in two merits, i.e., deeper trainable network architecture and better cross-layer extraction ability. Inspired by these insights, the proposed LARD block combines our local aware attention with multiple residual and dense connections, which is used to extract rich deep features from LR inputs. The LARD block can not only highlight the high-frequency components in the local view, i.e., within the sub-regions of each feature map, but also strengthen the model's extraction and representation ability.

8.3 SELF-ATTENTION AND VISION TRANSFORMERS

The Transformer model is the seq2seq model proposed by Google Brain at the end of 2017 [529]. The special thing about Transformer is that a special layer like Self-Attention is widely used in the model. In Self-Attention Layer, we first multiply each input a^i by 3 different matrices to obtain 3 different vectors, which are named q, k, and v respectively. The next thing to do is to use each query q to multiply each key k. Then use softmax to get $\hat{a}$, and then multiply and add the obtained $\hat{a}$ and v to get the output b^i. For b^i, the generated b^i has considered as the entire input.

Transformer first appeared in natural language processing (NLP) scenarios to process sequence information [529]. But as Transformer has achieved excellent results in NLP, it has also aroused the interest of the computer vision community [117], so starting in 2020, many researchers have begun to study their applications in computer vision problems. In the field of NLP, in addition to Transformer, there is also Long Short-Term Memory (LSTM). The advantage of Transformer over LSTM is that Transformer supports parallel processing of sequence data, so it is discovered and applied by computer vision.

Although the Transformer architecture has become the standard for NLP tasks, Vision Transformer (ViT) [117] was first proposed in the field of computer vision. ViT [117] was proposed by A. Dosovitskiy et al. The method adopted is to split the input image into patches, and label each patch to convert it into similar sequence information. In this way, image patches are processed in the same way as tokens in NLP, and image classification training can also be performed accordingly. However,

ViT [117] is not as effective as traditional CNN models, such as ResNet [200], when faced with small-scale datasets. But when the scale of the dataset becomes larger, the advantages of ViT [117] will gradually become apparent. In the model design, ViT [117] followed the original Transformer as much as possible. In order to process two-dimensional images, Transformer uses a constant hidden vector D on all layers, so the patches are flattened, and a trainable linear projection is used to map to the size of D. The output of this projection is called patch embedding. At the same time, position embedding is added to patch embedding to preserve position information. The Transformer's encoder consists of multi-head self-attention and MLP layers, and applies layernorm before each block, and uses residual linking after each block. In order to allow the model to classify images, ViT [117] also introduced the class token mechanism in BERT. The purpose is because the Transformer input is a series of patch embeddings, and the output is also a sequence of patch features of the same length, but in the end it must be summarized as a judge for classification. The author also introduced a class token, it can play as a flag, using its output features plus a linear classifier can achieve a good classification result.

ViT [117] also has many problems. For example, the use of a large number of self-attention modules leads to a large amount of parameters, which in turn leads to a large amount of calculation. The second thing is the large demand for data, mainly because CNN has a strong ability of inductive bias, which is something that self-attention cannot do.

In short, the emergence of ViT [117] and its excellent performance in the face of large-scale data defeated CNN, which is usually concerned by everyone in the computer vision field. Therefore, more and more researchers have begun to turn their attention to Transformer, and the methods based on Transformer have sprung up.

DeiT [518], as another Transformer-based method, was proposed by H. Touvron et al. to solve problems such as large amount of calculation caused by the vision transformer. They proposed that many Transformers used to solve visual problems have very expensive architectures and cannot be applied in real scenarios on a very large scale. But in DeiT [518], it uses knowledge distillation, adds a distillation token on the basis of ViT [117], and then continuously interacts with class token and patch token in self-attention layers. Distillation token is very similar to ViT's class token, but the goal of class token is to predict the real label, and the distillation token must be consistent with the label predicted by the teacher model. When training the model, use the loss of soft distillation or hard distillation for training. The author found that the convergence directions of class token and distillation token are different, indicating that they hope to get similar but different targets. At the same time, DeiT [518] optimizes data enhancement and regularization operations. Although it does not introduce any important framework, the training time of the model is greatly shortened through knowledge distillation, and the training accuracy of the model is also improved.

After the emergence of ViT [117] and DeiT [518], researchers began to use these recognition algorithms extensively. However, these recognition algorithms can only be used for recognition, and lack the ability as a backbone. The emergence of Swin Transformer [355] solves the problem that the previous Transformer-based model cannot be used as a backbone. This is a layered Transformer architecture and is calculated by using a sliding window. The sliding window operation includes non-overlapping local window and overlapping cross-window. Limiting the attention calculation to a window can introduce the locality of the CNN operation on the one hand, and save the amount of calculation on the other hand. The entire model adopts a hierarchical design, including a total of 4 stages, each stage will reduce the resolution of the input feature map, and expand the receptive field layer like CNN. Unlike ViT [117], Swin Transformer [355] uses the same avg-pooling as CNN for classification tasks. The idea of this paper has played a role in linking the previous and the next. For the first time, the computer vision field has a Transformer-based backbone, breaking the monopoly of CNN for computer vision feature extraction.

Transformer can not only be used in image classification, but also contribute its value in object detection. N. Carion et al. discovered the relationship between Transformer's encoder and decoder, and designed a new object detection model DETR [60]. The structure of the DETR [60] detection module is similar to that of Transformer. After the features obtained by backbone are flattened, position information is added and sent to the encoder of Transformer to obtain the features of candidates. Then the features of these candidates are sent to Transformer's decoder for parallel decoding, and finally the bounding box is obtained. The idea is that the decoder has two inputs, which are the feature results generated by the encoder. One is Object Query, which is the output of the previous decoder, and object encoder is a parameter that can be learned. During the training process, because different boxes need to be generated, Object queries will be forced to be different to reflect the information of position. In terms of performance, DETR [60] can reach or even surpass Faster RCNN [450]. In addition, it has another particularity in that it combines CNN and Transformer, uses CNN's backbone to extract image features, and then sends them to Transformer for detection.

In the field of image generation, many researchers have also begun to explore Transformer. TransGAN [249] is one of the representative methods. It uses two Transformers to generate a powerful Generative Adversarial Network (GAN), which does not include any convolution process. In terms of structure alone, TransGAN [249] is not very innovative for the encoder itself, but in the generator part, in order to save the GPU memory, the authors choose to be composed of multiple stages. As the stage increases, the resolution of the feature map is continuously increased until it is the same as the target resolution. Add a class token to the input tokens sequence part of the discriminator to determine whether it is a real picture. Although TransGAN [249] does not have much improvement over AutoGAN [160], it is a good attempt. At the same time, several tricks are proposed to reduce the amount of calculation and improve parameters. However, the author also found that using Transformer's encoder in the discriminator part cannot improve the overall performance of the model. Therefore, the use of Transformer for image generation still has a long way to go.

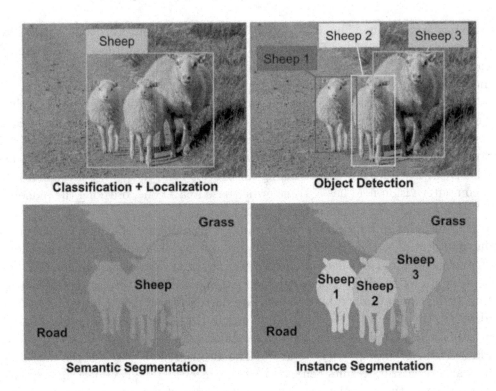

Figure 8.7 Differences between segmentation and object detection based on the architecture in [446].

8.4 ENVIRONMENT PERCEPTION: IMAGE SEGMENTATION AND OBJECT DETECTION

8.4.1 Object Detection

As shown in Figure 8.7, object detection is a very important task in the field of computer vision, which is used to detect specific object instances in images. Object detection forms the basis of many computer vision tasks, such as video tracking and segmentation. In recent years, the emergence of deep learning has enabled object detection to flourish. In this section, we will summarize object detection from two directions. That is, traditional object detection model and the deep network model.

8.4.1.1 Traditional Object Detection Model

In the early object detection models, due to the lack of understanding of the deep features of the image, most of the methods are based on the construction of manual features to achieve the detection procedure. These manual features are complicated to construct, time-consuming, and the quality of the generated features is not good enough. This makes the early object detection models unable to adapt to large-scale datasets and complex tasks.

In the year of 2000, P. Viola and M. Jones [532] realized face detection without any restriction for the first time. Compared with all algorithms at the time, the speed of this detector has been increased by dozens or even hundreds of times. The detection algorithm also uses a sliding window as a detection method, searching all possible positions in the image to see if any window contains a human face. In addition, VJ detector also incorporates three important technologies: "feature selection", "detection cascades" and "integral image". After this, some methods began to explore more accurate manual features, and try to use this feature to guide the detection of objects.

Histogram of Oriented Gradient (HOG) feature description was first proposed by N. Dalal and B. Triggs [101] in 2005. Compared with scale invariant feature transform (SIFT) and shape context feature transform, it is a huge improvement. HOG operates in the local cell area of the image, so it can maintain good invariance to image geometry and optical deformation. It is precisely because of this invariance that HOG features are mainly used for pedestrian detection. At the same time, the HOG feature detector has been the primary feature extraction method adopted by many object detectors for a long time.

Deformable Part-based Model (DPM) [137] is a deformable component model and a component-based detection algorithm. This method was proposed by P. Felzen-szwalb in 2008 and includes a root filter and a component filter. DPM adopts the improved HOG feature extraction, SVM classifier and sliding window detection ideas, and adopts a multi-component combination strategy for the multi-view problem of objects. Aiming at the problem of deformation of the object itself, a component model strategy based on graph structure is adopted. In addition, the class to which the sample belongs, the location of the component model, etc., are used as latent variables, and multi-instance learning is used to automatically determine it.

As several traditional models, they all have a certain degree of representative-ness. Although today's object detectors based on deep learning have far surpassed VJ [532] and DPM [137] in detection speed and accuracy, these models also have a profound impact on subsequent object detection methods. For example, R. Girshick, who proposed the RCNN series, extended a new hybrid model on the basis of DPM to deal with more changing real-world objects.

8.4.1.2 Deep Learning-Based Object Detection Model

As the performance of hand-made features becomes saturated, after the end of the first decade of the 21st century, the field of object detection has fallen into a bot-tleneck. More and more methods generally adopt the "manual feature extractor + classifier" model. But in 2012, with the emergence of AlexNet [273], convolutional neural networks (CNN) once again came into the eyes of researchers, that is, since deep convolutional neural networks can learn high-level feature representations of images, can they use such high-level feature representations and replace traditional hand-made features? R. Girshick et al. first proposed Regions CNN (RCNN) [157] for object detection tasks in 2014. Since then, object detection has entered the era of deep learning. In the era of deep learning, models are classified into "one-stage detection" and "two-stage detection". The following two types of models will be summarized.

The two-stage detection network follows the pattern of "from coarse to fine". As a pioneering method for two-stage detection, RCNN [157] has a very simple idea. First, use the selective search method for the input image to select candidate proposals, and then rescale each proposal to the same size and send it to the CNN model for training extract features. Finally, a support vector machine is used to identify the generated features and determine whether there is an object category in the candidate frame. Compared with the traditional manual feature method, the RCNN [157] method has a significant improvement in detection accuracy. The improvement on the Pascal VOC 2007 dataset [129] is as high as 20%. At the same time, this paper proves that the neural network can be applied to the bottom-up candidate area to classify and locate objects.

However, RCNN [157] still has many shortcomings. For example, RCNN needs to use selective search to extract multiple candidate frames in advance when extracting candidate regions, which is time-consuming. Candidate frames of different sizes extracted at the same time need to be fixed to the same size, which will cause the picture to be deformed and is not conducive to feature extraction. But this does not affect RCNN as a cross-age method.

In response to the above-mentioned problems, R. Girshick immediately put forward his new idea, namely Fast RCNN [156]. As the name suggests, compared to RCNN [157], Fast RCNN [156] solves the above-mentioned problems and proposes Regions of Interest (ROI) . The principle is to extract the potential regions from the selective search. After the image features are extracted by the convolutional network, the location the potential regions is selected on the feature map, and the pooling layer is used to unify the scale. Therefore, Fast RCNN [156] does not limit the input of data, which greatly improves the detection efficiency.

Although Fast RCNN has made great progress, ROI Pooling is not easy to operate because of the variable size of the candidate frames generated by selective search. Therefore, Faster RCNN [450] once again corrected the deficiencies of the first two tasks, and used the Regions Proposal Network (RPN) to detect the four steps of the object: that is, generating candidate regions, feature extraction, classification, and regression are all processed inside the neural network. Faster RCNN [450] uses RPN to complete the generation and extraction of candidate regions, and identify objects in the candidate region, then use anchors for positioning in the selected part of the candidate region. This greatly improves the speed and accuracy of detection, which is an example of a two-stage detection network.

The first-stage detection network pursues "one step". Compared with the "proposal detection + verification" of the second-stage detection network, its structure is simpler and more direct, and the detection speed is faster, but the detection accuracy is often not high.

You Only Look Once (YOLO) [448] was proposed by R. Joseph and was the first one-stage detector. Its core idea is to take the entire picture as input, and directly determine the position and class of the candidate frame in the feature output layer. In YOLO [448], for the input image, the image is first divided into grids of the same size, and each grid is set with a fixed number of bounding boxes, and each bounding box must predict the coordinates and confidence to predict the position of the object.

This one-step method is very simple to operate, can be real-time and has strong versatility. But the detection accuracy is not high, especially for small objects. These problems have been improved in subsequent versions. At present, YOLO [448] has produced 5 versions, which have become the representative of the one-stage detection network.

Single Shot Multibox Detector (SSD) [349] is another one-stage detection model proposed by W. Liu et al. Compared with YOLO [448], SSD [349] generates bounding boxes in feature maps of different scales, so it can capture the information of small objects. And because multi-scale feature maps will lead to an increase in bounding boxes, it is easier for SSD [349] to find candidate boxes close to ground truth.

Despite the tremendous efforts made by YOLO [448] and SSD [349], there was still a big gap between the accuracy of the first-stage detection network and the second-stage detection network at that time. T. -Y. Lin discovered that the real reason behind this is the imbalance between the foreground and the background, so he redesigned CE loss and named it Focal Loss [343]. It is a cross entropy loss that can be dynamically scaled, which effectively prevents the suppressing effect of a large number of easy negatives on the detector during training, and at the same time allows the model to focus more on hard negatives.

8.4.2 Image Segmentation

Image segmentation refers to dividing an image into several disjoint areas based on features such as gray-scale, color, spatial texture, and geometric shapes, so that these features show consistency or similarity in the same area. Image segmentation is a classic problem in the field of image processing. Since the 1970s, it has attracted the enthusiasm of many researchers and made great efforts for it, and many image segmentation algorithms have been proposed. However, since the objective criteria for the success of segmentation have not been resolved so far, the evaluation of the segmentation quality of image segmentation algorithms has become a subject of considerable research significance. Image segmentation is often divided into semantic segmentation, instance segmentation and panoramic segmentation. Semantic segmentation refers to the segmentation of objects of the same type by class, while instance segmentation combines object detection and semantic segmentation, and different instances of the same object on the map need to be marked.

8.4.2.1 Semantic Segmentation

Before the advent of deep learning technology, traditional image segmentation methods were divided into methods based on threshold, region growth, random forest, etc. The effect was not ideal. After the popularity of deep convolutional networks, methods based on deep learning have achieved a greater degree of improvement compared to traditional methods.

CNNs are very powerful visual models in the field of feature layering. The end-to-end, pixel-to-pixel training convolutional network can already be well applied in the field of image classification and detection. Therefore, J. Long et al. established a fully convolutional network (FCN) [358] , inputting any size, and generating an output of the corresponding size after effective learning. Fully convolution is used to solve the pixel-by-pixel prediction problem. By replacing the last few fully connected layers of the backbone network with convolutional layers, an image input of any size can be realized, and the output image size corresponds to the input. After the full convolution result is obtained, it needs to be up-sampled, so deconvolution is used to restore the image size and output the segmentation result. In addition, in the model design, FCN [358] also uses skip connection to improve the roughness of upsampling and make the output result more detailed.

After the FCN [358] was proposed, the resolution of the generated image was low due to the existence of the convolutional layer and the pooling layer. For this reason, G. Lin proposed RefineNet [336], a multi-path enhanced network. RefineNet [336] utilizes all the information of the down-sampling process and uses remote residuals to achieve high-resolution predictions. At this time, the perfect features of the shallow layer can be directly used to strengthen the high-level semantic features. RefineNet [336] includes Residual Conv Unit (RCU), and its structural design is roughly the same as ResNet [200]. Multi-resolution Fusion is to fuse the previous multi-resolution feature maps to obtain new feature maps of the same size, and use sum for fusion. Finally, there is a Chained Residual Pooling. The purpose of this module is to capture contextual information from a large background area. Multiple pooling windows can obtain effective features and use the learned weights for fusion.

Semantic segmentation not only exists in natural images, but also in medical images. Get the most widely used UNet [454] in medical images. The network structure of UNet [454] is similar to the English letter U. It has several changes relative to FCN [358]. First, UNet [454] is completely symmetric, and the structure of the down-sampling encoder and the up-sampling decoder are similar. Secondly, both UNet [454] and FCN [358] use the structure of skip connection, which can combine high-level semantics and low-level fine-grained information. Finally, the difference between UNet [454] and FCN [358] is that in skip connection, FCN [358] uses addition, while UNet [454] concats the channel, so that more information can be retained.

8.4.2.2 *Instance Segmentation*

Instance segmentation is the most difficult of all segmentation tasks. It combines semantic segmentation and target detection, and needs to distinguish different instances of the same category.

Mask RCNN [197] is a general object instance segmentation framework proposed by K. He and R. Girshick in 2017. It can not only detect objects in the image, but also provide a high-quality segmentation result for each instance. Mask RCNN [197] is an extension of Faster RCNN [450]. A new branch for generating object mask is added to the branch of bounding box recognition, which can provide segmentation results for objects. In addition, the author proposed ROI Align to replace ROI Pooling. Its operation is to avoid any quantification of the ROI boundary and use bilinear interpolation to calculate the precise value of the input feature at different sampling positions in each ROI block. And aggregate the results. Secondly, the generated bounding box and mask are independent of each other, and there will be no inter-class competition. In general, Mask RCNN combines the advantages of Faster RCNN [450] and FCN [358], but Mask RCNN [197] also has certain problems, that is, when the bounding box is not accurate, the generated segmentation results are not accurate.

In addition to the two-stage "detection and then segmentation" instance segmentation algorithm Mask RCNN [197], there are also many one-stage instance segmentation algorithms. Among them, YOLACT [44] is a typical representative. YOLACT [44] is also an anchor-based method, using the full connection layer (good at generating semantic vectors) and convolutional layer (good at generating spatial coherence masks) to generate "mask coefficients" and "prototype masks" respectively. It uses two parallel sub-networks to achieve instance segmentation. The Prediction Head sub-network is used to generate the class confidence of each anchor, the position regression parameters and the mask coefficient of the mask, while the Protonet [484] branch generates a set of prototype masks for each picture. In addition, the paper also proposes a new Fast-NMS algorithm, which greatly improves the speed of instance segmentation. Subsequently, the improved algorithm YOLACT++ [45] added deformable convolution on this basis, and replaced the rigid network sampling in the traditional CNN with free-form sampling. The sampling points obtained by the deformable convolution by learning the position offset are more in line with the shape and size of the object itself. In addition, YOLACT++ [45] adds the Mask Re-Scoring branch to the effect of the bounding box of Mask RCNN [197] on the mask. This branch uses the cropped prototype mask generated by YOLACT [44] as input and outputs the IoU corresponding to each category of GT-mask.

PolarMask [570] is another one-stage instance segmentation algorithm, which is an anchor free instance segmentation algorithm. Affected by the anchor free object detection algorithm FCOS [515] and semantic segmentation FCN [358], PolarMask [570] transforms the instance segmentation problem into an instance center point classification problem and a dense distance regression problem by finding the object's contour modeling based on the polar coordinate system. At the same time, the author also proposed Polar CenterNess and Polar IoU Loss to optimize the loss function optimization of High-Quality positive sample sampling and dense distance regression. The work of Polar Centerness is actually to give higher weight to the points of equilibrium and weaken the weight of unbalanced points. Polar IoU Loss approximately calculates the IoU of the predict mask and GT-mask, and better optimizes the regression of the mask through the IoU Loss.

8.4.2.3 Panoramic Segmentation

Different from the previously introduced semantic segmentation and instance segmentation, the panoramic segmentation task requires that each pixel in the image must be assigned a semantic label and an instance id. Among them, the semantic label refers to the class of the object, and the instance id corresponds to the different numbers of the similar objects. The realization of panoramic segmentation faces some difficulties. For example, compared with semantic segmentation, the difficulty of panoramic segmentation is to optimize the design of the fully connected network so that its network structure can distinguish different types of instances; compared with instance segmentation, because panoramic segmentation requires only one per pixel The category and id are labeled, so there can be no overlap in instance segmentation.

AUNet [320] is an end-to-end trained network for panoramic segmentation. The network tries to use the feature pyramid network (FPN) [342] to achieve the complementation of foreground and background information, and then divide the obtained multi-layer features into three branches, namely the foreground branch, the background branch and the RPN branch. In addition, the author introduced an attention mechanism to complement the foreground and background information, which are called Proposal Attention Module (PAM) and Mask Attention Module (MAM). The PAM attention module connects the RPN branch and the background branch, so that the segmentation task can focus more attention on the local object, so as to promote the accuracy of the background semantic segmentation. The MAM attention module connects the foreground and background branches and aims to complement the information of the two. This method accurately grasps the balance between the background and the foreground of the panoramic segmentation, and solves the actual problems through the branch network.

Panoptic FPN [264] is a new method used by A. Kirillov and others to solve panoramic segmentation. It combines FCN [358] and Mask RCNN [197], which are used for semantic segmentation and instance segmentation respectively, in structure, and is a simple, single-stage model. The main structure of the model is FPN [342], because FPN [342] can provide high-resolution and rich multi-scale features, taking into account rich semantic features and detailed image information. Then the model is divided into an instance segmentation branch based on Mask RCNN [197] and a semantic segmentation branch based on FCN [358], so that the network can handle both types of tasks. At the same time, the use of FPN [342] ensures that foreground information and background information are taken into account, so the task of panoramic segmentation is also well qualified.

All in all, as a classic problem in computer vision research, image segmentation has become a hot spot in the field of image understanding. It is also the foundation of computer vision and an important part of image understanding. Not only that, in daily life, image segmentation has very broad application prospects in fields such as autonomous driving, medical diagnosis, and resource searching. With the emergence and continuous development of deep learning, image segmentation will certainly receive more attention in the future.

8.5 CHAPTER SUMMARY

In this Chapter, we first discussed the general techniques for images classification covering from traditional methods to deep learning-based methods. Next, we introduced the image restoration and super-resolution techniques and further elaborate on a demo task for single image super-resolution. Last, we explained the image segmentation and object detection.

CHAPTER 9

Application: Video-Based Real-Time Processing

9.1 VIDEO RECOGNITION: EVOLVING FROM IMAGES

Video recognition applies advanced deep learning analysis and logic-based techniques to interpret video segments containing human action that must be classified into a specific category. Automatic video recognition tasks is of great significance in many real-world applications, such as surveillance, image retrieval, and medical diagnosis. We define video as collections of image sets organized in a certain sequence. Frames are a term used to describe a collection of images. The video recognition problem is different from image classification, where we do feature extraction using CNN and classify the images based on learned features. Video recognition tasks need to assign a particular category to a video segment, which is helpful if people want to know what activity is happening in the video clip. An excellent video recognition classifier not only supplies accurate categories but also describes the entire video information. In Figure 9.1, we provide various video segment with the corresponding action labels, including usual human daily activities such as shaking their hands or riding a bike.

There is a rapid development in the area of video recognition. DeepVideo [257] is one of the earliest attempts to deploy CNN models on large-scale video recognition tasks by using YouTube videos with 487 classes. The mainstream approach to video recognition involves three major trends. One popular trend is Two-Stream Networks (TSN) [480], which incorporates a spatial and a temporal network. The spatial network depicts the video objects and scenes information. The temporal network conveys the movement of the objects or camera. TSN received great success and inspired a large number of following literature, such as trajectory-pooled deep-convolutional descriptor (TDD) [543], Fusion [136], etc. Another trend is using 3D CNN kernels to extract the temporal feature of video, such as SlowFast [135], C3D [519], S3D [577], R3D [191], I3D [63], etc. The third trend concentrates on the aspect of computational efficiency to ensure that these models can be applied in real-time environment. For instance, Hidden TSN [633] and Temporal shift module (TSM) [339], etc.

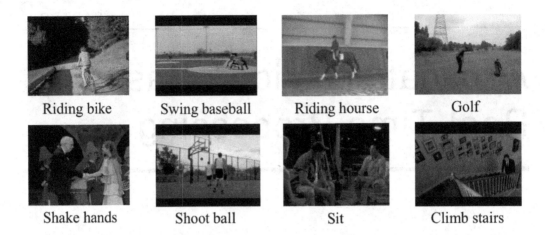

Figure 9.1 Visual examples of categories in popular video action datasets.

9.1.1 Challenges

There are some crucial challenges in designing and deploying practical video recognition algorithms. From the modeling point of view, video recognition requires a vast amount of video data and faces the same challenge as deep learning tasks. A small dataset is insufficient, and video data collection is highly time-consuming. The majority of datasets contain limited video types, which poorly perform on other classes. Besides, human actions vary between intra- and inter-class. For several steps, there are significant variations in performance. People can perform the same action at different speeds from various viewpoints. For instance, running activities can differ in stride length and rate. Also, there is anthropometric differentiation among different individuals. Similar characteristics can be made for the actions which are adapted to environment. For instance, people may point towards a particular direction or avoid obstacles while running. Some actions share similar patterns that are difficult to distinguish. An excellent video recognition method could be able to generalize over variations within the same class and determine actions of different categories. This will be difficult with the increasing number of action classes as the overlap between types increases.

Besides, analyzing video information needs simultaneous recognition of short-term action-related information and long-term temporal information. We require a well-designed model to process sophisticated perspectives rather than a single CNN structure. As a result, deep neural networks are known to perform better with a considerable amount of training data. However, many real-time environments lack sufficient data, even though several large-scale datasets have been used to fine-tune CNN models. To acquire hierarchical features from input videos, recurrent neural network (RNN) has been used to improve the performance of video recognition tasks that involve actions having long-term temporal dependencies. However, RNN modules increase network complexity. The computational cost for the training and inference process is high, hindering the deployment of video recognition models.

9.1.2 Methodologies

In this section, we will summarize DNN-based methods for video recognition tasks and introduce the previous work in the following text.

9.1.2.1 Two-Stream Networks

Since video recognition tasks require motion information, extracting the temporal information among video frames is of great importance to improve recognition performance. Optical flow [209] is a motion representation method, which can track the objects movement efficiently. To be precise, optical flow is the apparent motion of surfaces, edges, and image objects across different frame sequences caused by object or camera movement. It provides orthogonal features compared with the RGB image. It can remove the non-moving background and result in a more straightforward learning problem. In addition, optical flow shows to work well in video recognition.

Simonyan et al. [480] put forward a two-stream network for video recognition in 2014. Here we want to emphasize that the two-stream network is a general structure for video recognition tasks rather than a specific method. The two-stream network includes a partial stream and a temporal stream and each stream is implemented by a deep ConvNet. Two-stream networks based on the two-streams hypothesis [161]. The human visual cortex includes two parallel pathways: the ventral stream and the dorsal stream. The former performs object recognition, and the latter perceives movement.

The spatial stream absorbs raw frame sequences as input to acquire visual information in a two-stream network. The temporal stream takes optical flow images to capture motion features between stacked video frames. The output of two-stream networks corresponds to two optical flow images, and the final scores is acquired by averaging the prediction scores of each streams.

In fact, simonyan et al. [480] make some significant observations. First and foremost, although motion information is of great importance for human video recognition tasks, it is still an arduous task for convolutional neural networks to extract temporal features directly from video segments. Adopting pre-computing optical flow as the motion characteristics is an productive method for deep neural networks to perform well. As simonyan [480] narrowed the gap between deep learning methods and traditional handcrafted features, many follow-up papers on two-stream networks have emerged, greatly advancing the development of human video recognition. Here, we divide these literatures into several categories and describe them in detail.

Two-stream networks adopted a relatively shallow architecture [274]. Therefore, an extension of the two-stream network is to use a deeper network. However, simply using deeper networks does not lead to better performance due to overfitting on small video datasets. Wang et al. [544] was able to use a VGG16 model to train two-stream networks [481] which outperforms other methods [480] by a large degree on the UCF101 video dataset. Later, Wang et al. proposed Temporal Segment Networks (TSN) [545], a novel architecture for video-based recognition. TSN combines video-level supervision and a sparse temporal sampling strategy to achieve efficient and effective learning using whole action videos. TSN conducts a detailed evaluation of the influence of network architectures such as VGG16, ResNet, and Inception [500], concluding that for video recognition tasks, networks with deeper layers can often achieve higher recognition accuracy.

9.1.2.2 3D CNNs

Precomputing optical flow information requires relatively high computing and storage capabilities. Therefore, this method is not suitable for real-time environments and large-scale deployments. An alternative approach is to adopt a 3D tensor with two spatial and one time dimension to learn video information. Hence, this leads to the development of using 3D CNN as a processing unit to extract temporal information in videos.

We will introduce the 3D CNN-based video recognition literature separately below. In particular, we want to point out that 3D CNNs do not replace the two-stream model, nor are they mutually exclusive. They just model the temporal information in video clips in a different way.

Tran et al. [519] proposed a deep 3D CNNs architecture, termed C3D. It can be used to train, test, or fine-tune 3D ConvNets efficiently. The modular design of C3D inspired by [481], which could be view as a 3D extension of VGG16 model. C3D uses a homogeneous architecture consisting of $3 \times 3 \times 3$ convolution kernels followed by $2 \times 2 \times 2$ pooling modules at each layer. Although the C3D network does not perform satisfactorily on standard benchmarks, it exhibits excellent generalization performance. Therefore, C3D can be used as a feature extractor for multiple video recognition tasks [586]. However, a challenging problem of 3D CNNs is that they are hard to optimize. In order to improve the performance of 3D CNN models, we require a large-scale dataset with multiple video clips and categories. However, it is indicate that the C3D model takes several weeks to converge. Despite the popularity of the C3D model, most of the literature just embeds it as a feature extractor module into the entire network architecture, rather than fine-tuning the network. This is the reason why 2D CNN-based two-stream networks are still able to dominate video recognition tasks in the past few years.

In 2017, carreira et al. [63] put forward Two-Stream Inflated 3D ConvNet (I3D) based on 2D ConvNet inflation. I3D takes video clips as input, which are forwarded through stacked 3D CNN layers. Video clip is composed of a series of video frames, usually 16 or 32 frames. The main innovations of I3D are: 1) It adopts a well-performing image recognition architecture for 3D CNN; 2) For model weights, it applies a method dedicated to optical flow initialization in [544], Inflate the weights of the 2D model pretrained on ImageNet to the corresponding part in the 3D model. I3D solves the problem that 3D CNNs have to be trained from scratch. So far, I3D has pushed the field of video recognition to the next level. Over the next few years, 3D CNNs developed rapidly and achieved state-of-the-art performance on most benchmark datasets.

To improve the efficiency (i.e., model parameters and latency) of 3D CNNs, several variants of 3D CNNs begin to emerge. Channel-Separated Convolutional Network (CSN) [520] found that decomposing 3D convolutions by separating spatio-temporal and channel interactions is a good method, and is able to being 2 to 3 times faster than previous methods while obtain state-of-the-art accuracy. Later, feichtenhofer et al. [135] proposed SlowFast, which is an efficient network with both fast and slow pathways.

The slow pathway operates at a lower frame rate and can be used to extract detailed spatial information, while the fast pathway has a higher frame rate and can be adopted to capture rapidly changing motion. To incorporate motion information, SlowFast applies lateral connections to fuse each pathway. The overall efficiency of SlowFast is significantly improved compared to other methods, because the fast pathway enables lightweight deployment by reducing its channel capacity. While the SlowFast network also has two pathways, it differs from the two-stream network [480] because the two pathways are designed to model different temporal velocities rather than temporal and spatial modeling.

9.2 MOTION TRACKING: LEARN FROM TIME-SPATIAL SEQUENCES

Human motion tracking in video stream (sequences of images) is one of the most promising fields in computer vision. Generally speaking, the primary objective of human motion tracking is to generate real-time person trajectory that automatically represent the pose changes in video stream. Dynamical human motion tracking is a general requirement in varies real-time applications, such as human computer interaction (HCI), automatic smart security surveillance [391], medical rehabilitation [458], sport science, and 3D animation industries [399]. In the past several years, the research on pose estimation and human motion tracking has been continuously developing in such applications. However, human motion tracking is a quite challenging field, as the person in the video stream is a deformable target and has difference in size, scale, pose, and appearance. Many motion tracking methods have been proposed by researchers around the world, which have shown excellent performance.

There are several challenges that may affect the performance of pose tracking algorithms, such as complex backgrounds, changes in illumination conditions, cluttered scenes, abrupt motion, shadows, deformable characteristic of the object (scale and size), camera perspective view, close interaction of peoples, and occlusion. To tackle the above challenges of human motion tracking, optical flow tracking methods and CNN-based tracking algorithms have been proposed using different techniques. We will provide some related literature in the following sections.

9.2.1 Deep Learning-Based Tracking

In this section, we will introduce the literature overview about deep learning tracking approaches. Tracking-by-detection is a common approach applied in motion tracking algorithms. A set of detections are acquired from the video clips and are adopted to guide the tracking stage. For instance, bounding boxes are used to identify the targets in the video frames by associating them together and assigning the same ID to bounding boxes which belong to the same target. By doing so, many tracking methods regard the process as an assignment problem.

Modern detection architectures guarantee a excellent detection performance, and most methods concentrate on optimizing the association process. In fact, several tracking datasets provide a standard set of detectors that can be used by object tracking algorithms. Hence, the detection stage can be skipped. The target tracking algorithm can specifically compare the performance of the association algorithm, because the performance of the detector can seriously affect the tracking results.

Human motion tracking algorithms can be classified into online tracking and batch tracking. When the online algorithm predicts the current frame, it uses past and current information. This is a prerequisite for many real-time application scenarios, such as robotic navigation and autonomous driving. Batch tracking algorithms, on the contrary, are allowed to adopt future information of video stream when tracking the current object. Therefore, batch tracking algorithms usually learn global information, resulting in better tracking performance. Compared to batch tracking methods, online tracking methods tend to perform poorly because they cannot adjust past errors based on future information. At the same time, it is worth noting that although real-time algorithms are needed in online scenarios, in fact, with very few exceptions, online algorithms are still too slow to be used in real-time environments, especially for computationally intensive deep learning algorithm.

Despite the variety of approaches introduced in the literature, the majority of human pose tracking algorithms share the following steps.

- Detection stage: In the detection stage, the tracking algorithm analyzes each input video frame, and uses the bounding boxes to distinguish the category of the target object;

- Feature extraction/motion prediction stage: In this stage, the tracking algorithm analyzes the bounding boxes and the tracklets to extract the pose, motion, and appearance of targets. Typically, the next position of each tracked object can be predicted by a motion predictor;

- Affinity stage: motion predictions and features are adopted to compute distance/similarity values between pairs of tracklets and detections;

- Association stage: the distance/similarity values are used to associate tracklets and detections which belonging to the same target.

Although the stages can be performed sequentially, there are several ways to combine parts of these steps. Furthermore, some algorithms do not directly correlate detections together, but employ them to improve trajectory prediction, managing the initialization and termination of new trajectories. Still, even in this case, many of the proposed steps can be used.

9.2.2 Optical Flow-Based Tracking

Optical flow , one of the most successful motion estimation methods, has been widely investigated for computation of motion information from image sequences [524]. Two different way of optical flow was proposed in 1981 [209] [363]. As shown in Figure 9.2, the relative movement of a 3D scene observed with a camera leads to changes in the

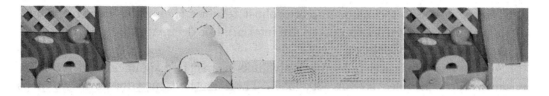

Figure 9.2 Examples for Optical Flow. Original Frame 1, color-coded flow, Vector plot flow, Original Frame 2 respectively.

2D projected images. The estimation of this motion comes down to the computation of a projection of the actual motion onto the image plane. In the past 40 years, optical flow has developed into several different techniques: differential based, region-based, feature-based, frequency-based and CNN-based techniques.

1. Differential Methods

Differential methods compute the velocity from spatial and temporal derivatives of the image brightness. However, one equation cannot uniquely determine two unknown components.

Overall, differential methods can be roughly divided into two mainstream ways, Global Differential Methods and Local Differential Methods, both aiming to solve the aperture problem, where motion direction of a contour is ambiguous due to the motion component paralleling to the line cannot be inferred based on the visual input. This means that a variety of contours of different orientations moving at different speeds can cause identical responses in a motion sensitive neuron in the visual system.

Global Differential methods assume that neighbour pixels are more likely belong to same object and consequently follow a similar motion. A typical global method [209] introduces a global regularization term to solve optical flow estimation problem by minimizing the associated Euler–Lagrange equations. In particular methods, there are various ways to solve the equation, like Successive Over-Relaxation (SOR) [51], efficient multi-grid methods [52], continuous optimization [28], variational method [209], etc.

Local Differential methods describe local neighbourhood pixels with a parametric model [363]. They derive an equation relating brightness and flow for each pixel in each local neighbourhood. Least-squares minimization helps solving a set of equations for all the pixels within the local neighborhood to estimate the optical flow. The most challenging part is controlling the size of neighborhood, as large neighbourhood may lose sufficient information to solve aperture problem, while small neighbourhood may conclude pixel from other motion. The local differential method also works worse in homogeneous regions and motion discontinue regions [32].

2. Region-Based Methods

Region-based methods extract temporal information by searching matching patches between two frames where optical flow is defined as the shift of two corresponding patches with largest correlation [15].

Three mainstream methods have been proposed to calculate corresponding patches, the sum of absolute differences (SAD) [414], the sum of squared differences (SSD) [209], and cross-correlation metrics [364].

The region-based technique is more robust to noise than differential techniques as they works well even when images are interlaced or decimated.

3. Feature-Based Methods

Feature-based method links and only links sparse but significant to recognize image features in video stream [39] [556]. These methods usually have two steps to go: feature detection and correspondence matching. Corners, edges, and other discriminative features as well as flat regions and other low-contrast features can be used to determine the optical flow [371]. However, this kind of methods usually ignore ambiguous area, thus they bring sparse but robust flow fields as well as two main drawbacks. First, the optical flow is too sparse when the background or the objects contain features that are not discriminative. Second, the selected features may not be reliable and disappear in subsequent frames [524].

4. Frequency-Based Methods

Frequency-based methods are optical estimation methods with velocity-tuned filters in the Fourier domain. Such motion-sensitive mechanisms operating on spatiotemporally oriented energy in the Fourier domain can estimate motion that cannot be estimated using matching approaches like Region-based methods and Feature-based methods [38]. Frequency-based methods can also be divided into two mainstream methods: Energy-based and Phase-based methods.

Energy-based methods are based on the output energy of the velocity-tuned filters [37] [202]. Optical flow is formulated as the least-squares fit of spatiotemporal energy to a plane in frequency space. A continuous translation in space cost energy that is concentrated on a plane in the spatiotemporal frequency domain with the orientation related to the velocity [553]. The first computational model for the perception of motion [60] consists of a quadrature Gabor filter pair was later extended to optical flow [8].

Phase-based methods defines the velocity component in the output of band pass velocity tuned Gabor filter [38] [140], based on the decomposition of the original image into band-pass channels. Multi-scale representations and more local constraints yielded from further decomposition are typically used for flow computation thus brings a generally higher Signal-Noise-Ratio (SNR). Compare to Energy-based methods, Phase-based methods usually have higher sub-pixel accuracy, have higher preserved velocity resolution and is more robust to changes in viewpoint and illumination [524].

5. CNN-Based Methods

As we have introduced before, Convolutional Neural Network (CNN) is widely used in image processing tasks. Recently, this trend has also affect Optical Flow estimation. In feature-based methods, most researchers used to use hand-crafted features to estimate Optical Flow. After CNN is widely used, many works start using CNN to extract such features [451]. Moreover, some works even used CNN to match these features in video-stream more recently [118] and thus used CNN in the whole optical flow process.

9.3 POSE ESTIMATION: KEY POINT EXTRACTION

Human Pose Estimation is one of significant problems in Computer Vision area, it can be applied in many scenarios such as medical rehabilitation, sports training, animation, and movie producing, etc. The aim of pose estimation is to segment human parts from images and videos and focus on the motion of human joints. Recent works that trained CNN networks to capture a topology of human joints out from a multi-viewpoint video or single-viewpoint videos have improved human pose estimation in accuracy and performance; however, occlusion-aware, and real-time on-device human pose estimation is still a challenging area which affected the popularity of human pose estimation on mobile devices at home.

9.3.1 2D-Based Extraction

When it comes to segment and recognize the human pose in one monocular image, 2D human estimation methods are proposed. 2D human pose can be diveded into two types, direct regression based and heat map based.

9.3.1.1 Single Person Estimation

1. Regression-Based Human Pose Estimation

Regression-based methods formulated human pose estimation as a regression task and proposed a cascaded DNN regressor to predict human key-points directly [516].However, mapping joints from directly regression with CNN model is still too difficult without other procedures as the direct regression of joint positions is highly non-linear [104,437]. To better estimate human pose by direct regression methods, self-correcting model [61], structure-aware compositional pose regression [495], key-point error distance based loss function and a context-based structure [367] are proposed, and some of them reached a state-of-art performance compared to heatmap-based methods, and they can be modified into 3D methods easily. However, regression based methods are hard to apply on multiple human scenarios compared to heatmap-based methods [104].

2. Heatmap-Based Human Pose Estimation

Heatmap-based methods generates heatmaps first and inferences keypoint location via heatmaps [104]. Graphical model with pairwise relations learned by DCNN [80] and training strategy of conditional Generative Adversarial Networks (GANs) are applied to heatmap-base framework respectively [82] after the proposal of heatmap-based human pose estimation. A most important construct of heatmap-based methods that was proven to be critical for improving human pose detection performance is stacked hourglass model [410]. Although heatmap-based methods have advantages in multiple human pose estimation, as heatmap is a 2D feature map, heatmap-based methods are difficult to extend to 3D space [104].

9.3.1.2 Multiple Human Estimation

When comes to multiple human estimation , how to accurately map the key-points to the right person becomes a problem. As shown in Figure 9.3, there are two mainstream methods aims to solve this problem as follows.

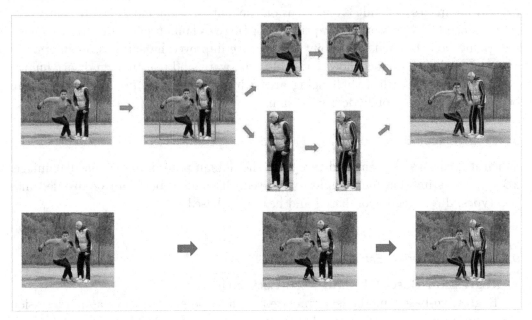

Figure 9.3 Comparison between Top-Down and Bottom-Up methods based on the architecture in [104].

1. Top-Down Methods

Top-down methods have a pipeline of detect a human bounding box and then estimate key-point in bounding box with single human pose estimation methods respectively [516].The simple approach is to incorporate a person detector first, followed by estimating the parts and then calculating the pose for each person. Usually a person detector could be a variation of Faster-RCNN [426].

2. Bottom-Up Methods

Another approach is to detect all parts in the image (i.e. parts of every person), followed by associating/grouping parts belonging to distinct persons. This method is known as the bottom-up approach. While usually Top-down methods have a better accuracy, as images only pass Bottom-up pipeline once, Bottom-up methods have a great advantage in speed.

3. Occluded Human Pose Estimation

When human pose estimation tasks are extended to multiple human estimation, occlusion became a critical challenge in this area. As shown in Figure 9.4, 2D human estimation occlusion detection and de-occlusion is a special case of amodal perception [622], but besides the challenges instance segmentation tasks have met, more challenges come out as human pose estimation is a very special work compared to traditional instance segmentation. (1) As humans are articulated non-rigid bodies [84], the main challenge is the ambiguity in occluded area and the huge state space [42]. Large number of degrees of freedom in the human body mechanics can lead to the frequent occurrence of parts occlusion which seldom occurs in rigid objects [26], thus their poses vary dramatically. (2) Human will possibly appear in any places on this planet thus the context relations between humans and backgrounds are relatively inferior to other common objects which are usually limited to specific scenes [26]. For example, forks and knives usually appears on the kitchen table, but human is not always eating in-door.

Figure 9.4 Example for heat map-based 2D human pose estimation.

9.3.2 3D-Based Extraction

3D human pose estimation is a new area of human pose estimation expanding human pose estimation to 3D space. Depending on the specific method applied, 3D human pose estimation may have several different challenges.

1. Stereo Matching

The main idea of stereo matching is to rebuild 3D model by matching two or more different viewpoint image [365] [74] [582]. However, the occluded regions are only visible in one view makes the matching difficult. The main challenges are ambiguous in scenes with low or repetitive textures and imperfect rectification as well as radiometric differences caused by that.

2. RGB-D Camera

This kind of methods implement a depth sensor to get depth information and rebuild the 3D model from the point cloud based on depth map [489]. However, the high cost of resolving the ambiguity occlusion brings is still a big problem. Modeling the mutual influence between human and object is usually neglected by researchers in this area, who relied more on specific pre-scanned object and scene templates to optimize the spatial arrangement thus caused limited reconstruction under the challenging occluded scenarios.

3. Monocular RGB Camera

Two methods [580, 591] mentioned before requires extra sensors or cameras to estimate 3D human pose, but more recent works try to extend 2D pose estimation to 3D space with one single RGB camera. (1) Because of the lack of depth information, this kind of works consume more computing power to get spatial information from temporal video sequence. (2) 2D detections are generally noisy and unreliable when motion blur and self-occlusion occurred in the captured video sequences while previous 2D detection works formulating the task as a coordinate regression problem still meet difficulties in fully utilizing human prior knowledge to resolve this issue. (3) Amodal perception is impossible to recover occludee in extreme severe occlusion when both side limbs are occluded [622].

4. Inertial Measurement Units

IMU-based methods are non-vision methods that aims to resolve the invisible area by implementing more motion information such as acceleration and motion orientation behind occluded area [533], however the combination of two different system of vision and non-vision is still challenging where improper calibration can degrade the precision of the results. Despite of the progress of many previous de-occlusion works in computer vision, one common challenge remains to be solved: Degraded precision in less occluded scenarios and higher computing power consumption in severe occluded scenarios [259, 288, 591, 601]. With the help of newly equipped 3D camera on mobile phone we can get a more precise 3D human model anywhere to track the patients' motion, however, due to limited computing resources on tiny mobile devices, some methods that aim to segment occlusion with a 3D camera like Microsoft Azure Kinect [3] is not able to run on-device due to the bottleneck of graphic RAM [9], thus we must reduce the model size as well as increase the throughput by reducing calculation consumption.

9.4 PRACTICE: REAL-TIME MOBILE HUMAN POSE TRACKING

Mobile human pose is the latest CVPR proceedings implementation of human pose estimation method on mobile devices, they provided an official GitHub source thus it worth a try for us to take a better understanding of human pose estimation on device. Figure 9.5 presents the visualization of human pose estimation applications.

9.4.1 Prerequisites and Data Preparation

The code is tested under Ubuntu 16.04, CUDA 11.2 environment with two NVIDIA RTX or V100 GPUs, according to the original author. We also applied the project under Ubuntu 20.04, CUDA 11.4 environment with single or dual NVIDIA RTX 3090, 2080Ti and A100 GPUs. In this Chapter, we do not require you to compile the project to mobile phone, but the project has been tested inference only under Android 10, TFLite with Samsung Galaxy S20 (Samsung Exynos 990) and iOS 13 with iPhone

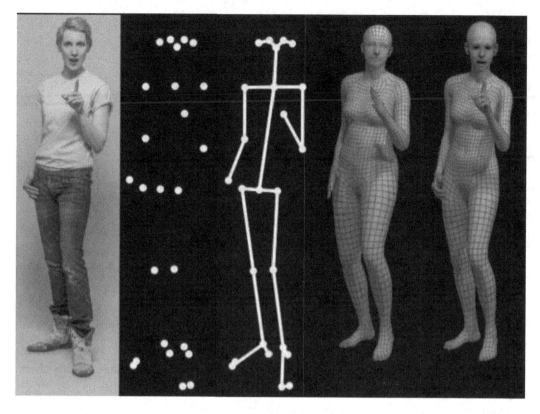

Figure 9.5 Example for 3D human pose estimation.

11 Pro (Apple A13), you can find more information on their official GitHub repo if you are interested.

First, clone the git hub repo from here: [56]

Second, download dataset from here (Human 3.6M and MPII for example):

Human 3.6M [235]:

Download data-set and annotation here [234]

MPII [16]:

Download images here [18]

Download Annotations here [17]

Create data folders as follows:

```
1 ${POSE_ROOT}
2 |-- data
3 |    |-- Human36M
4 |    |    |-- bbox_root
5 |    |    |    |-- bbox_root_human36m_output.json
6 |    |    |-- images
7 |    |    |-- annotations
8 |    |-- MPII
9 |    |    |-- images
10 |    |    |-- annotations
11 |    |-- MSCOCO
12 |    |    |-- bbox_root
```

```
13 |    |    |    |-- bbox_root_coco_output.json
14 |    |    |-- images
15 |    |    |    |-- train2017
16 |    |    |    |-- val2017
17 |    |    |-- annotations
18 |    |-- MuCo
19 |    |    |-- data
20 |    |    |    |-- augmented_set
21 |    |    |    |-- unaugmented_set
22 |    |    |    |-- MuCo-3DHP.json
23 |    |-- MuPoTS
24 |    |    |-- bbox_root
25 |    |    |    |-- bbox_mupots_output.json
26 |    |    |-- data
27 |    |    |    |-- MultiPersonTestSet
28 |    |    |    |-- MuPoTS-3D.json
```

Creating data folder as soft link form is recommended instead of folder form because it would take large storage capacity.

9.4.2   Hyper-Parameter Configuration and Model Training

The configuration file is located at ${POSE_ROOT}/main/config.py, you can change the epoch number, learning rate, dataset, batch size and other configurations there. The main program script is train.py. The running command could be:

```
1 python train.py --gpu 0 --backbone LPSKI
```

where –gpu regards the GPUs that you want to run the program on and – backbone means the backbone network it uses is LPNet with a skipping concatenating strategy, you can also use a backbone of LPNet without concatenating and LPNet with fully residual concatenating with LPWO and LPRES respectively. Add –continue argument if you want to continue training process when you had a model in ${POSE_ROOT}/output/model_dump already, the program will choose the latest snapshot according to the file name. Extension: If you want to modify the model, we recommend you create a new python script in ${POSE_ROOT}/common/backbone and match the arguments in ${POSE_ROOT}/main/model.py.

9.4.3   Realistic Inference and Performance Evaluation

After training, you will find several snapshot models in ${POSE_ROOT}/output/model _dump. Then, use this command to validate the model.

```
1 python test.py --gpu 0-1 --test_epoch 20-21 --backbone LPSKI
```

Same as trainning command, –gpu regards the GPUs that you want to run the program on and –backbone means the backbone network it uses is LPNet with a skipping concatenating strategy, you can also use a backbone of LPNet without concatenating and LPNet with fully residual concatenating with LPWO and LPRES respectively. Difference is an extra –test_epoch parameter targeting the specific snapshot model we want to evaluate. If you want to see the visualized result, go to ${POSE_ROOT}/main/test.py:69 change the variable vis to True.

9.5 CHAPTER SUMMARY

In this Chapter, we have discussed how video-based processing tasks are different from image-based tasks. We have introduced two main-stream method to extract information from temporal plane including optical flow and CNN, and further discussed how they can work together. We also introduced human pose estimation as a popular application in video tasks and several ways to achieve it. More importantly, we introduced how video-based methods can apply to tiny devices and gain a real-time performance, including quantization, residual skip and patch embedding. Finally, we provide a practice project Mobile Human Pose for exercise.

9.5 CHAPTER SUMMARY

CHAPTER 10

Application: Privacy, Security, Robustness and Trustworthiness in Edge AI

10.1 PRIVACY PROTECTION METHODS

As the mainstream machine learning algorithms and applications heavily rely on the data quantity and quality, the learning service providers are prone to continuously collecting data from the end users for model training and update [621]. Besides, it is common to mining the gathered data in-depth [442] to obtain financial benefits, such as boosting the accuracy rate of AI-driven advertisement recommendation system [68]. Thus, we can regard the data as the fuel of most existing AI system. While enjoying the power of machine learning and big data, the privacy concerns have recently become the critical issue [102].

In specific, from the training to inference phase, extensive private information leakage and abuse have posed severe threats to the existing AI systems. In practical, the training data can inevitably contain personal information like medical/financial records and portrait photos [407]. In order to encourage the sharing of such valuable while sensitive data, an essential measure it to preserve the data confidentiality or obfuscate it before processing. On one hand, during the training phase, especially the collaborative and federated learning (FL), the intermediate information like gradients, parameters can be exploited to reveal the original training data (e.g., gradient inverse attack) [150]. On the other hand, a certain scale of legitimate inference results can be leveraged to deduce the membership of training example (i.e.,. membership inference attack) [478]. Due to the space limitation, we cannot exhausted all the existing privacy attacks, interested readers are referred to [427].

We note that above privacy attacks are not only existed in traditional centralized or cloud-assisted learning systems, but also in the *federated* and *edge learning* setting [609]. Moreover, several new problems are caused since the training and inference are transplanted to the edge server and devices. A typical issue is that the edge devices are resource limited, which naturally requires the designed algorithms should be lightweight. In the following content, we firstly review the classical privacy

DOI: 10.1201/9781003340225-10

protection methods including homomorphic encryption, differential privacy, and (i.e., a customized MPC protocol) [427]. We start from introducing the basic concepts, algorithms of above primitives and then describe the representative schemes that are designed on which.

10.1.1 Homomorphic Encryption-Enabled Methods

A straightforward method to protect the privacy of the training data is to encrypt the examples or intermediate parameters with semantic secure crypto-systems like advanced encryption standard (AES), RSA, etc. [258]. However, the basic training computational operations will be totally forbidden over the ciphertext domain. Thus, the tension between privacy protection and model training needs to be relieved by using more advance cryptography techniques. is a widely used crypto methods that support computation over ciphertext without decryption [7]. Informally, given two or several encrypted data, we can obtain the addition or multiplicative results of the data without any decoding or decryption operation. Therefore, this technique can been applied to enable as well as inference [71]. In the following paragraphs, we first give the formal description of most used HE algorithms. Then, based on which, several typical approaches are elaborated. At last, we give a brief summary on the existing schemes and discuss the potential research directions to motivate future efforts.

HE can be constructed on symmetric primitives (private key encryption) or asymmetric primitives (public key encryption). Since very few works choose symmetric encryption as the building block [252], in this book, we mainly focus on the public key based schemes. Public key encryption generates a public and private key pair (PK, SK). PK is used to encrypt the data that could be published to the public. SK is the private key used to decrypt the ciphertext and should be only preserved by the data owner or any fully-trusted party. In terms of functionality, HE could be categorized into three types: , and . We use PHE, SHE and FHE for short. In the cipheretext domain, PHE scheme can only support one type of calculation: addition or multiplication [424]. SHE can support both addition and multiplication with limited homomorphic operation times [252]. FHE is more powerful that can conduct unlimited computation over ciphertext [531]. In the following paragraphs, we introduce three classical HE crypto-systems and then show that how they can be used to preserve the privacy in AI systems.

Paillier Encryption: is a recognized PHE crypto-system proposed by Paillier [424]. It is a probabilistic algorithm designed atop the *decisional composite residuosity problem* (DCRP) [424]. In another word, the security of Paillier relies on the hardness of DCRP. Given an integer a, it is difficult to determine the existence of an integer x makes $x^n \equiv a \bmod n^2$. We show the algorithm details as follows.

- P.KeyGen: This is the key pair generation algorithm. Given large prime p and q adhere to $gcd(pq, (p-1)(q-1)$. Compute $\lambda = lcm(p-1, q-1), n = pq$. Randomly select an integer $g \in \mathbb{Z}_{n^2}^*$ such that $gcd(n, L(g^{\lambda \bmod n^2}))$. For any $u \in \mathbb{Z}_{n^2}^*$, the function L is $L(u) = (u-1)/n$. The algorithm outputs the public and private key as $\{PK = (n, g), SK = (p, q)\}$.

- P.Enc: This is the encryption algorithm. Given the message m, and a random number r, the ciphertext c is calculated as $c = \mathsf{Enc}(m) = g^m r^n \bmod n^2$.

- P.Dec: This is the decryption algorithm. For any ciphertext such that $c < n^2$, take the private key (p, q) as the input, the plaintext message m is computed as:

$$m = \mathsf{Dec}(C) = \frac{L(c^\lambda \bmod n^2)}{L(g^\lambda \bmod n^2)} \bmod n.$$

The Paillier encryption can natually support the homomorphic addition and some other homomorphic operations over the ciphertext domain. In specific, given two message $m_1, m_2 \in \mathbb{Z}_{n^2}^*$, we have the following homomorpic properties: 1). $\mathsf{P.Enc}(m_1) * \mathsf{P.Enc}(m_2) = \mathsf{P.Enc}(m_1 + m_2)$; 2). $\mathsf{P.Enc}(m_1) * \mathsf{P.Enc}(m_2) \ (\bmod \ n^2) = \mathsf{P.Enc}(m_1 + m_2 \ (\bmod \ n))$; 3). $\mathsf{P.Enc}(m_1) * g^{m_2} \ (\bmod \ n^2) = \mathsf{P.Enc}(m_1 + m_2 \ (\bmod \ n))$; 4). $\mathsf{P.Enc}(m_1)^{m_2} \ (\bmod \ n^2) = \mathsf{P.Enc}(m_1 m_2 \ (\bmod \ n))$.

BGN Encryption: is a SHE crypto-system [47] that can support additive operation over the ciphertext domain (on a group) and one time multiplicative on anther group, on which, the arbitrary additive computation is supported. The details of BGN is shown as follows.

- BGN.KeyGen: This is the key pair generation algorithm. Let group G, G_1 are groups of order $n = pq$, where p, q are two large primes. e is a symmetric bilinear map $e : G \times G \to G_1$. Assume g and u are generators of group G, set $h = u^q$. Then, the public key is (n, G, G_1, e, g, h) and the private key is p.

- BGN.Enc: To encrypt a message m, given a random number $r \in \{0, 1, .., n-1\}$, the ciphertext is calculate as $c = \mathsf{BGN.Enc}(m) = g^m h^r \bmod n$.

- BGN.Dec: To decrypt the ciphertext c, compute $c' = c^p = (g^p)^m \bmod n$. Then, utilizing the private key p, the message can be recovered by solving the discrete logarithm problem. Thus, the message space should be small to enable efficient decryption.

We use two plaintext message m_1, m_2 as an example to describe the homomorphic properties of BGN. 1). Addition on group G: $\mathsf{BGN.Enc}(m_1) * \mathsf{BGN.Enc}(m_2) = \mathsf{BGN.Enc}(m_1 + m_2) \in G$; 2). Multiplication on group G_1: $e(\mathsf{BGN.Enc}(m_1), \mathsf{BGN.Enc}(m_2)) = \mathsf{BGN.Enc}(m_1 * m_2) \in G_1$; 3). Addition on group G_1: the computation is exactly the same as in group G. BGN can efficiently support inner product of two encrypted vectors without decryption, while Paillier encryption can not.

Paillier and BGN including some other classical homomorphic encryption algorithms such as El-Gamal, OU, RSA [258] are designed atop groups. Therefore,the functionality is inevitable limited, and can hardly be used to train or to conduct inference on the complex models especially the widely applied deep neural networks (DNN) [499]. For simple example, intensive matrix multiplication operations are needed to process DNN forward propagation. To handle such complex computation, the advanced encryption FHE is needed [531].

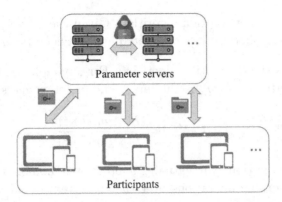

Parameter servers

Participants

Figure 10.1 A Conceptual Model for Secure FL using PHE/SHE.

Informally, FHE encompass all the crypto-systems that allow unlimited additive and multiplicative homomorphic operations over the ciphertext space. Distinct from the conventional HE schemes, classical FHE schemes such as BFV [131] and BGV [50] are constructed using polynomial ring and lattice. The security of BFV and BGV is guaranteed by ring learning with error (RLWE) [131] problem, and learning with error (LWE) [50] problem, respectively. To boost the encryption, decryption, packing, and evaluation efficiency, CKKS [86] are proposed to achieve large-scale approximate linear computation on the ciphertext. Due to the complexity and space limitation, we omit the detailed description of FHE algorithms. In the following content, we first conduct a case study to illustrate that how the Pillier and BGN encyption can be used to support secure FL, which is a widely applied special edge learning. Afterwards, we give a brief introduction on how the FHE schemes are used to support deep learning and inference.

Case study for PHE/SHE enabled FL: Due to the limitation of PHE and SHE, they cannot support the training and inference services for the current mainstream deep learning model. Considering the inherent properties of PHE/SHE, researchers find that they can be applied to support secure aggregation for FL [602]. In the Figure 10.1, a typical parameter server assisted FL conceptual model is shown. We first recall the basic work flow of FL. The parameter server initiates an globe model and distributes it to the online participants. Each participant then trains the model using local data and updates it to the parameter server for aggregation. The server uses the aggregated updates gradients or the parameters to update the globe model. This is a typical one iteration round of FL. Although FL is original proposed to protect the local data from the public server, the updated gradients and parameters can still be abused to inference the raw local data [407]. To address such concern, Paillier and BGN encryption can be applied to support privacy-preserving FL aggregation. Let $\{P_1, P_2, ..., P_N\}$ be the N participants, PS be the parameter server. $P_i, i \in \{1, ..., N\}$ computes the updated gradients (or parameters) W_i, then encrypts it using Paillier encryption as $\widehat{W_i} = \mathsf{P.Enc}(W_i)$. Note that W_i is a vector, P_i can trivially encrypt each element one by one. To boost the efficiency, P_i can also apply the advanced packetization technique to compress the encryption overhead.

Interested readers can refer to [48]. Given all the participants' update $\{\widehat{W_1}, ..., \widehat{W_N}\}$, PS calculates $\prod_{i=1}^{N} \widehat{W_i}$. Due to the homomorphic property of Paillier, $\prod_{i=1}^{N} \widehat{W_i}$ is the encryption of $\sum_{i=1}^{N} W_i$. Thus, PS just shares the encrypted aggregated gradients to the participants for decryption and local update.

In above case, only private simple average aggregation is supported. This could be a limitation of Paillier, if we consider the weighted aggregation [439]. The weights normally are determined by the trusted third party rather than the local participant, which should not be disclosed to PS neither. Thus, for private weighted aggregation, PS needs to compute the inner product of weights and updated gradients on the ciphertext. As discussed above, BGN encryption can support such calculation. For simplicity, assume that the generated BGN encrypted weights are $\{\widehat{\alpha_1}, ..., \widehat{\alpha_N}\}$, and the encrypted gradients are $\widehat{G_i}, ..., \widehat{G_N}$. For P_i, PS first uses the bilinear pairing to obtain the encrypted multiplication of the gradient and weight as $e(\widehat{\alpha_i}, \widehat{G_i}) \in G_1$. Afterwards, PS computes the weighted aggregation as $\prod_{i=1}^{N} e(\widehat{\alpha_i}, \widehat{G_i}) \in G_1$. Same as the simple average aggregation, the participants then decrypt the result and update the local model. Since the decryption of BGN needs to solve the discrete logarithm problem, which is time-consuming, quantization of the gradients/parameters to reduce the message space could be a potential mitigation solution.

Advanced issues: Above case study has proven that PHE/SHE can well-preserve the privacy of updated data while enable the basic FL aggregation function. Besides, some other security and privacy risks should also be carefully considered. Here, we mainly discuss two critical issues. The first concern is the security of private key. Each round of learning iteration, the local participant has to access the private key to decrypt the aggregated result. Thus, all the participants have to share the same private key, which puts the whole secure protocol onto risks. Recent work [351] attempt to address this issue using threshold-Paillier encryption [103]. The decryption of the result involves a certain number of participants, say t. Therefore, only if the number of malicious participants is equal or larger than t, the ciphertext can then be decrypted. As a result, the robustness of the protocol is enhanced. How to handle $N - 1$ malicious participants is still an open problem in this setting. The second concern is the data poisoning attack [351], that the participant maliciously tamper the updated data to undermine the performance of globe model. In the plaintext domain, numerous defense methods are proposed [472]. However, the existing methods are incompatible with the HE enabled FL. For example, if PS attempts to resist the scale attack [412], PS has to compare the received data with the defined boundary, which can solely hardly supported by HE. A straightforward method is using the two non-collusion servers (they do not exchange information without permission) [393]. As shown in Figure 10.1, one of the server homomorphically computes the encrypted differences between the data boundary and updated data. The other server then reveal the differences using the private key. In doing so, the updated data is filtered over the ciphertext. However, in this setting, the private key is share with one of the server, which could be a potential security risk. Thus, some critical issues remains unsolved, interested readers may refer to [351].

FHE for private learning and inference: Theoretically, we can conduct arbitrary homomorphic evaluation over the FHE encrypted messages [531]. However, the computational overhead is magnitudes larger than PHE/SHE so is the ciphertext expansion. Thus, normally, we do not choose such heavy tool to implement the simple tasks like secure aggregation for FL. For centralized learning (training process is carried by single entity), especially the outsourced scenario (e.g., public cloud server), the data owner may encrypt all the dataset using FHE. Then, the data owner transfer the encrypted data to cloud server for training. This setting is the typical private centralized training [294]. Note that, the non-linear layer (e.g., ReLu) needs to be converted to polynomial fitting function to be compatible with FHE. Due to the relative high encryption and decryption cost, there is still no scheme implement FHE for resource limited cross-device FL. Therefore, researchers are considering utilizing the state-of-art FHE schemes [398] to enable strong privacy-preserving FHE for cross-silo FL [463]. In [463], the authors for the first time propose [398] (named as MFHE) to support private FL among several enterprises, who have powerful servers and are forbidden to use the raw data for learning as to be compliant with the regulations like GDPR [183]. In another word, the raw data on the local servers are also encrypted, which is the primary difference between common FL setting. The authors assume that the raw data are collected from individual users, that needs strong privacy guarantee (i.e., encrypt before use). The enterprises use the same public key to encrypt the local data and train the model on it. In each round, for each enterprise, only encrypted gradients are shared. The secret key is shared (additive sharing) among the participants. Thus, they need to collaboratively conduct the bootstrap process (remove noise for decryption), which needs to take the private key as input. The sharing of private key brings a significant security benefit, that is the *malicious majority security*. Assume that there are N participants, even if $N - 1$ parties are malicious, they can still not reveal any additional information. Such strong security setting can remove the current concerns about the big data private among the enterprises. However, there is no free launch for privacy protection. On one hand, the communication and computation overheads are significantly increased. On the other hand, the protocol has to reboot (re-train) when new participants comes, which is extreme time-consuming. Thus, how to enable efficient and practical cross-silo FL using FHE remains an open problem.

Conclusion: In the above paragraphs, we give a brief introduction to the basic concepts of classical HE schemes and describe the corresponding HE properties. Then, we describe how PHE/SHE can be applied to preserve the privacy of FL. The cross-silo FL that each participant can bear computation intensive tasks while the privacy concerns are urgent, has great potential to adopt FHE crypto-system. Thus, we also describe the state-of-art method for private cross-silo federated deep learning. To motivate the future research, the advantages and limitations of current results are discussed in terms of efficiency, security properties and the functionality. As a conclusion, HE driven private learning enjoys proven secure and versatile functionality. However, in the edge learning setting, intensive study is urgently needed to diminish the high cost for tiny edge devices.

10.1.2   Differential Privacy-Enabled Methods

In this part, we will explore the de facto standard privacy protection method, . In 2006, Dwork *et al.* [123] for the first time proposed the mathematical definitions and instantiate methods for DP. Informally, a DP algorithm aims to protect the individual's data records through adding calibrated random noises into the output. Therefore, any DP mechanism can be regarded as a probabilistic algorithm. The scale of the added noise, the privacy protection level and the utility of the obfuscated algorithm can be mathematically characterized by the DP parameters. Thus, as a new privacy protection paradigm, the advent of DP breaks away from the empiricism, and foster versatile theory and application advancement. In the following content, we first describe the definitions of DP, then show that how DP can be applied for deep learning, and FL/edge learning. Afterwards, the advantages and limitation of the current research results are discussed to motivate the future study.

If tiny difference is injected into the input, the output of the algorithm is indistinguishable, then the algorithm follows the DP style. Formally, given arbitrary database instance D, the set of the neighboring databases is denoted as $nbrs(D)$. Given $D' \in nbrs(D)$, the equation $|(D - D') \cup (D' - D)| = 1$ holds, that indicates any two neighboring databases have at most one different record. The formal definition of DP algorithm is as follows. For all instances D, that $D' \in nbrs(D)$, and any subset of the outputs $S \subseteq Range(\mathcal{A})$, we say an randomized algorithm $\mathcal{A}$ is ϵ-differentially private if the following inequality holds:

$$Pr[\mathcal{A}(D) \in S] \leq \exp(\epsilon) \times Pr[\mathcal{A}(D') \in S],$$

where ϵ is privacy budget, that can be manual preset.

Based on the above definition, any DP mechanism has the following two *composition properties*. 1). *Sequential Composition*: Given n independent algorithms: $\mathcal{A}_1, \ldots, \mathcal{A}_n$ with the privacy budgets $\epsilon_1, \ldots, \epsilon_n$, then any composition function $\mathcal{K}$ of them: $\mathcal{K}(\mathcal{A}_1, \ldots, \mathcal{A}_n)$ is $\sum_{i=1}^{n} \epsilon_i$ -differentially private. 2). *Parallel Composition* : If all the algorithms are computed on the disjoint subsets of the dataset, then the function $\mathcal{K}$ is $\max\{\epsilon_i\}$-differentially private. The composition properties are the theoretical basis for DP mechanisms that needs to invoke sub-DP-algorithms.

The noise scale is bounded by the privacy budget ϵ and the sensitivity of the original algorithm output (i.e., the algorithm without noise). Formally, given an algorithm f, the sensitivity of f, denoted ΔQ, is: $\Delta f = \max \|f(D) - f(D')\|_1$. For simplicity, in this book, we use parameter λ to represent the noise scale, which is the function of Δf and ϵ. For example, if the noise is sampled from the Laplace distribution [124], we use $\mathsf{Lap}(\lambda)$ to indicate the noise randomly sampled from the Laplace distribution. Similarly, $\mathcal{N}(\lambda)$ is the gaussian noise.

DP for Deep Learning: DP enabled private deep learning (DL) aims to train a noisy model that can preserve the privacy of the training dataset [6] in the inference phase. Before diving into the technical details, we briefly review the DL [291]. DL adopts the deep neural networks (DNN) to extract the features of the raw data (e.g., image, vedio, etc.). The number of the neurons in each layer, the connection way between different layers, the network depth, and some other information can be preset as the hyperparameters. The weights of the connections, and the bias are obtained through training. One round training of all the dataset is called one epoch. In each epoch, all the batches (randomly sampled from the dataset) are trained once as one iteration. In each iteration, the model computes the loss function (forward propagation) and then conducts the backward propagation to update the parameters. The common used optimization algorithm is stochastic gradient descent (SGD). As mentioned above, to determine the noise scale, we need to figure out the sensitivity of the function. However, it is challenging to find the sensitivity of DL (consider DL model as a function). It seams out of reach to solve such open problem. Thus, the researchers choose to add the noise into the gradients [6]. They first truncate the gradient into a specific range (adopted as the sensitivity degree), then add the noises. Such method is named as [6], which is widely adopted in literatures [181].

Algorithm 4 Primary DP-SGD outline

Input: Training examples $\{x_1, ..., x_N\}$, loss function $\mathcal{L}(\theta) = \frac{1}{N} \sum_{i=1}^{N} \mathcal{L}(\theta, x_i)$, batch size B, noise scale λ, gradient clipping bound C, learning rate η.

Initialize θ_0 randomly.

for $t \in [T]$ **do**

    Randomly sample B_t with the probability B/N.

    Compute gradient: for each $i \in B_t$, compute $g_t(x_i) \leftarrow \nabla_{\theta_t} \mathcal{L}(\theta_t, x_i)$.

    Clip gradient: $\bar{g}_t(x_i) \leftarrow g_t(x_i)/max(1, \frac{\|g_t(x_i)\|_2}{C})$.

    Add noise: $\tilde{g}_t \leftarrow \frac{1}{B} \sum_{i=1}^{N} (\bar{g}_t(x_i) + \mathcal{N}(\lambda))$.

    Descent: $\theta_{t+1} \leftarrow \theta_t - \eta \tilde{g}_t$.

endfor

Output: Model θ_T.

The primary DP-SGD outline is shown in Algorithm 4. Base on a randomly initialized model, the training process is quite similar to the common DL. Two complementary operations are to enable DP protection. First, the calculated gradients need to be clipped into a bounded range. As mentioned above, the sensitivity of the function (SGD) needs to be calculated to calibrate the noise scale. However, how a single example can qualitatively effect the SGD results is challenging to figure out due to the large output range. Thus, researchers propose a mitigation method that is to clip the SGD [6] then the sensitivity of SGD should be no larger then the clipping range. Second, base on the SGD range and the given privacy budget, the noise scale is determined. The remain training processing is exactly the same as non-DP paradigm.

Advanced DP-SGD methods: Algorithm 4 is the classical while quite basic DP-SGD algorithm. Several optimization methods are presented to boost the accuracy [592] or enrich the security properties [411]. In paper [592], the authors point out that equally adding the same scale noises to the SGD introduce unnecessary privacy budget consuming. As we know, the different training epoches contribute different in model convergence. Therefore, the corresponding update scale changes with the training process goes on. For instance, in the final rounds, the differences introduced by the updated gradients are mild. Considering this, the privacy budget assignment method needs to be adapted along with the training process. In paper [592], the authors have proposed four dynamic privacy budget assignment functions. The experimental results demonstrate that all the new functions bring lower accuracy decrease given the same total privacy budget. The details of the functions and the utility analysis are referred to [592]. Note that, most advanced DP-SGD schemes are designed over the DP algorithms with relaxations (e.g., $\acute{R}enyi$ DP [385]).

DP-SGD methods can be easily applied for FL and edge learning [554]. Different from the centralized scenario, the noises are added locally by the participants. In this setting, the commonly used DP mechanism is named as LDP [95]. Since all the noises are added locally, the privacy protection is enhanced. However, compared to centralized DP, LDP based schemes decrease the prediction accuracy [241]. To mitigate such dilemma, several crypto-assisted DP mechanisms are proposed. They either leverage HE [456], or secure multi-party computation [43]. In doing so, the model accuracy is boosted without relying on a trusted central server. To achieve this appealing benefit, additional computation and communication costs among the involved servers are needed.

In addition to privacy protection, DP-SGD is proved to be effective to defend some attacks against learning system [411]. Several literatures have applied DP-SGD to defend membership inference attack [478] (the attackers aim to figure out whether an example belongs to the training set). According the experimental results, the noises injected into models can significantly reduce the success rate of attack (SRA) [411]. When it comes to FL, the latest work [411] also adopts dynamic (the noise scale changes with the distribution of updated gradients) DP-SGD to mitigate backdoor attack [413], which is pretty intricate to defend in FL system. The malicious participant can stealthily add triggers into the training examples. However, the aggregator can hardly distinguish the poisoned update from the benign ones. Thus, it is more challenging to resist backdoor attack in FL setting since the local training data is totally not accessible. Indeed, using DP-SGD for data poisoning defense other than privacy protection is quite novel and inspiring. Here, we encourage readers to explore other effective applications of DP-SGD.

Conclusion: In the above paragraphs, we first review the definition, and the properties of DP. Afterwards, we show how DP noises can be injected into the deep learning model as to preserve the training data privacy. The detailed algorithm DP-SGD is described in Algorithm 4, which is widely used for centralized and federated/edge private deep learning. Besides, we also introduce the advanced issues of DP-SGD, including boosting the model accuracy and enhancing the model robustness. In sum, DP-SGD can not only protect the data privacy but also defense the poisoning attack, which has great potential in future secure and private learning research.

10.1.3 Secure Multi-Party Computation

In edge AI, end devices are often required to calculate different functions for specific purposes. For example, in federated learning, end devices are required to collaboratively train a global model with their own (personal) data. With privacy concerns, each party is not willing to share its private data with others.

Secure multi-party computation (MPC) techniques enable multiple participants, each having a private input, to jointly compute a function secretly. By adopting MPC techniques, each participant utilizes his/her private data to calculate a result without leaking any private information. As a result, the MPC techniques are often utilized in edge AI for balancing the trade-off between security and utility. Specifically, the MPC techniques often include secret sharing, oblivious transfer, garbled circuit, zero-knowledge proof, etc. We briefly introduce the aforementioned MPC techniques as follows.

Secret Sharing. Secret sharing (SS) protocols enable a data owner to split a secret (a value or a document) into shares and deliver these shares to participants with functionalities that any qualified set of participants can jointly calculate a function or rebuild the secret from their shares, while any unqualified set of participants knows nothing about the secret. Since secret sharing techniques have homomorphic properties, each participant can separately perform additive or multiplicative operations on his/her share, and send each calculated share to a receiver, who aggregates all calculated shares and obtains the secret result. In the process of SS, each participant cannot obtain any private information, and the receiver only knows the calculated results. As a result, SS can not only prevent the leakage of sensitive data, but calculate the desired results.

A representative secret sharing protocol is Shamir's secret sharing, which was proposed by Adi Shamir in 1979 [471]. The Shamir's SS protocol is a (t, n)-threshold scheme, which can be utilized to divide a secret S into n shares, i.e., $S_1, S_2, \ldots, S_n$, where t and n are two integer, such that $t \leq n$. The shares satisfies that any t shares can easily reconstruct the secret S, but less than t shares cannot rebuild the secret S. Let $\mathcal{P} = \{\mathcal{P}_1, \mathcal{P}_2, \ldots, \mathcal{P}_n\}$ be n participants, and $\mathcal{P}_0$ shares the secret S to $\mathcal{P}$. Let $\mathbb{G}_q$ be a finite field with q elements, where q is a prime such that $q > n$ and $S \in \mathbb{G}_q$. The Shamir's secret sharing protocol contains two stages, i.e., secret allocation and secret reconstruction. In the secret allocation stage, $\mathcal{P}_0$ selects $t - 1$ random elements in $\mathbb{G}_q$, i.e., $a_1, \ldots, a_{t-1}$, and divides S into n pieces by utilizing the following polynomial, i.e.,

$$f(x) = S + a_1 \cdot x^1 + a_2 \cdot x^2 + \cdots + a_{t-1} \cdot x^{t-1}. \tag{10.1}$$

For each piece S_i, $\mathcal{P}_0$ sets $S_i = f(i)$. Finally, $\mathcal{P}_0$ allocates $S_1, S_2, \ldots, S_n$ to $\mathcal{P}_1, \mathcal{P}_2, \ldots, \mathcal{P}_n$, respectively. In the secret reconstruction stage, any t participants can reconstruct the secret S by utilizing the aforementioned S_i values. Specifically, t participants jointly calculate the coefficients of $f(x)$ by interpolation, and obtain the secret S by evaluating $S = f(0)$. The security analysis can be referred to [471].

Oblivious Transfer. Oblivious transfer (OT) protocols enable a receiver to select k of n messages from a sender, while the sender knows nothing about which messages the receiver have chosen. The OT protocols are secure two-party protocols, which ensure that the receiver only knows the content of selected messages but nothing about other messages, while the sender cannot know the selected messages. The OT protocols can be utilized for building many secure computation protocols. For example, the OT protocols can be utilized in calculating the intersection of two datasets.

Numerous oblivious transfer protocols have been proposed in a semi-honest security model for solving the 1-out-of-N oblivious transfer problem, the k-out-of-N oblivious transfer problem, and the oblivious polynomial evaluation problem with efficiency [403, 404]. Naor and Pinkas designed an efficient 1-out-of-2 OT protocol, which is secure under the Decisional Diffie-Hellman (DDH) assumption [405]. The 1-out-of-2 OT protocol [405] includes a sender $\mathcal{S}$ and a receiver $\mathcal{R}$, where $\mathcal{S}$ inputs two l-bit string (i.e., x_0 and x_1) and $\mathcal{R}$ inputs a bit $r \in \{0, 1\}$. Let p and q are large prime, where $q|p-1$. Let Z_q be a subgroup of Z_p^* with order q. Let g be a generator of Z_q. The efficient 1-out-of-2 OT protocol is described as follows.

1. $\mathcal{S}$ randomly selects an element $C \in Z_q$ and sends it to $\mathcal{R}$.

2. $\mathcal{R}$ randomly selects a value k, where $1 \leq k \leq q$. Then, $\mathcal{R}$ calculates $K_\alpha = g^k$ and $K_{1-\alpha} = C/K_\alpha$, where $\alpha \in 0, 1$ indicates the chosen string x_α. Finally, $\mathcal{R}$ sends K_0 to $\mathcal{S}$.

3. $\mathcal{S}$ calculates $K_1 = C/K_0$ and selects two random value $r_0, r_1 \in Z_q$. Then, $\mathcal{S}$ computes

$$E_0 = \langle g^{r_0}, H(K_0^{r_0}) \oplus x_0 \rangle, \tag{10.2}$$

$$E_1 = \langle g^{r_1}, H(K_1^{r_1}) \oplus x_1 \rangle, \tag{10.3}$$

where $H(\cdot)$ is a random oracle. Finally, $\mathcal{S}$ sends both E_0 and E_1 to $\mathcal{R}$.

4. $\mathcal{R}$ calculates $H((g^{r_\alpha})^k) = H(K_\alpha^{r_\alpha})$, and obtains the desired $x_\alpha = E_\alpha \oplus H(K_\alpha^{r_\alpha})$.

Garbled Circuit. Garbled circuits (GC) are boolean circuits for secure two-party computation. Since any computational functionality can be transformed to boolean circuits, the GC techniques encrypt and random permutate the value of the truth table of each gate of the computational circuit, which ensures the confidentiality of data. Specifically, the GC protocol normally includes two parties, i.e., Alice and Bob. Specifically, Alice first generates a circuit for a specific function, encrypts and randomly permutates all values of the truth table of the circuit. Then, Bob leverages OT protocols to get desired values from Alice, and calculates all garbled tables by utilizing his/her values. Finally, Bob decrypts the final values and obtains the result of the circuit. By utilizing GC techniques, Alice knows nothing about Bob while Bob only knows the computation results.

10.1.4 Lightweight Private Computation Techniques for Edge AI

With the proliferation of the Internet of Things (IoTs) and AI technologies, more and more real-world applications match the emerging trend that enables remote decision services for edge devices. For instance, in health monitoring systems, wearable devices collect remote users' real-time medical data and monitor the users' health conditions periodically. With limited computational and storage resources, a potential workflow is the wearable devices periodically collect the users' medical features, and receive the clinical decision from a remote server by submitting the collected medical features. Such a workflow has been adopted in many smart city applications, which makes resource-constrained edge sensors and end-devices more "intelligent", and therefore can make real-time decisions for specific purposes via AI techniques.

From the perspective of data privacy, sensitive data and decision models should be well protected when making the edge nodes more intelligent. The aforementioned homomorphic encryption (HE) and secure multi-party computation (MPC) techniques can definitely ensure data confidentiality while enabling any functions secretly. However, such private computation techniques may incur prohibitive computational or communication costs to resource-limited edge devices. As a result, designing *lightweight* private computation techniques for specific services have been a new trend for edge AI, especially on resource-constrained edge sensors and end devices.

Recent lightweight privacy computation techniques for edge AI are mainly designed based on matrix transformation (MT) [220,485,557], order-preserving encryption (OPE) [328], randomized Bloom filters [329], and searchable symmetric encryption (SSE) [330–332]. MT-based schemes and OPE-based schemes are lightweight in terms of computation, communication and storage costs. Yet, MT-based schemes may reveal the distribution of data [220] and OPE-based schemes will leak the numerical orders of data [328], which may incur privacy leakage against static adversaries. Randomized Bloom filter-based schemes [329] protect the confidentiality of data with computational and communication efficiency. However, Bloom filter techniques inevitably introduce false positives to the decision model, which may decrease the decision accuracies. It seems that SSE is a potential private computation technique for building secure edge AI, which ensures security, efficiency and accuracy simultaneously [330–332].

To design SSE-based private computation techniques for edge AI, the key problem is to transform the AI functionalities to specific search properties [330]. For instance, some recent works transform the decision tree classification functionality to the keyword-document matching property [330] and the subset matching property [331]. Another example is that some recent works transform the support vector machine (SVM) classification functionality to the range query property [328] and the subset matching property [329,332]. All the aforementioned examples show that it is promising to design lightweight SSE-based private computation techniques for edge AI by transforming specific AI functionalities to specific search properties.

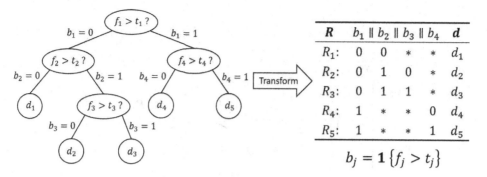

Figure 10.2 An example of decision tree rule extraction.

10.1.4.1 Example 1: Lightweight and Secure Decision Tree Classification

Liang *et al.* designed the first secure decision tree classification scheme in 2019 [330]. Since the decision tree classifier is an interpretable decision model, decision rules can be extracted by traversing all decision paths from the root node to the leaf node. As shown in Figure 10.2, a decision tree classifier can be transformed to a rule-based index, where $t = \{t_1, t_2, \ldots, t_j, \ldots, t_n\}$ is a set of thresholds associated with all internal nodes, $d = \{d_1, d_2, \ldots, d_i, \ldots, d_m\}$ be a set of decisions associated with all leaf nodes, and $f = \{f_1, f_2, \ldots, f_j, \ldots, f_n\}$ is an n-dimensional input feature vector. With such an idea, Liang *et al.* built searchable indexes and designed an SSE-based scheme (SDTC) with $\mathcal{O}(1)$ computational complexity and only 1 round communication interaction [330]. Although the scheme in [330] significantly reduces the time costs compared with HE-based and MPC-based schemes, it inevitably introduce high storage costs when the decision tree model is complex (with more inner nodes and higher depths), because the size of indexes in [330] are exponential to the depth of decision tree classifier.

To address the challenge of huge size indexes, an improved privacy-preserving decision tree classification scheme (named privacy-preserving decision tree classification, PPDT) is developed [331]. Different from the scheme in [330], PPDT built searchable indexes by utilizing boolean vectors, which can be later encrypted by designing a variant of symmetric hidden vector encryption (SHVE) [282]. Compared with the scheme in [330], the PPDT reduced the size of indexes from exponential to polynomial to the size of the decision tree, and therefore boosted the performance in terms of computational, communication, and storage costs when the depth of the decision tree classifier grows large.

10.1.4.2 Example 2: Lightweight and Secure SVM Classification

Some recent approaches focus on building lightweight and secure SVM classification for edge AI. The starting points of these schemes are designing secure SVM classification schemes without HE and MPC commitments, which is computational friendly to resource-limited edge nodes. To design SSE-based secure SVM classification, a key problem is to transform the SVM classifier to interpretable rules, which

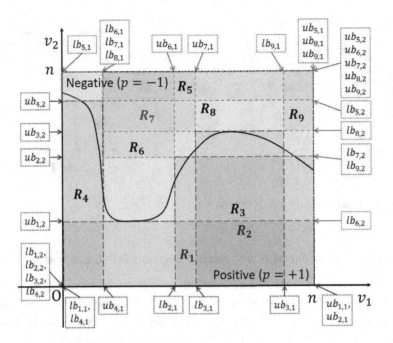

Figure 10.3 An Example of SVM Rule Extraction.

can be further utilized for building encrypted indexes. Fu *et al.* provided a potential solution for SVM rule extraction, which utilized hyper-rectangles to represent the SVM model [143]. As shown in Figure 10.3, an SVM classifier can be represented by a set of hyper-rectangles, whose boundary can be treated as the decision rules of the SVM model. In Fig. 10.3, let $v = \{v_1, v_2, \ldots, v_m\}$ be an m-dimensional input feature ($m = 2$ and $v = \{v_1, v_2\}$), which are normalized to the interval $[0, n]$. Let $p = \{-1, +1\}$ be the negative and positive decisions, respectively. For each dimension ($i \in [1, 2]$ of each extracted hyper-rectangles R_t ($t \in [1, 9]$), let $lb_{t,i}$ and $ub_{t,i}$ be the lower boundary and the upper boundary of R_t, respectively. Then the SVM classifier in Fig. 10.3 can be transformed to a set of decision rules in Table 10.1. Detailed information of the SVM rule extraction and rule usage can be found in [143, 332].

With extracted rules, an SVM classifier can be transformed to different indexes. Recent approaches utilized range query property [328], subset matching property [329], and conjunctively query property [332] to represent the SVM classifier. Among these schemes, the scheme in [332] (named verifiable and secure SVM classification, **VSSVMC**) is an SSE-based scheme with competitive performance against a malicious adversary setting. Specifically, **VSSVMC** first transform the outsourced SVM classification functionality to a function of conjunctively searching whether a feature vector is located in a multi-dimensional hyper-rectangle (interval). Then, efficient querying indexes are constructed via boolean vectors for the extracted SVM rules. After that, symmetric encryption, pseudo-random functions and permutations are leveraged to encrypt the boolean vectors and produce verifiable strings. Finally, the efficient, trustworthy, and secure outsourced SVM classification scheme for edge

Table 10.1   Extracted rules for the example in Fig. 10.3.

Rules	Conditions	Predictions
R_1	$lb_{1,1} \leq v_1 \leq ub_{1,1}$ and $lb_{1,2} \leq v_2 \leq ub_{1,2}$	Positive
R_2	$lb_{2,1} \leq v_1 \leq ub_{2,1}$ and $lb_{2,2} \leq v_2 \leq ub_{2,2}$	Positive
R_3	$lb_{3,1} \leq v_1 \leq ub_{3,1}$ and $lb_{3,2} \leq v_2 \leq ub_{3,2}$	Positive
R_4	$lb_{4,1} \leq v_1 \leq ub_{4,1}$ and $lb_{4,2} \leq v_2 \leq ub_{4,2}$	Positive
R_5	$lb_{5,1} \leq v_1 \leq ub_{5,1}$ and $lb_{5,2} \leq v_2 \leq ub_{5,2}$	Negative
R_6	$lb_{6,1} \leq v_1 \leq ub_{6,1}$ and $lb_{6,2} \leq v_2 \leq ub_{6,2}$	Negative
R_7	$lb_{7,1} \leq v_1 \leq ub_{7,1}$ and $lb_{7,2} \leq v_2 \leq ub_{7,2}$	Negative
R_8	$lb_{8,1} \leq v_1 \leq ub_{8,1}$ and $lb_{8,2} \leq v_2 \leq ub_{8,2}$	Negative
R_9	$lb_{9,1} \leq v_1 \leq ub_{9,1}$ and $lb_{9,2} \leq v_2 \leq ub_{9,2}$	Negative

resource-limited nodes is implemented by querying the outsourced encrypted indexes and testing the verifiable strings. Detail description of VSSVMC is given as follows.

Detail description of VSSVMC. VSSVMC focuses on a outsourced SVM classification scenario, where a service provider ($\mathcal{SP}$) outsources a pre-trained SVM model to a cloud server ($\mathcal{CS}$), which later provides SVM decision services to remote edge users ($\mathcal{EU}$). VSSVMC contains two protocols, i.e., model initialization (Init) and feature evaluation (Eva).

In the model initialization protocol, $\mathcal{SP}$ first transforms an SVM decision model to a rule-set $\boldsymbol{R} = \{R_1, \ldots, R_i, \ldots, R_t\}$, where $R_i = \{R_{i,1}, \ldots, R_{i,j}, \ldots, R_{i,m}, p_i\}$ is the i-th rule, $p_i \in \boldsymbol{p} = \{p_1, \ldots, p_t\}$ is the prediction of R_i, and $R_{i,j} = \{lb_{i,j}, ub_{i,j}\}$ are the corresponding lower and upper boundaries of R_i in dimension j, respectively. Then $\mathcal{SP}$ utilizes $t \times m$ n-element boolean vectors $\boldsymbol{I} = \{\boldsymbol{I}_{1,1}, \ldots, \boldsymbol{I}_{i,j}, \ldots, \boldsymbol{I}_{t,m}\}$ to represent $\boldsymbol{R}$. After that, $\mathcal{SP}$ generates a security parameter κ to generate a set of keys for pseudo-random functions $F_0(\cdot)$ and $F_1(\cdot)$, pseudo-random permutations $H_0(\cdot)$ and $H_1(\cdot)$, and symmetric key encryption Sym, and allocates these keys to authorized $\mathcal{EU}$. Finally, $\mathcal{SP}$ encrypts $\boldsymbol{I}$ as T_0, encrypts $\boldsymbol{p}$ as $\boldsymbol{c}$, produces the corresponding verification messages $\boldsymbol{vc}$ for $\boldsymbol{c}$ and stores $\boldsymbol{c}$ and $\boldsymbol{vc}$ in T_0, which is later outsourced to $\mathcal{CS}$. The Init protocol is illustrated in Fig. 5.

In the feature evaluation protocol, $\mathcal{EU}$ generates a set of tokens $\boldsymbol{TK}(\boldsymbol{v}) = \{TK_1(\boldsymbol{v}), \ldots, TK_t(\boldsymbol{v})\}$ for a feature vector $\boldsymbol{v}$, and submits $\boldsymbol{TK}(\boldsymbol{v})$ to $\mathcal{CS}$. Then, $\mathcal{CS}$ utilizes $\boldsymbol{TK}(\boldsymbol{v})$ to search corresponding encrypted predictions on T_0 and T_1. After that, $\mathcal{CS}$ returns the encrypted predictions $\boldsymbol{c}(\boldsymbol{v})$ and the verification messages PF to $\mathcal{EU}$. Finally, $\mathcal{EU}$ verifies $\boldsymbol{c}(\boldsymbol{v})$ by utilizing PF, and obtains the corresponding prediction of $\boldsymbol{v}$ by decrypting $\boldsymbol{c}(\boldsymbol{v})$. The VSSVMC.Eva protocol is illustrated in Fig. 6.

Algorithm 5 Detail Construction of VSSVMC.Init.

The Model Initialization Protocol (VSSVMC.Init)

Inputs: κ, $\boldsymbol{R}$.
Outputs: K_{f_0}, K_{f_1}, K_{h_0}, K_{h_1}, K_0, T_0, T_1.

1: $\mathcal{SP}$: $\mathcal{SP}$ transforms an SVM classifier to ruleset $\boldsymbol{R}$.
2: $\mathcal{SP}$: For each $i \in [t]$, $j \in [m]$, $k \in [n]$, $\mathcal{SP}$ sets:

$$I_{i,j}[k] \leftarrow \begin{cases} 1, & \text{if } lb_{i,j} \leq k \leq ub_{i,j}; \\ 0, & \text{otherwise.} \end{cases}$$

3: $\mathcal{SP} \rightarrow \mathcal{EU}$: $\mathcal{SP}$ chooses a security parameter κ and samples:

$$K_{f_0}, K_{f_1}, K_{h_0}, K_{h_1} \xleftarrow{\$} \{0,1\}^\kappa,$$
$$K_0 \leftarrow \text{Sym.Gen}(1^\kappa).$$

Then, $\mathcal{SP}$ allocates the keys to authorized $\mathcal{EU}$.
4: $\mathcal{SP}$: For each $i \in [t]$, $j \in [m]$, and $k \in [n]$, $\mathcal{SP}$ sets:

$$T_0\left[H_0\left(i||j||k\right)\right] \leftarrow F_0\left(I_{i,j}[k]||i||j||k\right).$$

5: $\mathcal{SP}$: For each $i \in [t]$, $\mathcal{SP}$ calculates:

$$c_i \leftarrow \text{Sym.Enc}(K_0, p_i),$$
$$vc_i \leftarrow F_1(H_1(i)||c_i),$$

where $p_i \in \boldsymbol{p}$, and sets:

$$T_1[H_1(i)] \leftarrow c_i||vc_i.$$

6: $\mathcal{SP} \rightarrow \mathcal{CS}$: $\mathcal{SP}$ outsources T_0 and T_1 to $\mathcal{CS}$.

10.2 SECURITY AND ROBUSTNESS

10.2.1 Practical Issues

Deep learning uses neural network to extract and learn features of data. The excellent feature extraction ability of neural network makes the application of deep learning obviously superior to previous machine learning technology in many fields, especially the convolutional neural networks (CNNs), which has outstanding advantages in image and word processing and recognition. Neural network-based models have played an important role in image recognition, speech processing, machine translation, games fields, and face recognition, automatic driving and other real scenes. Compared with the reasoning process of traditional machine learning algorithm, the training of deep neural network needs to go through more steps, including data collection, data preprocessing, model selection and design, model training, model storage, model deployment and other steps. More steps give the attacker more opportunities to attack. It is well known that training deep neural networks often requires lots of time and computing resources, which are too expensive for most users. Therefore,

---

Algorithm 6 Detail Construction of VSSVMC.Eva.

The Feature Evaluation Protocol (VSSVMC.Eva)

Inputs: K_{f_0}, K_{f_1}, K_{h_0}, K_{h_1}, K_0, $\boldsymbol{v}$, T_0, T_1.
Outputs: $\perp$ or $\boldsymbol{p(v)}$.

1: $\mathcal{EU}$: $\mathcal{EU}$ randomly samples:

$$K_1, K_2, \ldots, K_t \leftarrow \texttt{Sym.Gen}(1^\kappa).$$

2: $\mathcal{EU}$: $\mathcal{EU}$ produces $\boldsymbol{TK(v)} = \{TK_1(\boldsymbol{v}), \ldots, TK_t(\boldsymbol{v})\}$ for the input feature vector $\boldsymbol{v}$.
Each token $TK_i(\boldsymbol{v}) \in \boldsymbol{TK(v)}$ is $TK_i(\boldsymbol{v}) = (\alpha_i, \beta_i, \gamma_i, \boldsymbol{L}_i)$, whose values are calculated as follows.

$$\alpha_i = \oplus_{j \in \mathbb{Z}_m} (F_0(1||i||j||v_j)) \oplus K_i,$$
$$\beta_i = \texttt{Sym.Enc}(K_i, 0^\kappa),$$
$$\gamma_i = \texttt{Sym.Enc}(K_i, H_1(i)),$$
$$\boldsymbol{L}_i = \{H_0(i||j||v_j)\}_{j \in \mathbb{Z}_m}.$$

3: $\mathcal{EU} \rightarrow \mathcal{CS}$: $\mathcal{EU}$ submits $\boldsymbol{TK(v)}$ to $\mathcal{CS}$.
4: $\mathcal{CS}$: $\mathcal{CS}$ initializes $\boldsymbol{c(v)} \leftarrow \emptyset$.
5: $\mathcal{CS}$: For each $TK_i(\boldsymbol{v}) \in \boldsymbol{TK(v)}$, $\mathcal{CS}$ calculates:

$$K_i' = \oplus_{j \in [m]} (T_0 [H_0(i||j||v_j)]) \oplus \alpha_i.$$

1. If $\texttt{Sym.Dec}(K_i', \beta_i) = 0^\kappa$, then $\mathcal{CS}$ searches $T_1 [\texttt{Sym.Dec}(K_i', \gamma_i)]$ and obtains $c_i||vc_i$. Later, $\mathcal{CS}$ adds c_i to $\boldsymbol{c(v)}$ and produces PF_i, i.e.,

$$\boldsymbol{c(v)} \leftarrow \boldsymbol{c(v)} \cup \{c_i\},$$
$$\text{PF}_i \leftarrow K_i' \,||\, vc_i.$$

2. Else if $\texttt{Sym.Dec}(K_i', \beta_i) \neq 0^\kappa$, then $\mathcal{CS}$ adds $\emptyset$ to $\boldsymbol{c(v)}$ and produces PF_i, i.e.,

$$\boldsymbol{c(v)} \leftarrow \boldsymbol{c(v)} \cup \emptyset,$$
$$\text{PF}_i \leftarrow \{T_0[H_0(i||j||v_j)]\}_{j \in [m]}.$$

6: $\mathcal{CS} \rightarrow \mathcal{EU}$: $\mathcal{CS}$ returns $\boldsymbol{c(v)}$ and $\textbf{PF} = \{\text{PF}_1, \ldots, \text{PF}_t\}$ to $\mathcal{EU}$.
7: $\mathcal{EU}$: For each $i \in [t]$, $\mathcal{EU}$ considers the following two cases for $\boldsymbol{c(v)}$ and $\textbf{PF}$:

1. If $c_i \in \boldsymbol{c(v)}$, then $\mathcal{EU}$ verifies K_i' and vc_i, i.e., if $K_i \neq K_i'$ or $F_1(H_1(i)||c_i) \neq vc_i$, then outputs $\perp$.

2. Else if $c_i \notin \boldsymbol{c(v)}$, then $\mathcal{EU}$ verifies PF_i, i.e., if $\forall v_j \in \boldsymbol{v}$, $F_0(0||i||j||v_j) \neq T_0[H_0(i||j||v_j)]$, then outputs $\perp$.

8: $\mathcal{EU}$: If for each $i \in [t]$, $\mathcal{EU}$ didn't outputs $\perp$, then for each $c_i \in \boldsymbol{c(v)}$, $\mathcal{EU}$ calculates

$$\boldsymbol{p(v)} = \{p_i \mid p_i = \texttt{Sym.Dec}(K_0, c_i), c_i \in \boldsymbol{c(v)}\}.$$

The majority prediction of $\boldsymbol{p(v)}$ is the corresponding prediction of $\boldsymbol{v}$.

in order to reduce training costs, many people choose to use third-party datasets, third-party platforms to train their models, or third-party models directly. However, although this way of using third-party resources makes deep learning more widely used, it also brings some security risks. One of the threats is the backdoor attacks, which this paper focuses on in image recognition.

Gu et al. [167] were the first to introduce the threat of backdoor attacks (BA). In general, the backdoor attack will embed the potential backdoor into the deep neural network, which makes the model show similar performance to the normal model with benign samples. However, when an attacker uses a backdoor trigger to activate the attack, the infected samples end up being predicted with the attacker's target label. Therefore, for deep neural network, backdoor attack is a great threat, while Data Poisoning is still by far the most direct method of backdoor attack [353].

Accordingly, the safety of deep learning has also received more and more attention, especially in real scenes such as face recognition, automatic driving and other real scenes. Once a security vulnerability occurs, it will bring serious personal injury and property loss. With the development of federated learning research, how to protect the security and privacy of models and data has become an important issue in cooperative learning. With the increasingly extensive research and application of deep learning, its own training process faces more and more security threats, especially the threat of backdoor attack. In this case, future DNNs applications will put forward higher security and privacy requirements. Given these challenges, we need to develop new methods to evaluate the security of models and provide protection for training privacy-sensitive data. In future, we need to explore the benign application of backdoor attack in federated learning scenarios, contributing to the interpretability of neural networks and collaborative learning data sharing.

10.2.2 Backdoor Attacks

Data-poisoning backdoor attacks. As shown in Figure 10.4, Badnets [167] is a classical backdoor attack, using a pure color block posted on the picture and its label is changed to a target label. Then, a dataset containing poisoned samples is used to train the model to embed the backdoor into the model. Chen et al. [81] proposed blended attack, which carries out a more stealthier attack by using a blended backdoor trigger. Zhong et al. [333] used a similar approach to adversarial attack [396] to frame triggers to minimize the L-2 norm. Li et al. [316] used the L-P norm as a limit when optimizing triggers. Recently, Li et al. [323] inveted a novel invisible backdoor attack method with the help of image steganography. The attack mentioned above changed the labels of poisoning samples to target label while poisoning them, making the subsequent model learn the association between triggers and target label. However, such label changes could be easily detected by people. Turner et al. [527] explored clean tag attacks first, and make the model learn robust features by superimposing small perturbations and then performing invisible backdoor attacks to ensure that the model can be activated by triggers. However, the attack success rate of the clean-label attack is usually only half of the Badnets. Physical world attacks have also been studied. [81, 321]

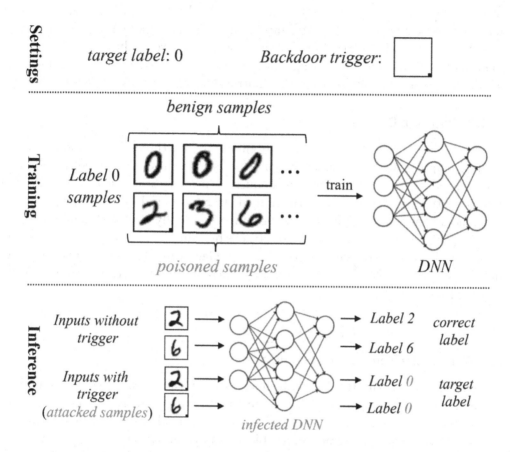

Figure 10.4 An overview for backdoor attack, where the visualized images are from the open dataset MNIST [323].

Model-changing backdoor attacks. These attacks do not rely on data poisoning to change model parameters, but instead builds backdoors at other stages of model training. Dumford et al. [122] firstly explore a backdoor attack of face recognition task by searching the whole model through greedy algorithm to modify the weight of model parameters. Rakin et al. [443] discussed a method of injecting a hidden backdoor without a training process called Target Bit Trogan. Guo et al. [169] proposed TrojanNet, which was designed to activate backdoors in infected DNNs models by secret weights.

In cooperative learning, such as federated learning scenarios, there is also a threat of backdoor attacks. Federated learning aggregates multiple local models into a federated model, and the local models are trained separately by multiple participants. At the same time, the security aggregation mechanism is adopted in federated learning to protect the privacy of local trainers including local training data. On the one hand, this mechanism allows aggregation models to be trained with sensitive private data, and on the other hand, it prevents aggregators from detecting local models submitted by participants, making it unable to detect malicious models. Bagdasaryan et al. [30]

introduced backdoor attacks into federated learning by amplifying the toxic gradient of node servers. Xie et al. [569] introduced a distributed backdoor attack method for federated learning. Recently, Wanget al. [538] had theoretically demonstrated that under the condition of federal learning moderation, models are vulnerable to backdoor attacks if they are vulnerable to adversal attacks.

10.2.3 Backdoor Defences

Several defenses have been designed to eliminate the threat of backdoor attacks. Existing approaches focus on backdoor attacks using the idea of data poisoning. Liu et al. [354] use pretreatment techniques to process samples. Doan et al. [113] used potential trigger region substitution to clear triggers. Liu et al. [348] proposed to defend against backdoor attacks by pruning abnormally activated neurons. Neural Cleanse [536] defends against backdoor attacks by using exception detectors to detect triggers and then synthesize potential triggers. Gao et al. [145] distinguished benign and malignant samples by superimposing different image patterns to observe the predicted results.

10.3 TRUSTWORTHINESS

10.3.1 Blockchain and Swarm Learning

Blockchain is a distributed ledger technology that can keep the data immutability, integrity, and transparency between untrusted parties, which draws tremendous attention from academia and industry in recent years. Characterized with trustworthiness, transparency, and traceability, blockchain technologies have been integrated into a significant amount of areas, such as cryptocurrency, supply chain, international trade, etc. In the following, we first briefly introduce the blockchain technique.

Blockchain Overview. As shown in Figure 10.5, blockchain was originally derived from Bitcoin [402], a decentralized peer-to-peer cryptocurrency. As an append-only ledger, a blockchain consists of a volume of blocks to record all transactions uploaded by multiple participants. Due to the decentralized nature of the blockchain, not all participants are honest, and some of them want to maliciously modify the content of the block. Therefore, to ensure the immutability, each block points to the previous block via a tamper-proof hash value of its previous block, timestamp, and transactions of this block. In a peer-to-peer blockchain network, the nodes can be various devices in daily life, such as mobile phones, smart watch, and other IoT devices.

Block Structure. Since there are a volume of transactions stored on a single block, all the transaction hash values in the block also need to be hashed to speed up the verification process of them. A hash tree, or a Merkle tree [384], enables the quick verification of blockchain data through a Merkle proof which contains hash values on the critical path that can reconstruct the root hash value of the tree. Therefore, the light clients who only maintain the Merkle root can verify the legality of the transaction through the local Merkle root and the Merkle proof from the full node who has an entire Merkle tree.

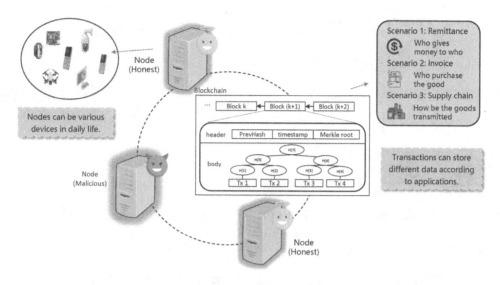

Figure 10.5 An overview for a blockchain system and its application.

Consensus. In order to add a new block to the end of blockchain, all participants need to reach a consensus on whether transactions should be accepted or rejected, and in which order. A plethora of consensus protocols exist—such as proof-of-work (PoW) mechanism on Bitcoin [402] and Practical Byzantine Fault Tolerance (PBFT) on Hyperledger Fabric [20], which through probabilistic consensus to committee-based that repurposes classical protocols to the blockchain setting. All the consensus mechanisms decide a member to execute the transactions and pack them into a new block which will be broadcast to the blockchain network. hong

Smart Contract. For the blockchains for cryptocurrency such as Bitcoin, transactions may be more than just transfers between users. To enrich the trading functions, a set of rules is stored on the blockchain and executed automatically, which called *smart contract* [558]. Smart contracts are usually written in some Turing-complete programming languages and allow everyone to deploy them to the blockchain system in a public manner. In a smart contract, there can be as many clauses as possible for the participants to complete the task to their satisfaction.

Depending on the aforementioned characteristics of decentralization, transparency, traceability, and immutability, blockchain is promising to enhance the trustworthiness among participants in an AI application (e.g., data owners, cloud vendors, AI developers, and customers.) Next, we will introduce several existing blockchain applications in trustworthy AI as follows.

As shown in Figure 10.6, Swarm Learning (SL) is a novel blockchain-empowered distributed learning architecture first proposed in [551] and is designed to support trustworthy distributed learning. As shown in Fig. 10.6(a), for a traditional distributed learning technology such as federated learning, there is a dedicated parameter server responsible for distributing local learning tasks to the workers and aggregating their results. However, such a centralized architecture poses a challenge for trustworthiness because a malicious server can easily tamper with the training

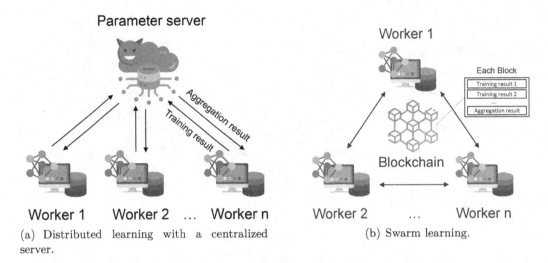

(a) Distributed learning with a centralized server.

(b) Swarm learning.

Figure 10.6 Difference between distributed learning and swarm learning.

process. Therefore, to dispense with a dedicated server and provide trustworthy training, the idea of SL is proposed. It is based on a blockchain platform in which the workers are the consensus participants and can commit and receive transactions related to the learning. As shown in Fig. 10.6(b), in each round, a worker can download the latest global model from the blockchain. Next, the worker performs local model training until defined conditions for synchronization (e.g., time for merge) are met. The current model parameters in each worker can be shared to the blockchain network in the form of transactions. The consensus leader in the current round is responsible to merge the local model parameters in the blockchain for a new global model. Thus, the blockchain consensus can guarantee the trustworthiness of the model aggregation in distributed learning. Furthermore, to illustrate the feasibility of SL, the authors develop several disease classifiers based on the distributed clinical data. The result shows SL not only outperforms the classifiers developed at individual sites instead of distributed data, but also fulfils the trustworthiness requirement in a distributed setting.

There are a set of works that share a similar idea, i.e., guaranteeing the trustworthiness of distributed learning via blockchain, with SL. In particular, Bao *et al.* propose a blockchain-based auditable federated learning system called FLchain [36]. The system stores trainer information and verifiable training details for public auditability. Depending on the history documented by FLchain, the honest trainer gain fairly partitioned profit according to its contribution while the malicious can be timely detected and heavily punished. Similarly, Weng *et al.* design a blockchain-based collaborative deep learning system named Deepchain [555] which adopts homomorphic encryption technique to protect the local gradients stored in the blockchain transactions. Moreover, DeepChain enables any third party to audit the collaborative training process based on a tool of non-interactive zero-knowledge proof.

In the above, we present various blockchain applications in trustworthy AI. However, we found little studies on how to leverage blockchain to construct a trustworthy

TinyML. In the following, we attempt to push our effort forward above by discussing the challenges of applying blockchain in TinyML and present some possible solutions for a blockchain-empowered trustworthy TinyML.

The first challenge is that the weak hardware in TinyML devices cannot meet the high requirement of the existing blockchain consensuses. First, each blockchain node is required to store a full copy of the blockchain, which may occupy a huge storage space such as about 1 TB in Ethereum. Second, during the consensus, the nodes need to receive and validate new transactions and blocks, which consumes both network bandwidth and CPU computation power. Thus, these requirements of blockchain place a burden on TinyML with the limited resource.

The second challenge is that the weak scalability of existing blockchain systems cannot support the massive number of TinyML devices. In particular, Hyperledger Fabric achieves end-to-end throughput of more than 3500 transactions per second (TPS) but its network scale is less than 100, while Bitcoin and Ethereum can support thousands of nodes but only process 7 and 15 TPS, respectively. In comparison, most TinyML applications involves the edge environment composed of thousands of user devices, e.g., mobile and IoT equipment.

For the above two challenges, sharding architecture is a potential solution which improves the scalability of blockchain and has been used in some blockchain systems, e.g., [13, 208, 269, 599]. It partitions blockchain nodes into multiple shards to allow transactions to be executed in different shards in parallel. The high scalability of blockchain sharding motivates us to use sharding blockchains for the above challenges. First, sharding architecture can alleviate the hardware requirement pressure of the TinyML device. It is because the ledger is divided into different shards and each node only needs to store a partial copy of the blockchain ledger and participate in less consensus process. Second, sharding can increase the transaction throughput and network scale simultaneously, which supports a large number of TinyML devices participating in the system. Moreover, there are several different sharding architectures including dynamic sharding [608], geographic location-based sharding [13], etc. To implement a TinyML-oriented sharding, we can design a ML task-based sharding architecture in which the TinyML devices are assigned to different shards based on their training tasks. For example, the devices for CV are distributed into the shard for CV, and nodes with microphones are distributed into the shard for NLP. Through the task-based method, the resources of each device can be used to the maximum.

10.3.2 Trusted Execution Environment and Federated Learning

As a secure environment maintained by each main processor, Trusted Execution Environment (TEE) protects the data and code from attackers with respect of confidentiality and integrity through memory isolation. As shown in Figure 10.7, it guarantees that the execution of applications can be executed correctly in outsourced environments in which the hosts may be malicious, such as outsourced computation and outsourced database [626]. Typical examples of TEE implementation include Software Guard eXtensions (SGX) [233] for Intel CPU, and Trustzone [11] for ARM processors.

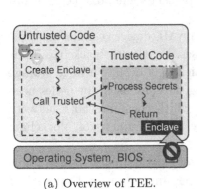

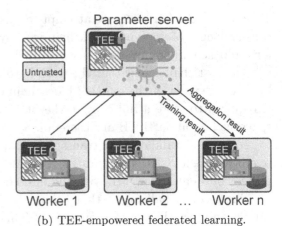

(a) Overview of TEE.

(b) TEE-empowered federated learning.

Figure 10.7 Illustration for trusted execution environment and trusted execution environment-empowered federated learning.

We take Intel SGX as an example as follows. There is a virtual container named *enclave* in each Intel processor with SGX support. As shown in Figure 10.7, it live in an isolated virtual address space of a conventional user process, in which both the data and code are maintained in a special memory area named *enclave page cache* (EPC). The other components of the host such as operating system (OS) cannot access the EPC, which thus guarantees the confidentiality and integrity of any storage and computation within the EPC. Next, SGX supports *remote attestation* which creates an attestation report based on a hardware-based root of trust. The clients can verify the report via the local or remote attestation mechanism in SGX, to show the unmodified enclave code/data on an untrusted host. In addition, the attestation mechanism can also be used to establish an encrypted communication channel between different TEEs, by which some credible data can be provisioned directly to each TEE. However, there are several limitations in TEE, such as limited memory space, expensive authenticated library calls, and rollback attacks, which need to be considered in the application of TEE.

Depending on the aforementioned characteristics, TEE is promising to guarantee the integrity, verifiability, and confidentiality of the learning process in other untrusted servers for the trustworthiness in AI applications. Next, based on federated learning, we first describe a basic model for TEE-empowered federated learning.

For a TEE-empowered federated learning system, the parameter server and workers with TEE support can deploy enclaves for learning. The enclaves deployed in different parties can introduce different advantages. Specifically, the enclave in a worker can input the private data of data owners and run data processing codes such as gradient computation for model updates. The enclave in the parameter server can collect and aggregate updates from the workers. The attestation mechanism of TEE can guarantee the model updates in the enclaves of the workers and the model aggregation in the enclave of the server. There have been several works to adopt TEE in FL as follows.

Zhang *et al.* present a collaborative machine learning system named Citadel [603] that adopts TEE to protect both data privacy and model confidentiality when training a model in untrusted machines. Each data or model owner can deploy an enclave in the untrusted cloud instance. The enclaves deployed by data owners are called *training enclaves* and those deployed by model owners are called *aggregator enclaves*. Then, the training workload is divided into two parts. The first one is used to handle data and the second one is used to update models, which are run in training enclaves and aggregator enclaves, respectively. Thus, the training and aggregation can be protected by TEE. Moreover, to guarantee that the codes used to handle models cannot recover the private data of the data owner, the system proposes two designs, i.e., zero-sum masking and hierarchical aggregation, to rigidly separate these two parts.

Mo *et al.* present a TEE-empowered federated learning frametwork for DNN [390]. In the framework, both workers and parameter servers own the TEE hardware for local training and global aggregation, respectively. Because the memory of TEE is limited, neither the workers nor servers cannot place the whole DNN into their TEEs. Considering this constraint, the proposed framework first splits each model into layers, places each layer in the TEE each time, and finally trains the model in a layer-wise manner until the convergence of the model. In other words, the framework greedily trains one layer of the DNN model each time within the TEE. The experimental evaluation shows that the proposed framework can provide a similar accuracy performance with a tolerable delay compared with the traditional federated learning that trains through the complete model.

10.4 CHAPTER SUMMARY

In this chapter, we have comprehensively reviewed the secure, private and trustworthy learning methods from diverse perspectives. Motivated by the security and privacy issues, we first present the real data disclosure risks, attack scenarios and vulnerabilities of the current learning systems. Afterwards, the mainstream mitigation methods proposed to use differential privacy, homomorphic encryption, lightweight secure multi-party encryption, blockchain and trusted execution environment are reviewed by introducing the core algorithms and protocols. Following the tone of classical textbook writing style, in each sub-chapter, the advantages and limitations of the current schemes are discussed. Besides, we argue that the adoption of single technique such as cryptograph brings about significant drawbacks. Therefore, the deep fusion of reviewed methods is promising research and practicing route to design secure while efficient learning protocols. We hope that the knowledge and insights shared in the chapter can motivate future efforts from our readers.

Bibliography

[1] Cifar-10 dataset. https://www.cs.toronto.edu/~kriz/cifar.html.

[2] Imagenet dataset. http://image-net.org/.

[3] Microsoft azure. https://azure.microsoft.com.

[4] Prashanth L. A. and Mohammad Ghavamzadeh. Actor-critic algorithms for risk-sensitive mdps. In *Proceedings of the Annual Conference on Neural Information Processing Systems (NeurIPS)*, pages 252–260, 2013.

[5] Martín Abadi, Paul Barham, Jianmin Chen, Zhifeng Chen, Andy Davis, Jeffrey Dean, Matthieu Devin, Sanjay Ghemawat, Geoffrey Irving, Michael Isard, Manjunath Kudlur, Josh Levenberg, Rajat Monga, Sherry Moore, Derek Gordon Murray, Benoit Steiner, Paul A. Tucker, Vijay Vasudevan, Pete Warden, Martin Wicke, Yuan Yu, and Xiaoqiang Zheng. Tensorflow: A system for large-scale machine learning. In *Proceedings of the USENIX Symposium on Operating Systems Design and Implementation (OSDI)*, 2016.

[6] Martin Abadi, Andy Chu, Ian Goodfellow, H Brendan McMahan, Ilya Mironov, Kunal Talwar, and Li Zhang. Deep learning with differential privacy. In *Proceedings of the ACM SIGSAC Conference on Computer and Communications Security*, pages 308–318, 2016.

[7] Abbas Acar, Hidayet Aksu, A Selcuk Uluagac, and Mauro Conti. A survey on homomorphic encryption schemes: Theory and implementation. *ACM Computing Surveys*, 51(4):1–35, 2018.

[8] Edward H Adelson and James R Bergen. Spatiotemporal energy models for the perception of motion. *Josa A*, 2(2):284–299, 1985.

[9] Gojko Adzic and Robert Chatley. Serverless computing: economic and architectural impact. In *Proceedings of the 2017 11th joint meeting on foundations of software engineering*, pages 884–889, Paderborn, Germany, September 4-8, 2017.

[10] Mohammad Al-Fares, Alexander Loukissas, and Amin Vahdat. A scalable, commodity data center network architecture. In *Proceedings of the ACM Conference on Applications, Technologies, Architectures, and Protocols for Computer Communications (SIGCOMM)*, 2008.

[11] Thaynara Alves. Trustzone : Integrated hardware and software security. *White Paper*, 2004.

[12] Marcelo Amaral, Jorda Polo, David Carrera, Seetharami R. Seelam, and Malgorzata Steinder. Topology-aware GPU scheduling for learning workloads in cloud environments. In Bernd Mohr and Padma Raghavan, editors, In *Proceedings of the International Conference for High Performance Computing, Networking, Storage and Analysis (SC)*, pages 17:1–17:12, 2017.

[13] Mohammad Javad Amiri, Divyakant Agrawal, and Amr El Abbadi. Sharper: Sharding permissioned blockchains over network clusters. In *Proceedings of the 2021 International Conference on Management of Data*, pages 76–88, 2021.

[14] Mohammad Mohammadi Amiri, Deniz Gunduz, Sanjeev R Kulkarni, and H Vincent Poor. Update aware device scheduling for federated learning at the wireless edge. *arXiv preprint arXiv:2001.10402*, 2020.

[15] Padmanabhan Anandan. A computational framework and an algorithm for the measurement of visual motion. *International Journal of Computer Vision*, 2(3):283–310, 1989.

[16] Mykhaylo Andriluka, Leonid Pishchulin, Peter Gehler, and Bernt Schiele. 2d human pose estimation: New benchmark and state of the art analysis. In *IEEE Conference on Computer Vision and Pattern Recognition (CVPR)*, June 2014.

[17] Mykhaylo Andriluka, Leonid Pishchulin, Peter Gehler, and Bernt Schiele. Mpii annotation: Download. `https://drive.google.com/drive/folders/1MmQ2FRP0coxHGk0Ntj0JOGv9OxSNuCfK`, 2014.

[18] Mykhaylo Andriluka, Leonid Pishchulin, Peter Gehler, and Bernt Schiele. Mpii dataset: Download. `http://human-pose.mpi-inf.mpg.de/`, 2014.

[19] Evgeny Andriyash, Arash Vahdat, and William G. Macready. Improved gradient-based optimization over discrete distributions. *arXiv preprint*, abs/1810.00116, 2018.

[20] Elli Androulaki, Artem Barger, Vita Bortnikov, Christian Cachin, Konstantinos Christidis, Angelo De Caro, David Enyeart, Christopher Ferris, Gennady Laventman, Yacov Manevich, et al. Hyperledger fabric: a distributed operating system for permissioned blockchains. In *Proceedings of the thirteenth EuroSys conference*, pages 1–15, 2018.

[21] Apple Animoji. `https://support.apple.com/en-gb/HT208190`, 2020.

[22] Sajid Anwar, Kyuyeon Hwang, and Wonyong Sung. Structured pruning of deep convolutional neural networks. *ACM J. Emerg. Technol. Comput. Syst.*, 13(3):32:1–32:18, 2017.

[23] NVIDIA Ampere Architecture. `https://www.nvidia.com/en-us/data-center/nvidia-ampere-gpu-architecture/`, 2020.

[24] Arturo Argueta and David Chiang. Accelerating sparse matrix operations in neural networks on graphics processing units. In *Proceedings of the Conference of the Association for Computational Linguistics (ACL)*, pages 6215–6224, 2019.

[25] Manoj Ghuhan Arivazhagan, Vinay Aggarwal, Aaditya Kumar Singh, and Sunav Choudhary. Federated learning with personalization layers. *arXiv preprint arXiv:1912.00818*, 2019.

[26] Bruno Artacho and Andreas Savakis. Unipose: Unified human pose estimation in single images and videos. In *Proceedings of the IEEE/CVF conference on computer vision and pattern recognition*, pages 7035–7044, 2020.

[27] Nouman Ashraf, Ammar Hasan, Hassaan Khaliq Qureshi, and Marios Lestas. Combined data rate and energy management in harvesting enabled tactile iot sensing devices. *IEEE Trans. Industrial Informatics*, 15(5):3006–3015, 2019.

[28] Gilles Aubert, Rachid Deriche, and Pierre Kornprobst. Computing optical flow via variational techniques. *SIAM Journal on Applied Mathematics*, 60(1):156–182, 1999.

[29] Hossein Azizpour, Ali Sharif Razavian, Josephine Sullivan, Atsuto Maki, and Stefan Carlsson. Factors of transferability for a generic convnet representation. *IEEE Trans. Pattern Anal. Mach. Intell.*, 38(9):1790–1802, 2016.

[30] Eugene Bagdasaryan, Andreas Veit, Yiqing Hua, Deborah Estrin, and Vitaly Shmatikov. How to backdoor federated learning. In *International Conference on Artificial Intelligence and Statistics*, pages 2938–2948. PMLR, 2020.

[31] Simon Baker and Takeo Kanade. Limits on super-resolution and how to break them. *IEEE Transactions on Pattern Analysis & Machine Intelligence*, (9):1167–1183, 2002.

[32] Simon Baker and Iain Matthews. Lucas-kanade 20 years on: A unifying framework. *International journal of computer vision*, 56(3):221–255, 2004.

[33] Ioana Baldini, Paul Castro, Kerry Chang, Perry Cheng, Stephen Fink, Vatche Ishakian, Nick Mitchell, Vinod Muthusamy, Rodric Rabbah, Aleksander Slominski, et al. Serverless computing: Current trends and open problems. In *Research advances in cloud computing*, pages 1–20. Springer, 2017.

[34] Ron Banner, Itay Hubara, Elad Hoffer, and Daniel Soudry. Scalable methods for 8-bit training of neural networks. In *Proceedings of the Advances in Neural Information Processing Systems (NeurIPS)*, pages 5151–5159, Montréal, Canada, 2018.

[35] Ron Banner, Yury Nahshan, Elad Hoffer, and Daniel Soudry. ACIQ: analytical clipping for integer quantization of neural networks. *arXiv preprint*, abs/1810.05723, 2018.

[36] Xianglin Bao, Cheng Su, Yan Xiong, Wenchao Huang, and Yifei Hu. Flchain: A blockchain for auditable federated learning with trust and incentive. In *2019 5th International Conference on Big Data Computing and Communications (BIGCOM)*, pages 151–159, 2019.

[37] John L Barron, David J Fleet, and Steven S Beauchemin. Performance of optical flow techniques. *International journal of computer vision*, 12(1):43–77, 1994.

[38] Steven S. Beauchemin and John L. Barron. The computation of optical flow. *ACM computing surveys (CSUR)*, 27(3):433–466, 1995.

[39] Zakaria Belhachmi and Frédéric Hecht. Control of the effects of regularization on variational optic flow computations. *Journal of Mathematical Imaging and Vision*, 40(1):1–19, 2011.

[40] Pawel Benecki, Michal Kawulok, Daniel Kostrzewa, and Lukasz Skonieczny. Evaluating super-resolution reconstruction of satellite images. *Acta Astronautica*, 153:15–25, 2018.

[41] Irving Biederman. Recognition-by-components: a theory of human image understanding. *Psychological review*, 94(2):115, 1987.

[42] Aaron F Bobick and Stephen S Intille. Large occlusion stereo. *International Journal of Computer Vision*, 33(3):181–200, 1999.

[43] Jonas Bohler and Florian Kerschbaum. Secure multi-party computation of differentially private median. In *Proceedings of the USENIX Security Symposium*, pages 2147–2164, Republic of Korea, November 15–19, 2021.

[44] Daniel Bolya, Chong Zhou, Fanyi Xiao, and Yong Jae Lee. Yolact: Real-time instance segmentation. In *Proceedings of the IEEE/CVF international conference on computer vision*, pages 9157–9166, 2019.

[45] Daniel Bolya, Chong Zhou, Fanyi Xiao, and Yong Jae Lee. Yolact++: Better real-time instance segmentation. *IEEE transactions on pattern analysis and machine intelligence*, 2020.

[46] Yelysei Bondarenko, Markus Nagel, and Tijmen Blankevoort. Understanding and overcoming the challenges of efficient transformer quantization. In *Proceedings of the 2021 Conference on Empirical Methods in Natural Language Processing*, pages 7947–7969, Online and Punta Cana, Dominican Republic, November 2021. Association for Computational Linguistics.

[47] Dan Boneh, Eu-Jin Goh, and Kobbi Nissim. Evaluating 2-dnf formulas on ciphertexts. In *Proceedings of the Theory of cryptography conference*, pages 325–341. Springer, 2005.

[48] Florian Bourse, Michele Minelli, Matthias Minihold, and Pascal Paillier. Fast homomorphic evaluation of deep discretized neural networks. In *Proceedings of the Annual International Cryptology Conference*, pages 483–512. Springer, 2018.

[49] Bozhong Liu. Single image super-resolution challenge. https://towards datascience.com/single-image-super-resolution-challenge-6f4835e5a156, 2021.

[50] Zvika Brakerski, Craig Gentry, and Vinod Vaikuntanathan. (leveled) fully homomorphic encryption without bootstrapping. *ACM Transactions on Computation Theory*, 6(3):1–36, 2014.

[51] Thomas Brox, Andrés Bruhn, Nils Papenberg, and Joachim Weickert. High accuracy optical flow estimation based on a theory for warping. In *European Conference on Computer Vision*, pages 25–36. Springer, 2004.

[52] Andrés Bruhn, Joachim Weickert, and Christoph Schnörr. Lucas/kanade meets horn/schunck: Combining local and global optic flow methods. In *Proceedings of the IEEE/CVF Conference on Computer Vision and Pattern Recognition (CVPR)*, 61(3):211–231, 2005.

[53] Maxime Bucher, Stéphane Herbin, and Frédéric Jurie. Improving semantic embedding consistency by metric learning for zero-shot classiffication. In *European Conference on Computer Vision*, pages 730–746. Springer, 2016.

[54] Cristian Bucila, Rich Caruana, and Alexandru Niculescu-Mizil. Model compression. In *Proceedings of the ACM International Conference on Knowledge Discovery and Data Mining (KDD)*, pages 535–541, 2006.

[55] Duc Bui, Kshitiz Malik, Jack Goetz, Honglei Liu, Seungwhan Moon, Anuj Kumar, and Kang G Shin. Federated user representation learning. *arXiv preprint arXiv:1909.12535*, 2019.

[56] Choi Sang Bum. https://github.com/SangbumChoi/MobileHuman Pose, 2022.

[57] Bolun Cai, Xiangmin Xu, Kui Jia, Chunmei Qing, and Dacheng Tao. Dehazenet: An end-to-end system for single image haze removal. *IEEE Transactions on Image Processing*, 25(11):5187–5198, 2016.

[58] Han Cai, Chuang Gan, Tianzhe Wang, Zhekai Zhang, and Song Han. Once-for-all: Train one network and specialize it for efficient deployment. In *Proceedings of the International Conference on Learning Representations (ICLR)*, 2020.

[59] Han Cai, Chuang Gan, Ligeng Zhu, and Song Han. Tinytl: Reduce memory, not parameters for efficient on-device learning. In *Proceedings of the Advances in Neural Information Processing Systems (NeurIPS)*, December 6–12, 2020, virtual event.

[60] Nicolas Carion, Francisco Massa, Gabriel Synnaeve, Nicolas Usunier, Alexander Kirillov, and Sergey Zagoruyko. End-to-end object detection with transformers. In *European conference on computer vision*, pages 213–229. Springer, 2020.

[61] Joao Carreira, Pulkit Agrawal, Katerina Fragkiadaki, and Jitendra Malik. Human pose estimation with iterative error feedback. In *Proceedings of the IEEE Conference on Computer Vision and Pattern Recognition*, pages 4733–4742, 2016.

[62] Joao Carreira, Pedro Fonseca, Alexey Tumanov, Andrew Zhang, and Randy Katz. A case for serverless machine learning. In *Workshop on Systems for ML and Open Source Software at NeurIPS*, volume 2018, Montreal, Quebec, Canada, December 2–8, 2018.

[63] Joao Carreira and Andrew Zisserman. Quo vadis, action recognition? a new model and the kinetics dataset. In *Proceedings of the IEEE Conference on Computer Vision and Pattern Recognition*, pages 6299–6308, 2017.

[64] Hongyan Chang, Virat Shejwalkar, Reza Shokri, and Amir Houmansadr. Cronus: Robust and heterogeneous collaborative learning with black-box knowledge transfer. *arXiv preprint arXiv:1912.11279*, 2019.

[65] Sung-En Chang, Yanyu Li, Mengshu Sun, Weiwen Jiang, Sijia Liu, Yanzhi Wang, and Xue Lin. RMSMP: A novel deep neural network quantization framework with row-wise mixed schemes and multiple precisions. *arXiv preprint*, abs/2111.00153, 2021.

[66] Soravit Changpinyo, Wei-Lun Chao, Boqing Gong, and Fei Sha. Synthesized classifiers for zero-shot learning. In *Proceedings of the IEEE Conference on Computer Vision and Pattern Recognition*, pages 5327–5336, 2016.

[67] Saqib Rasool Chaudhry, Andrei Palade, Aqeel Kazmi, and Siobhán Clarke. Improved qos at the edge using serverless computing to deploy virtual network functions. *IEEE Internet of Things Journal*, 7(10):10673–10683, 2020.

[68] Chaochao Chen, Jun Zhou, Li Wang, Xibin Wu, Wenjing Fang, Jin Tan, Lei Wang, Alex X Liu, Hao Wang, and Cheng Hong. When homomorphic encryption marries secret sharing: Secure large-scale sparse logistic regression and applications in risk control. In *Proceedings of the ACM International Conference on Knowledge Discovery and Data Mining (KDD)*, pages 2652–2662, Singapore, August 14–18, 2021.

[69] Chen Chen, Qizhen Weng, Wei Wang, Baochun Li, and Bo Li. Fast distributed deep learning via worker-adaptive batch sizing. In *Proceedings of the ACM Symposium on Cloud Computing (SoCC)*, 2018.

[70] Duan Chen, Arturo S. Leon, Samuel P. Engle, Claudio Fuentes, and Qiuwen Chen. Offline training for improving online performance of a genetic algorithm based optimization model for hourly multi-reservoir operation. *Environ. Model. Softw.*, 96:46–57, 2017.

[71] Hao Chen, Wei Dai, Miran Kim, and Yongsoo Song. Efficient multi-key homomorphic encryption with packed ciphertexts with application to oblivious neural network inference. In *Proceedings of the ACM SIGSAC Conference on Computer and Communications Security*, pages 395–412, London, UK, November 11–15, 2019.

[72] Hong-You Chen and Wei-Lun Chao. Fedbe: Making bayesian model ensemble applicable to federated learning. In *9th International Conference on Learning Representations, ICLR 2021, Virtual Event, Austria, May 3-7, 2021*. OpenReview.net, 2021.

[73] Jianmin Chen, Rajat Monga, Samy Bengio, and Rafal Józefowicz. Revisiting distributed synchronous SGD. *arXiv preprint*, abs/1604.00981, 2016.

[74] Long Chen, Haizhou Ai, Rui Chen, Zijie Zhuang, and Shuang Liu. Cross-view tracking for multi-human 3d pose estimation at over 100 fps. In *Proceedings of the IEEE/CVF Conference on Computer Vision and Pattern Recognition*, pages 3279–3288, 2020.

[75] Mengyu Chen, Weifa Liang, and Jing Li. Energy-efficient data collection maximization for uav-assisted wireless sensor networks. In *2021 IEEE Wireless Communications and Networking Conference (WCNC)*, pages 1–7. IEEE, 2021.

[76] Qiang Chen, Junshi Huang, Rogério Schmidt Feris, Lisa M. Brown, Jian Dong, and Shuicheng Yan. Deep domain adaptation for describing people based on fine-grained clothing attributes. In *Proceedings of the IEEE/CVF Conference on Computer Vision and Pattern Recognition (CVPR)*, pages 5315–5324, 2015.

[77] Tianqi Chen, Mu Li, Yutian Li, Min Lin, Naiyan Wang, Minjie Wang, Tianjun Xiao, Bing Xu, Chiyuan Zhang, and Zheng Zhang. Mxnet: A flexible and efficient machine learning library for heterogeneous distributed systems. *arXiv preprint*, abs/1512.01274, 2015.

[78] Tianqi Chen, Thierry Moreau, Ziheng Jiang, Lianmin Zheng, Eddie Q. Yan, Haichen Shen, Meghan Cowan, Leyuan Wang, Yuwei Hu, Luis Ceze, Carlos Guestrin, and Arvind Krishnamurthy. TVM: an automated end-to-end optimizing compiler for deep learning. In *Proceedings of the USENIX Symposium on Operating Systems Design and Implementation (OSDI)*, pages 578–594, Carlsbad, USA, 2018.

[79] Tianshi Chen, Zidong Du, Ninghui Sun, Jia Wang, Chengyong Wu, Yunji Chen, and Olivier Temam. Diannao: a small-footprint high-throughput accelerator for ubiquitous machine-learning. In *Proceedings of the Architectural Support for Programming Languages and Operating Systems (ASPLOS)*, pages 269–284, 2014.

[80] Xianjie Chen and Alan L Yuille. Articulated pose estimation by a graphical model with image dependent pairwise relations. *Advances in neural information processing systems*, 27, 2014.

[81] Xinyun Chen, Chang Liu, Bo Li, Kimberly Lu, and Dawn Song. Targeted backdoor attacks on deep learning systems using data poisoning. *arXiv preprint arXiv:1712.05526*, 2017.

[82] Yu Chen, Chunhua Shen, Xiu-Shen Wei, Lingqiao Liu, and Jian Yang. Adversarial posenet: A structure-aware convolutional network for human pose estimation. In *Proceedings of the IEEE International Conference on Computer Vision*, pages 1212–1221, 2017.

[83] Yunji Chen, Tao Luo, Shaoli Liu, Shijin Zhang, Liqiang He, Jia Wang, Ling Li, Tianshi Chen, Zhiwei Xu, Ninghui Sun, and Olivier Temam. Dadiannao: A machine-learning supercomputer. In *Proceedings of the Annual IEEE/ACM International Symposium on Microarchitecture (MICRO)*, pages 609–622, 2014.

[84] Yu Cheng, Bo Yang, Bo Wang, Wending Yan, and Robby T Tan. Occlusion-aware networks for 3d human pose estimation in video. In *Proceedings of the IEEE/CVF International Conference on Computer Vision*, pages 723–732, 2019.

[85] Zezhou Cheng, Qingxiong Yang, and Bin Sheng. Deep colorization. In *Proceedings of the IEEE/CVF Conference on Computer Vision and Pattern Recognition (CVPR)*, pages 415–423, 2015.

[86] Jung Hee Cheon, Andrey Kim, Miran Kim, and Yongsoo Song. Homomorphic encryption for arithmetic of approximate numbers. In *Proceedings of the International Conference on the Theory and Application of Cryptology and Information Security*, pages 409–437, Hong Kong, China, December 3–7, 2017, Springer, 2017.

[87] Rewon Child, Scott Gray, Alec Radford, and Ilya Sutskever. Generating long sequences with sparse transformers. *arXiv preprint arXiv:1904.10509*, 2019.

[88] Trishul M. Chilimbi, Yutaka Suzue, Johnson Apacible, and Karthik Kalyanaraman. Project adam: Building an efficient and scalable deep learning training system. In *Proceedings of the USENIX Symposium on Operating Systems Design and Implementation (OSDI)*, 2014.

[89] Jungwook Choi, Zhuo Wang, Swagath Venkataramani, Pierce I-Jen Chuang, Vijayalakshmi Srinivasan, and Kailash Gopalakrishnan. PACT: parameterized clipping activation for quantized neural networks. *arXiv preprint*, abs/1805.06085, 2018.

[90] Grace Chu, Okan Arikan, Gabriel Bender, Weijun Wang, Achille Brighton, Pieter-Jan Kindermans, Hanxiao Liu, Berkin Akin, Suyog Gupta, and Andrew Howard. Discovering multi-hardware mobile models via architecture search. In *Proceedings of the IEEE/CVF Conference on Computer Vision and Pattern Recognition*, pages 3022–3031, 2021.

[91] Dan Claudiu Ciresan, Ueli Meier, Jonathan Masci, Luca Maria Gambardella, and Jürgen Schmidhuber. Flexible, high performance convolutional neural networks for image classification. In *Twenty-Second International Joint Conference on Artificial Intelligence*, Barcelona, Catalonia, Spain, July 16–22, 2011.

[92] Liam Collins, Hamed Hassani, Aryan Mokhtari, and Sanjay Shakkottai. Exploiting shared representations for personalized federated learning. In Marina Meila and Tong Zhang, editors, *Proceedings of the 38th In Proceedings of the International Conference on Machine Learning*, pages 2089–2099, 18–24 July 2021, Virtual Event, PMLR, 2021.

[93] Ronan Collobert, Jason Weston, Léon Bottou, Michael Karlen, Koray Kavukcuoglu, and Pavel Kuksa. Natural language processing (almost) from scratch. *Journal of Machine Learning Research*, 12(ARTICLE):2493–2537, 2011.

[94] Ronan Collobert, Jason Weston, Léon Bottou, Michael Karlen, Koray Kavukcuoglu, and Pavel P. Kuksa. Natural language processing (almost) from scratch. *J. Mach. Learn. Res.*, 12:2493–2537, 2011.

[95] Graham Cormode, Somesh Jha, Tejas Kulkarni, Ninghui Li, Divesh Srivastava, and Tianhao Wang. Privacy at scale: Local differential privacy in practice. In *Proceedings of the ACM SIGMOD International Conference on Management of Data*, pages 1655–1658, Houston, TX, USA, June 10–15, 2018.

[96] Graham Cormode and S. Muthukrishnan. An improved data stream summary: the count-min sketch and its applications. *J. Algorithms*, 55(1):58–75, 2005.

[97] Matthieu Courbariaux, Yoshua Bengio, and Jean-Pierre David. Binaryconnect: Training deep neural networks with binary weights during propagations. In *Proceedings of the Annual Conference on Neural Information Processing Systems (NeurIPS)*, pages 3123–3131, 2015.

[98] Henggang Cui, James Cipar, Qirong Ho, Jin Kyu Kim, Seunghak Lee, Abhimanu Kumar, Jinliang Wei, Wei Dai, Gregory R. Ganger, Phillip B. Gibbons, Garth A. Gibson, and Eric P. Xing. Exploiting bounded staleness to speed up big data analytics. In *Proceedings of the USENIX Annual Technical Conferenc (ATC)*, 2014.

[99] Harshit Daga, Patrick K. Nicholson, Ada Gavrilovska, and Diego Lugones. Cartel: A system for collaborative transfer learning at the edge. *Proceedings of the ACM Symposium on Cloud Computing*, Santa Cruz, CA, USA, November 20–23, 2019.

[100] Xiaoliang Dai, Peizhao Zhang, Bichen Wu, Hongxu Yin, Fei Sun, Yanghan Wang, Marat Dukhan, Yunqing Hu, Yiming Wu, Yangqing Jia, et al. Chamnet: Towards efficient network design through platform-aware model adaptation. In *Proceedings of the IEEE/CVF Conference on Computer Vision and Pattern Recognition*, pages 11398–11407, Long Beach, CA, USA, June 16–20, 2019.

[101] Navneet Dalal and Bill Triggs. Histograms of oriented gradients for human detection. In *Proceedings of the IEEE/CVF Conference on Computer Vision and Pattern Recognition (CVPR)*, volume 1, pages 886–893. Ieee, 2005.

[102] Ivan Damgård, Daniel Escudero, Tore Frederiksen, Marcel Keller, Peter Scholl, and Nikolaj Volgushev. New primitives for actively-secure mpc over rings with applications to private machine learning. In *Proceedings of the IEEE Symposium on Security and Privacy*, pages 1102–1120. IEEE, 2019.

[103] Ivan Damgård and Jesper Buus Nielsen. Universally composable efficient multi-party computation from threshold homomorphic encryption. In *Proceedings of the Annual International Cryptology Conference*, pages 247–264. Springer, 2003.

[104] Qi Dang, Jianqin Yin, Bin Wang, and Wenqing Zheng. Deep learning based 2d human pose estimation: A survey. *Tsinghua Science and Technology*, 24(6):663–676, 2019.

[105] MNIST Dataset. Mnist dataset. `http://yann.lecun.com/exdb/mnist`, 2013.

[106] Jeffrey Dean, Greg S. Corrado, Rajat Monga, Kai Chen, Matthieu Devin, Quoc V. Le, Mark Z. Mao, Marc'Aurelio Ranzato, Andrew Senior, Paul Tucker, Ke Yang, and Andrew Y. Ng. Large scale distributed deep networks. In *Proceedings of the Annual Conference on Neural Information Processing Systems (NeurIPS)*, 2012.

[107] Ofer Dekel, Ran Gilad-Bachrach, Ohad Shamir, and Lin Xiao. Optimal distributed online prediction using mini-batches. *J. Mach. Learn. Res.*, 13:165–202, 2012.

[108] Jia Deng, Wei Dong, Richard Socher, Li-Jia Li, Kai Li, and Fei-Fei Li. Imagenet: A large-scale hierarchical image database. In *Proceedings of the IEEE/CVF Conference on Computer Vision and Pattern Recognition (CVPR)*, pages 248–255, 2009.

[109] Yuyang Deng, Mohammad Mahdi Kamani, and Mehrdad Mahdavi. Adaptive personalized federated learning. *arXiv preprint arXiv:2003.13461*, 2020.

[110] Rohit R. Deshmukh, Makarand Sudhakar Ballal, Hiralal M. Suryawanshi, and Mahesh K. Mishra. An adaptive approach for effective power management in DC microgrid based on virtual generation in distributed energy sources. *IEEE Trans. Industrial Informatics*, 16(1):362–372, 2020.

[111] Jacob Devlin, Ming-Wei Chang, Kenton Lee, and Kristina Toutanova. Bert: Pre-training of deep bidirectional transformers for language understanding. *arXiv preprint arXiv:1810.04805*, 2018.

[112] Sauptik Dhar, Junyao Guo, Jiayi Liu, Samarth Tripathi, Unmesh Kurup, and Mohak Shah. On-device machine learning: An algorithms and learning theory perspective. *arXiv preprint*, abs/1911.00623, 2019.

[113] Bao Gia Doan, Ehsan Abbasnejad, and Damith C Ranasinghe. Februus: Input purification defense against trojan attacks on deep neural network systems. In *Annual Computer Security Applications Conference*, pages 897–912, 2020.

[114] Chao Dong, Chen Change Loy, Kaiming He, and Xiaoou Tang. Image super-resolution using deep convolutional networks. *IEEE Transactions on Pattern Analysis and Machine Intelligence*, 38(2):295–307, 2016.

[115] Chao Dong, Chen Change Loy, and Xiaoou Tang. Accelerating the super-resolution convolutional neural network. In *European Conference on Computer Vision*, pages 391–407. Springer, 2016.

[116] Xin Dong, Shangyu Chen, and Sinno Jialin Pan. Learning to prune deep neural networks via layer-wise optimal brain surgeon. In *Proceedings of the Annual Conference on Neural Information Processing Systems (NeurIPS)*, pages 4857–4867, 2017.

[117] Alexey Dosovitskiy, Lucas Beyer, Alexander Kolesnikov, Dirk Weissenborn, Xiaohua Zhai, Thomas Unterthiner, Mostafa Dehghani, Matthias Minderer, Georg Heigold, Sylvain Gelly, Jakob Uszkoreit, and Neil Houlsby. An image is worth 16x16 words: Transformers for image recognition at scale. In *Proceedings of the International Conference on Learning Representations (ICLR)*, 2021.

[118] Alexey Dosovitskiy, Philipp Fischer, Eddy Ilg, Philip Hausser, Caner Hazirbas, Vladimir Golkov, Patrick Van Der Smagt, Daniel Cremers, and Thomas Brox. Flownet: Learning optical flow with convolutional networks. In *Proceedings of the IEEE/CVF Conference on Computer Vision and Pattern Recognition (CVPR)*, pages 2758–2766, 2015.

[119] Dong Du, Tianyi Yu, Yubin Xia, Binyu Zang, Guanglu Yan, Chenggang Qin, Qixuan Wu, and Haibo Chen. Catalyzer: Sub-millisecond startup for serverless computing with initialization-less booting. In *Proceedings of the Twenty-Fifth International Conference on Architectural Support for Programming Languages and Operating Systems*, pages 467–481, Lausanne, Switzerland, March 16–20, 2020.

[120] Moming Duan, Duo Liu, Xianzhang Chen, Renping Liu, Yujuan Tan, and Liang Liang. Self-balancing federated learning with global imbalanced data in mobile systems. *IEEE Transactions on Parallel and Distributed Systems*, 32(1):59–71, 2020.

[121] Yan Duan, Xi Chen, Rein Houthooft, John Schulman, and Pieter Abbeel. Benchmarking deep reinforcement learning for continuous control. In Maria-Florina Balcan and Kilian Q. Weinberger, editors, In *Proceedings of the International Conference on Machine Learning (ICML)*, volume 48, pages 1329–1338, 2016.

[122] Jacob Dumford and Walter Scheirer. Backdooring convolutional neural networks via targeted weight perturbations. In *2020 IEEE International Joint Conference on Biometrics (IJCB)*, pages 1–9. IEEE, Houston, TX, USA, September 28 - October 1, 2020.

[123] Cynthia Dwork. Differential privacy: A survey of results. In *Proceedings of the International Conference on Theory and Applications of Models of Computation*, pages 1–19. Springer, 2008.

[124] Cynthia Dwork, Frank McSherry, Kobbi Nissim, and Adam Smith. Calibrating noise to sensitivity in private data analysis. In *Proceedings of the Theory of Cryptography*, pages 265–284. Springer, 2006.

[125] Ascend 310 AI Processor: Energy efficiency and high integration for edges. https://e.huawei.com/se/products/cloud-computing-dc/atlas/ascend-310, 2021.

[126] Kieren J Egan, Ángel C Pinto-Bruno, Irene Bighelli, Marla Berg-Weger, Annemieke van Straten, Emiliano Albanese, and Anne-Margriet Pot. Online training and support programs designed to improve mental health and reduce burden among caregivers of people with dementia: a systematic review. *Journal of the American Medical Directors Association*, 19(3):200–206, 2018.

[127] Apple Neural Engine. https://developer.apple.com/machine-learning/, 2020.

[128] Martin Ester, Hans-Peter Kriegel, Jörg Sander, and Xiaowei Xu. A density-based algorithm for discovering clusters in large spatial databases with noise. In *Proceedings of the ACM International Conference on Knowledge Discovery and Data Mining (KDD)*, 1996.

[129] Mark Everingham, L Van Gool, Christopher KI Williams, John Winn, and Andrew Zisserman. The pascal visual object classes challenge 2007 (voc 2007) results (2007), 2008.

[130] Alireza Fallah, Aryan Mokhtari, and Asuman E. Ozdaglar. Personalized federated learning with theoretical guarantees: A model-agnostic meta-learning approach. In Hugo Larochelle, Marc'Aurelio Ranzato, Raia Hadsell, Maria-Florina Balcan, and Hsuan-Tien Lin, editors, In *Proceedings of the Annual Conference on Neural Information Processing Systems (NeurIPS) December 6–12, 2020, virtual event*.

[131] Junfeng Fan and Frederik Vercauteren. Somewhat practical fully homomorphic encryption. *Cryptology ePrint Archive*, 2012.

[132] Biyi Fang, Xiao Zeng, and Mi Zhang. Nestdnn: Resource-aware multi-tenant on-device deep learning for continuous mobile vision. In *Proceedings of the Annual International Conference on Mobile Computing and Networking (MobiCom)*, pages 115–127, 2018.

[133] Biyi Fang, Xiao Zeng, and Mi Zhang. Nestdnn: Resource-aware multi-tenant on-device deep learning for continuous mobile vision. *Proceedings of the 24th Annual International Conference on Mobile Computing and Networking*, 2018.

[134] Iman Faraji, Seyed Hessam Mirsadeghi, and Ahmad Afsahi. Topology-aware GPU selection on multi-gpu nodes. In *Proceedings of the IEEE International Parallel and Distributed Processing Symposium (IPDPS)*, pages 712–720, 2016.

[135] Christoph Feichtenhofer, Haoqi Fan, Jitendra Malik, and Kaiming He. Slowfast networks for video recognition. In *Proceedings of the IEEE/CVF International Conference on Computer Vision (ICCV)*, pages 6202–6211, 2019.

[136] Christoph Feichtenhofer, Axel Pinz, and Andrew Zisserman. Convolutional two-stream network fusion for video action recognition. In *Proceedings of the IEEE/CVF Conference on Computer Vision and Pattern Recognition (CVPR)*, pages 1933–1941, 2016.

[137] Pedro Felzenszwalb, David McAllester, and Deva Ramanan. A discriminatively trained, multiscale, deformable part model. In *Proceedings of the IEEE/CVF Conference on Computer Vision and Pattern Recognition (CVPR)*, pages 1–8. Ieee, 2008.

[138] Lang Feng, Prabhakar Kudva, Dilma Da Silva, and Jiang Hu. Exploring serverless computing for neural network training. In *Proceedings of the IEEE International Conference on Cloud Computing (CLOUD)*, pages 334–341. IEEE, 2018.

[139] Chelsea Finn, Pieter Abbeel, and Sergey Levine. Model-agnostic meta-learning for fast adaptation of deep networks. In *Proceedings of the International Conference on Machine Learning (ICML)*, pages 1126–1135. PMLR, Sydney, NSW, Australia, 6-11 August 2017.

[140] David J Fleet and Allan D Jepson. Computation of component image velocity from local phase information. *International Journal of Computer Vision*, 5(1):77–104, 1990.

[141] Denis Foley and John Danskin. Ultra-performance pascal gpu and nvlink interconnect. In *Proceedings of the Annual IEEE/ACM International Symposium on Microarchitecture (MICRO)*, 37:7–17, 2017.

[142] Andrea Frome, Greg S Corrado, Jon Shlens, Samy Bengio, Jeff Dean, Tomas Mikolov, et al. Devise: A deep visual-semantic embedding model. In *Proceedings of the Annual Conference on Neural Information Processing Systems (NeurIPS)*, pages 2121–2129, 2013.

[143] Xiuju Fu, ChongJin Ong, Sathiya Keerthi, Gih Guang Hung, and Liping Goh. Extracting the knowledge embedded in support vector machines. In *Proc. of IEEE IJCNN*, volume 1, pages 291–296, 2004.

[144] Min Gao, Kun Wang, and Lei He. Probabilistic model checking and scheduling implementation of an energy router system in energy internet for green cities. *IEEE Trans. Industrial Informatics*, 14(4):1501–1510, 2018.

[145] Yansong Gao, Change Xu, Derui Wang, Shiping Chen, Damith C Ranasinghe, and Surya Nepal. Strip: A defence against trojan attacks on deep neural networks. In *Proceedings of the 35th Annual Computer Security Applications Conference*, pages 113–125, San Juan, PR, USA, December 09–13, 2019.

[146] Yuanxiang Gao, Li Chen, and Baochun Li. Spotlight: Optimizing device placement for training deep neural networks. In *Proceedings of the International Conference on Machine Learning (ICML)*, volume 80, pages 1662–1670, 2018.

[147] Alex Gaunt, Matthew Johnson, Maik Riechert, Daniel Tarlow, Ryota Tomioka, Dimitrios Vytiniotis, and Sam Webster. Ampnet: Asynchronous model-parallel training for dynamic neural networks. *arXiv preprint*, abs/1705.09786, 2017.

[148] Weifeng Ge and Yizhou Yu. Borrowing treasures from the wealthy: Deep transfer learning through selective joint fine-tuning. In *Proceedings of the IEEE/CVF Conference on Computer Vision and Pattern Recognition (CVPR)*, pages 10–19, 2017.

[149] Jonas Gehring, Michael Auli, David Grangier, Denis Yarats, and Yann N Dauphin. Convolutional sequence to sequence learning. In *International Conference on Machine Learning*, pages 1243–1252. PMLR, 2017.

[150] Jonas Geiping, Hartmut Bauermeister, Hannah Dröge, and Michael Moeller. Inverting gradients-how easy is it to break privacy in federated learning? In *Proceedings of the Annual Conference on Neural Information Processing Systems (NeurIPS)*, 33:16937–16947, 2020.

[151] Yeli Geng, Yi Yang, and Guohong Cao. Energy-efficient computation offloading for multicore-based mobile devices. In *Proceedings of the IEEE International Conference on Computer Communications (INFOCOM)*, pages 46–54, 2018.

[152] Yeli Geng, Yi Yang, and Guohong Cao. Energy-efficient computation offloading for multicore-based mobile devices. In *Proceedings of the IEEE International Conference on Computer Communications (INFOCOM)*, pages 46–54, 2018.

[153] Saeed Ghadimi and Guanghui Lan. Stochastic first- and zeroth-order methods for nonconvex stochastic programming. *SIAM Journal on Optimization*, 23(4):2341–2368, 2013.

[154] Golnaz Ghiasi, Tsung-Yi Lin, and Quoc V Le. Nas-fpn: Learning scalable feature pyramid architecture for object detection. In *Proceedings of the IEEE/CVF Conference on Computer Vision and Pattern Recognition*, pages 7036–7045, 2019.

[155] Avishek Ghosh, Jichan Chung, Dong Yin, and Kannan Ramchandran. An efficient framework for clustered federated learning. In Hugo Larochelle, Marc'Aurelio Ranzato, Raia Hadsell, Maria-Florina Balcan, and Hsuan-Tien

Lin, editors, *Advances in Neural Information Processing Systems 33: Annual Conference on Neural Information Processing Systems 2020, NeurIPS 2020,* December 6–12, 2020, virtual event.

[156] Ross Girshick. Fast r-cnn. In *Proceedings of the IEEE/CVF International Conference on Computer Vision (ICCV)*, pages 1440–1448, 2015.

[157] Ross Girshick, Jeff Donahue, Trevor Darrell, and Jitendra Malik. Rich feature hierarchies for accurate object detection and semantic segmentation. In *Proceedings of the IEEE/CVF Conference on Computer Vision and Pattern Recognition (CVPR)*, pages 580–587, 2014.

[158] Daniel Glasner, Shai Bagon, and Michal Irani. Super-resolution from a single image. In *2009 IEEE 12th International Conference on Computer Vision (ICCV)*, pages 349–356. IEEE, 2009.

[159] Mevludin Glavic. (deep) reinforcement learning for electric power system control and related problems: A short review and perspectives. *Annu. Rev. Control.*, 48:22–35, 2019.

[160] Xinyu Gong, Shiyu Chang, Yifan Jiang, and Zhangyang Wang. Autogan: Neural architecture search for generative adversarial networks. In *Proceedings of the IEEE/CVF International Conference on Computer Vision*, pages 3224–3234, 2019.

[161] Melvyn A Goodale and A David Milner. Separate visual pathways for perception and action. *Trends in Neurosciences*, 15(1):20–25, 1992.

[162] Ian Goodfellow, Yoshua Bengio, and Aaron Courville. *Deep learning.* MIT press, 2016.

[163] Grzegorz Góra and Arkadiusz Wojna. Riona: A classifier combining rule induction and k-nn method with automated selection of optimal neighbourhood. In *European Conference on Machine Learning*, pages 111–123. Springer, 2002.

[164] Benjamin Graham, Alaaeldin El-Nouby, Hugo Touvron, Pierre Stock, Armand Joulin, Herve Jegou, and Matthijs Douze. Levit: A vision transformer in convnet's clothing for faster inference. In *Proceedings of the IEEE/CVF International Conference on Computer Vision (ICCV)*, pages 12259–12269, October 2021.

[165] Michael Greenwald and Sanjeev Khanna. Space-efficient online computation of quantile summaries. In *Proceedings of the International Conference on Management of Data (SIGMOD)*, pages 58–66, 2001.

[166] Juncheng Gu, Mosharaf Chowdhury, Kang G. Shin, Yibo Zhu, Myeongjae Jeon, Junjie Qian, Hongqiang Harry Liu, and Chuanxiong Guo. Tiresias: A GPU cluster manager for distributed deep learning. In *Proceedings of the USENIX Symposium on Networked Systems Design and Implementation (NSDI)*, pages 485–500, 2019.

[167] Tianyu Gu, Kang Liu, Brendan Dolan-Gavitt, and Siddharth Garg. Badnets: Evaluating backdooring attacks on deep neural networks. *IEEE Access*, 7:47230–47244, 2019.

[168] Neel Guha, Ameet Talwalkar, and Virginia Smith. One-shot federated learning. *arXiv preprint*, abs/1902.11175, 2019.

[169] Chuan Guo, Ruihan Wu, and Kilian Q Weinberger. Trojannet: Embedding hidden trojan horse models in neural networks. *arXiv preprint arXiv:2002.10078*, 2020.

[170] Chuanxiong Guo, Guohan Lu, Dan Li, Haitao Wu, Xuan Zhang, Yunfeng Shi, Chen Tian, Yongguang Zhang, and Songwu Lu. Bcube: A high performance, server-centric network architecture for modular data centers. In *Proceedings of the ACM Conference on Applications, Technologies, Architectures, and Protocols for Computer Communications (SIGCOMM)*, 2009.

[171] Gongde Guo, Hui Wang, David Bell, Yaxin Bi, and Kieran Greer. Knn model-based approach in classification. In *OTM Confederated International Conferences" On the Move to Meaningful Internet Systems"*, pages 986–996. Springer, 2003.

[172] Jingcai Guo. An improved incremental training approach for large scaled dataset based on support vector machine. In *2016 IEEE/ACM 3rd International Conference on Big Data Computing Applications and Technologies (BDCAT)*, pages 149–157. IEEE, 2016.

[173] Jingcai Guo and Song Guo. Adaptive adjustment with semantic feature space for zero-shot recognition. In *ICASSP 2019-2019 IEEE International Conference on Acoustics, Speech and Signal Processing (ICASSP)*, pages 3287–3291. IEEE, 2019.

[174] Jingcai Guo and Song Guo. Ams-sfe: Towards an alignment of manifold structures via semantic feature expansion for zero-shot learning. In *2019 IEEE International Conference on Multimedia and Expo (ICME)*, pages 73–78. IEEE, 2019.

[175] Jingcai Guo and Song Guo. Ee-ae: An exclusivity enhanced unsupervised feature learning approach. In *ICASSP 2019-2019 IEEE International Conference on Acoustics, Speech and Signal Processing (ICASSP)*, pages 3517–3521. IEEE, 2019.

[176] Jingcai Guo and Song Guo. A novel perspective to zero-shot learning: Towards an alignment of manifold structures via semantic feature expansion. *IEEE Transactions on Multimedia*, 23:524–537, 2020.

[177] Jingcai Guo, Shiheng Ma, Jie Zhang, Qihua Zhou, and Song Guo. Dual-view attention networks for single image super-resolution. In *Proceedings of the 28th ACM International Conference on Multimedia*, pages 2728–2736, 2020.

[178] Yiwen Guo, Anbang Yao, and Yurong Chen. Dynamic network surgery for efficient dnns. In *Proceedings of the Annual Conference on Neural Information Processing Systems (NeurIPS)*, pages 1379–1387, 2016.

[179] Suyog Gupta, Ankur Agrawal, Kailash Gopalakrishnan, and Pritish Narayanan. Deep learning with limited numerical precision. In *Proceedings of the International Conference on Machine Learning (ICML)*, volume 37, pages 1737–1746, 2015.

[180] Philipp Gysel, Jon J. Pimentel, Mohammad Motamedi, and Soheil Ghiasi. Ristretto: A framework for empirical study of resource-efficient inference in convolutional neural networks. *IEEE Trans. Neural Networks Learn. Syst.*, 29(11):5784–5789, 2018.

[181] Trung Ha, Tran Khanh Dang, Tran Tri Dang, Tuan Anh Truong, and Manh Tuan Nguyen. Differential privacy in deep learning: an overview. In *Proceedings of the International Conference on Advanced Computing and Applications*, pages 97–102. IEEE, Nha Trang, Vietnam, 27–29 November 2019.

[182] Stefan Hadjis, Ce Zhang, Ioannis Mitliagkas, and Christopher Ré. Omnivore: An optimizer for multi-device deep learning on cpus and gpus. *arXiv preprint*, abs/1606.04487, 2016.

[183] Rajaa El Hamdani, Majd Mustapha, David Restrepo Amariles, Aurore Troussel, Sébastien Meeùs, and Katsiaryna Krasnashchok. A combined rule-based and machine learning approach for automated gdpr compliance checking. In *Proceedings of the International Conference on Artificial Intelligence and Law*, pages 40–49, Sao Paulo Brazil, June 21–25, 2021.

[184] Song Han, Huizi Mao, and William J. Dally. Deep compression: Compressing deep neural network with pruning, trained quantization and huffman coding. *arXiv preprint*, abs/1510.00149, 2016.

[185] Song Han, Huizi Mao, and William J. Dally. Deep compression: Compressing deep neural network with pruning, trained quantization and huffman coding. In *Proceedings of the International Conference on Learning Representations (ICLR)*, San Juan, Puerto Rico, 2016.

[186] Song Han, Jeff Pool, Sharan Narang, Huizi Mao, Enhao Gong, Shijian Tang, Erich Elsen, Peter Vajda, Manohar Paluri, John Tran, Bryan Catanzaro, and William J. Dally. DSD: dense-sparse-dense training for deep neural networks. In *Proceedings of the International Conference on Learning Representations (ICLR)*, 2017.

[187] Song Han, Jeff Pool, John Tran, and William J. Dally. Learning both weights and connections for efficient neural network. In *Proceedings of the Annual Conference on Neural Information Processing Systems (NeurIPS)*, pages 1135–1143, 2015.

[188] Song Han, Jeff Pool, John Tran, and William J. Dally. Learning both weights and connections for efficient neural networks. *arXiv preprint*, abs/1506.02626, 2015.

[189] Filip Hanzely, Slavomír Hanzely, Samuel Horváth, and Peter Richtárik. Lower bounds and optimal algorithms for personalized federated learning. In *Proceedings of the Annual Conference on Neural Information Processing Systems (NeurIPS)*, December 6–12, 2020, virtual event.

[190] Filip Hanzely and Peter Richtárik. Federated learning of a mixture of global and local models. *arXiv preprint arXiv:2002.05516*, 2020.

[191] Kensho Hara, Hirokatsu Kataoka, and Yutaka Satoh. Can spatiotemporal 3d cnns retrace the history of 2d cnns and imagenet? In *Proceedings of the IEEE/CVF Conference on Computer Vision and Pattern Recognition (CVPR)*, pages 6546–6555, 2018.

[192] Muhammad Haris, Gregory Shakhnarovich, and Norimichi Ukita. Deep back-projection networks for super-resolution. In *Proceedings of the IEEE/CVF Conference on Computer Vision and Pattern Recognition (CVPR)*, pages 1664–1673, 2018.

[193] Aaron Harlap, Henggang Cui, Wei Dai, Jinliang Wei, Gregory R. Ganger, Phillip B. Gibbons, Garth A. Gibson, and Eric P. Xing. Addressing the straggler problem for iterative convergent parallel ml. In *Proceedings of the ACM Symposium on Cloud Computing (SoCC)*, 2016.

[194] Aaron Harlap, Deepak Narayanan, Amar Phanishayee, Vivek Seshadri, Nikhil R. Devanur, Gregory R. Ganger, and Phillip B. Gibbons. Pipedream: Fast and efficient pipeline parallel DNN training. *arXiv preprint*, abs/1806.03377, 2018.

[195] Chaoyang He, Salman Avestimehr, and Murali Annavaram. Group knowledge transfer: Collaborative training of large cnns on the edge. *arXiv preprint arXiv:2007.14513*, 2020.

[196] Jiong He, Yao Chen, Tom Z. J. Fu, Xin Long, Marianne Winslett, Liang You, and Zhenjie Zhang. Haas: Cloud-based real-time data analytics with heterogeneity-aware scheduling. In *Proceedings of the IEEE International Conference on Distributed Computing Systems (ICDCS)*, pages 1017–1028, 2018.

[197] Kaiming He, Georgia Gkioxari, Piotr Dollár, and Ross Girshick. Mask r-cnn. In *Proceedings of the IEEE/CVF International Conference on Computer Vision (ICCV)*, pages 2961–2969, 2017.

[198] Kaiming He, Xiangyu Zhang, Shaoqing Ren, and Jian Sun. Deep residual learning for image recognition. In *Proceedings of the IEEE/CVF Conference on Computer Vision and Pattern Recognition (CVPR)*, pages 770–778, 2016.

[199] Kaiming He, Xiangyu Zhang, Shaoqing Ren, and Jian Sun. Deep residual learning for image recognition. In *Proceedings of the IEEE Conference on Computer Vision and Pattern Recognition (CVPR)*, June 2016.

[200] Kaiming He, Xiangyu Zhang, Shaoqing Ren, and Jian Sun. Deep residual learning for image recognition. In *Proceedings of the IEEE/CVF Conference on Computer Vision and Pattern Recognition (CVPR)*, pages 770–778, 2016.

[201] Yang He, Ping Liu, Ziwei Wang, Zhilan Hu, and Yi Yang. Filter pruning via geometric median for deep convolutional neural networks acceleration. In *Proceedings of the IEEE/CVF Conference on Computer Vision and Pattern Recognition (CVPR)*, pages 4340–4349, 2019.

[202] David J Heeger. Optical flow using spatiotemporal filters. *International Journal of Computer Vision*, 1(4):279–302, 1988.

[203] Matteo Hessel, Joseph Modayil, Hado van Hasselt, Tom Schaul, Georg Ostrovski, Will Dabney, Dan Horgan, Bilal Piot, Mohammad Gheshlaghi Azar, and David Silver. Rainbow: Combining improvements in deep reinforcement learning. In *Proceedings of the AAAI Conference on Artificial Intelligence (AAAI)*, 2018.

[204] Geoffrey Hinton, Li Deng, Dong Yu, George E Dahl, Abdel-rahman Mohamed, Navdeep Jaitly, Andrew Senior, Vincent Vanhoucke, Patrick Nguyen, Tara N Sainath, et al. Deep neural networks for acoustic modeling in speech recognition: The shared views of four research groups. *IEEE Signal processing magazine*, 29(6):82–97, 2012.

[205] Geoffrey E. Hinton, Oriol Vinyals, and Jeffrey Dean. Distilling the knowledge in a neural network. *arXiv preprint*, abs/1503.02531, 2015.

[206] Qirong Ho, James Cipar, Henggang Cui, Jin Kyu Kim, Seunghak Lee, Phillip B. Gibbons, Garth A. Gibson, Gregory R. Ganger, and Eric P. Xing. More effective distributed ml via a stale synchronous parallel parameter server. In *Proceedings of the Annual Conference on Neural Information Processing Systems (NeurIPS)*, 2013.

[207] Sepp Hochreiter and Jürgen Schmidhuber. Long short-term memory. *Neural Computation*, 9(8):1735–1780, 1997.

[208] Zicong Hong, Song Guo, Peng Li, and Wuhui Chen. Pyramid: A layered sharding blockchain system. In *IEEE INFOCOM 2021-IEEE Conference on Computer Communications*, pages 1–10. IEEE, 2021.

[209] Berthold KP Horn and Brian G Schunck. Determining optical flow. *Artificial Intelligence*, 17(1-3):185–203, 1981.

[210] David W. Hosmer and Stanley Lemeshow. Applied logistic regression. 1989.

[211] Andrew Howard, Mark Sandler, Grace Chu, Liang-Chieh Chen, Bo Chen, Mingxing Tan, Weijun Wang, Yukun Zhu, Ruoming Pang, Vijay Vasudevan, et al. Searching for mobilenetv3. In *Proceedings of the IEEE/CVF International Conference on Computer Vision*, pages 1314–1324, Seoul, Korea (South), October 27 - November 2, 2019.

[212] Andrew G. Howard, Menglong Zhu, Bo Chen, Dmitry Kalenichenko, Weijun Wang, Tobias Weyand, Marco Andreetto, and Hartwig Adam. Mobilenets: Efficient convolutional neural networks for mobile vision applications. *arXiv preprint*, abs/1704.04861, 2017.

[213] Kevin Hsieh, Aaron Harlap, Nandita Vijaykumar, Dimitris Konomis, Gregory R. Ganger, Phillip B. Gibbons, and Onur Mutlu. Gaia: Geo-distributed machine learning approaching LAN speeds. In *Proceedings of the USENIX Symposium on Networked Systems Design and Implementation (NSDI)*, 2017.

[214] Kevin Hsieh, Aaron Harlap, Nandita Vijaykumar, Dimitris Konomis, Gregory R. Ganger, Phillip B. Gibbons, and Onur Mutlu. Gaia: Geo-distributed machine learning approaching lan speeds. In *Proceedings of the USENIX Symposium on Networked Systems Design and Implementation (NSDI)*, 2017.

[215] Kevin Hsieh, Aaron Harlap, Nandita Vijaykumar, Dimitris Konomis, Gregory R Ganger, Phillip B Gibbons, and Onur Mutlu. Gaia: Geo-distributed machine learning approaching *LAN* speeds. In *Proceedings of the USENIX Symposium on Networked Systems Design and Implementation (NSDI)*, pages 629–647, 2017.

[216] Kevin Hsieh, Amar Phanishayee, Onur Mutlu, and Phillip Gibbons. The non-iid data quagmire of decentralized machine learning. In *International Conference on Machine Learning*, pages 4387–4398. PMLR, 13-18 July 2020, Virtual Event.

[217] Tzu-Ming Harry Hsu, Hang Qi, and Matthew Brown. Measuring the effects of non-identical data distribution for federated visual classification. *arXiv preprint arXiv:1909.06335*, 2019.

[218] Hanpeng Hu, Dan Wang, and Chuan Wu. Distributed machine learning through heterogeneous edge systems. In *Proceedings of the AAAI Conference on Artificial Intelligence (AAAI)*, pages 7179–7186, 2020.

[219] Jie Hu, Li Shen, and Gang Sun. Squeeze-and-excitation networks. In *Proceedings of the IEEE/CVF Conference on Computer Vision and Pattern Recognition (CVPR)*, pages 7132–7141, 2018.

[220] Yunhong Hu, Liang Fang, and Guoping He. Privacy-preserving svm classification on vertically partitioned data without secure multi-party computation. In *Proceedings of the International Conference on Natural Computation (ICNC)*, pages 543–546, 2009.

[221] Fu Jie Huang and Yann LeCun. Large-scale learning with svm and convolutional for generic object categorization. In *Proceedings of the IEEE/CVF Conference on Computer Vision and Pattern Recognition (CVPR)*, volume 1, pages 284–291. IEEE, 2006.

[222] Gao Huang, Zhuang Liu, Laurens van der Maaten, and Kilian Q. Weinberger. Densely connected convolutional networks. In *Proceedings of the IEEE/CVF Conference on Computer Vision and Pattern Recognition (CVPR)*, pages 2261–2269, 2017.

[223] Gao Huang, Zhuang Liu, Laurens Van Der Maaten, and Kilian Q Weinberger. Densely connected convolutional networks. In *Proceedings of the IEEE/CVF Conference on Computer Vision and Pattern Recognition (CVPR)*, pages 4700–4708, 2017.

[224] Li Huang, Yifeng Yin, Zeng Fu, Shifa Zhang, Hao Deng, and Dianbo Liu. Loadaboost: Loss-based adaboost federated machine learning on medical data. *arXiv preprint arXiv:1811.12629*, 2018.

[225] Tao Huang, Baoliu Ye, Zhihao Qu, Bin Tang, Lie Xie, and Sanglu Lu. Physical-layer arithmetic for federated learning in uplink MU-MIMO enabled wireless networks. In *Proceedings of the IEEE International Conference on Computer Communications (INFOCOM)*, 2020.

[226] Yan Huang, Wei Wang, and Liang Wang. Video super-resolution via bidirectional recurrent convolutional networks. *IEEE Transactions on Pattern Analysis and Machine Intelligence (TPAMI), IEEE Trans. Pattern Anal. Mach. Intell.*, 40(4):1015–1028, 2018.

[227] Yanping Huang, Yonglong Cheng, Dehao Chen, HyoukJoong Lee, Jiquan Ngiam, Quoc V. Le, and Zhifeng Chen. Gpipe: Efficient training of giant neural networks using pipeline parallelism. In *Proceedings of the Annual Conference on Neural Information Processing Systems (NeurIPS)*, 2019.

[228] Yanping Huang, Youlong Cheng, Ankur Bapna, Orhan Firat, Dehao Chen, Mia Xu Chen, HyoukJoong Lee, Jiquan Ngiam, Quoc V. Le, Yonghui Wu, and Zhifeng Chen. Gpipe: Efficient training of giant neural networks using pipeline parallelism. In *Proceedings of the Annual Conference on Neural Information Processing Systems (NeurIPS)*, pages 103–112, 2019.

[229] Yutao Huang, Lingyang Chu, Zirui Zhou, Lanjun Wang, Jiangchuan Liu, Jian Pei, and Yong Zhang. Personalized cross-silo federated learning on non-iid data. In *Proceedings of the AAAI Conference on Artificial Intelligence*, volume 35, pages 7865–7873, 2021.

[230] Yuzhen Huang, Tatiana Jin, Yidi Wu, Zhenkun Cai, Xiao Yan, Fan Yang, Jinfeng Li, Yuying Guo, and James Cheng. Flexps: Flexible parallelism control in parameter server architecture. In *Proceedings of the VLDB Endowment (VLDB)*, 2018.

[231] Zehao Huang and Naiyan Wang. Like what you like: Knowledge distill via neuron selectivity transfer. *arXiv preprint*, abs/1707.01219, 2017.

[232] Forrest N. Iandola, Matthew W. Moskewicz, Khalid Ashraf, and Kurt Keutzer. Firecaffe: Near-linear acceleration of deep neural network training on compute clusters. In *Proceedings of the IEEE/CVF Conference on Computer Vision and Pattern Recognition (CVPR)*, pages 2592–2600, 2016.

[233] Intel. Intel sgx platform services. https://software.intel.com/sites/default/files/managed/1b/a2/Intel-SGX-Platform-Services.pdf.

[234] Catalin Ionescu, Dragos Papava, Vlad Olaru, and Cristian Sminchisescu. Human3.6m: Download. https://drive.google.com/drive/folders/1kgVH-GugrLoc9XyvP6nRoaFpw3TmM5xK, 2014.

[235] Catalin Ionescu, Dragos Papava, Vlad Olaru, and Cristian Sminchisescu. Human3.6m: Large scale datasets and predictive methods for 3d human sensing in natural environments. *IEEE Transactions on Pattern Analysis and Machine Intelligence*, 36(7):1325–1339, jul 2014.

[236] Md Zahidul Islam. Explore: A novel decision tree classification algorithm. In *British National Conference on Databases*, pages 55–71. Springer, 2010.

[237] Sohei Itahara, Takayuki Nishio, Yusuke Koda, Masahiro Morikura, and Koji Yamamoto. Distillation-based semi-supervised federated learning for communication-efficient collaborative training with non-iid private data. *arXiv preprint arXiv:2008.06180*, 2020.

[238] Nikita Ivkin, Daniel Rothchild, Enayat Ullah, Vladimir Braverman, Ion Stoica, and Raman Arora. Communication-efficient distributed SGD with sketching. In *Proceedings of the Annual Conference on Neural Information Processing Systems (NeurIPS)*, pages 13144–13154, 2019.

[239] Benoit Jacob, Skirmantas Kligys, Bo Chen, Menglong Zhu, Matthew Tang, Andrew G. Howard, Hartwig Adam, and Dmitry Kalenichenko. Quantization and training of neural networks for efficient integer-arithmetic-only inference. In *Proceedings of the IEEE/CVF Conference on Computer Vision and Pattern Recognition (CVPR)*, pages 2704–2713, 2018.

[240] Martin Jaggi, Virginia Smith, Martin Takác, Jonathan Terhorst, Sanjay Krishnan, Thomas Hofmann, and Michael I. Jordan. Communication-efficient distributed dual coordinate ascent. In *Proceedings of the Annual Conference on Neural Information Processing Systems (NeurIPS)*, 2014.

[241] Bargav Jayaraman and David Evans. Evaluating differentially private machine learning in practice. In *Proceedings of the USENIX Security Symposium*, pages 1895–1912, Santa Clara, CA, USA, August 14–16, 2019.

[242] Eunjeong Jeong, Seungeun Oh, Hyesung Kim, Jihong Park, Mehdi Bennis, and Seong-Lyun Kim. Communication-efficient on-device machine learning: Federated distillation and augmentation under non-iid private data. *arXiv preprint arXiv:1811.11479*, 2018.

[243] Pengyi Jia, Xianbin Wang, and Kan Zheng. Distributed clock synchronization based on intelligent clustering in local area industrial iot systems. *IEEE Trans. Industrial Informatics*, 16(6):3697–3707, 2020.

[244] Jiawei Jiang, Bin Cui, Ce Zhang, and Lele Yu. Heterogeneity-aware distributed parameter servers. In *Proceedings of the International Conference on Management of Data (SIGMOD)*, 2017.

[245] Jiawei Jiang, Fangcheng Fu, Tong Yang, and Bin Cui. Sketchml: Accelerating distributed machine learning with data sketches. In *Proceedings of the International Conference on Management of Data (SIGMOD)*, pages 1269–1284, 2018.

[246] Jiawei Jiang, Shaoduo Gan, Yue Liu, Fanlin Wang, Gustavo Alonso, Ana Klimovic, Ankit Singla, Wentao Wu, and Ce Zhang. Towards demystifying serverless machine learning training. In *Proceedings of the 2021 International Conference on Management of Data*, pages 857–871, Virtual Event, June 20–25, 2021.

[247] Jie Jiang, Lele Yu, Jiawei Jiang, Yuhong Liu, and Bin Cui. Angel: a new large-scale machine learning system. *National Science Review*, 5(2):216–236, 2018.

[248] Weiwen Jiang, Xinyi Zhang, Edwin H-M Sha, Lei Yang, Qingfeng Zhuge, Yiyu Shi, and Jingtong Hu. Accuracy vs. efficiency: Achieving both through fpga-implementation aware neural architecture search. In *Proceedings of the 56th Annual Design Automation Conference 2019*, pages 1–6, 2019.

[249] Yifan Jiang, Shiyu Chang, and Zhangyang Wang. Transgan: Two pure transformers can make one strong gan, and that can scale up. *Advances in Neural Information Processing Systems*, 34, 2021.

[250] Yihan Jiang, Jakub Konečný, Keith Rush, and Sreeram Kannan. Improving federated learning personalization via model agnostic meta learning. *arXiv preprint arXiv:1909.12488*, 2019.

[251] Yuhang Jiang, Xin Wang, and Wenwu Zhu. Hardware-aware transformable architecture search with efficient search space. In *2020 IEEE International Conference on Multimedia and Expo (ICME)*, pages 1–6. IEEE, 2020.

[252] Zhifeng Jiang, Wei Wang, and Yang Liu. Flashe: Additively symmetric homomorphic encryption for cross-silo federated learning. *arXiv preprint arXiv:2109.00675*, 2021.

[253] Eric Jonas, Johann Schleier-Smith, Vikram Sreekanti, Chia-Che Tsai, Anurag Khandelwal, Qifan Pu, Vaishaal Shankar, Joao Carreira, Karl Krauth, Neeraja Yadwadkar, et al. Cloud programming simplified: A berkeley view on serverless computing. *arXiv preprint arXiv:1902.03383*, 2019.

[254] Norman P. Jouppi, Cliff Young, Nishant Patil, David A. Patterson, Gaurav Agrawal, Raminder Bajwa, Sarah Bates, Suresh Bhatia, Nan Boden, Al Borchers, Rick Boyle, Pierre-luc Cantin, Clifford Chao, Chris Clark, Jeremy Coriell, Mike Daley, Matt Dau, Jeffrey Dean, Ben Gelb, Tara Vazir Ghaemmaghami, Rajendra Gottipati, William Gulland, Robert Hagmann, C. Richard Ho, Doug Hogberg, John Hu, Robert Hundt, Dan Hurt, Julian Ibarz, Aaron Jaffey, Alek Jaworski, Alexander Kaplan, Harshit Khaitan, Daniel Killebrew, Andy Koch, Naveen Kumar, Steve Lacy, James Laudon, James Law, Diemthu Le, Chris Leary, Zhuyuan Liu, Kyle Lucke, Alan Lundin, Gordon MacKean, Adriana Maggiore, Maire Mahony, Kieran Miller, Rahul Nagarajan, Ravi Narayanaswami, Ray Ni, Kathy Nix, Thomas Norrie, Mark Omernick, Narayana Penukonda, Andy Phelps, Jonathan Ross, Matt Ross, Amir Salek, Emad Samadiani, Chris Severn, Gregory Sizikov, Matthew Snelham, Jed Souter, Dan Steinberg, Andy Swing, Mercedes Tan, Gregory Thorson, Bo Tian, Horia Toma, Erick Tuttle, Vijay Vasudevan, Richard Walter, Walter Wang, Eric Wilcox, and Doe Hyun Yoon. In-datacenter performance analysis of a tensor processing unit. In *Proceedings of the Annual International Symposium on Computer Architecture (ISCA)*, pages 1–12, 2017.

[255] Sangil Jung, Changyong Son, Seohyung Lee, JinWoo Son, Jae-Joon Han, Youngjun Kwak, Sung Ju Hwang, and Changkyu Choi. Learning to quantize deep networks by optimizing quantization intervals with task loss. In *Proceedings of the IEEE Conference on Computer Vision and Pattern Recognition (CVPR)*, pages 4350–4359, Long Beach, USA, 2019.

[256] Peter Kairouz, H. Brendan McMahan, Brendan Avent, Aurélien Bellet, Mehdi Bennis, Arjun Nitin Bhagoji, Keith Bonawitz, Zachary Charles, Graham Cormode, Rachel Cummings, Rafael G. L. D'Oliveira, Salim El Rouayheb, David Evans, Josh Gardner, Zachary Garrett, Adrià Gascón, Badih Ghazi, Phillip B. Gibbons, Marco Gruteser, Zaïd Harchaoui, Chaoyang He, Lie He, Zhouyuan Huo, Ben Hutchinson, Justin Hsu, Martin Jaggi, Tara Javidi, Gauri Joshi, Mikhail Khodak, Jakub Konecný, Aleksandra Korolova, Farinaz Koushanfar, Sanmi Koyejo, Tancrède Lepoint, Yang Liu, Prateek Mittal, Mehryar Mohri, Richard Nock, Ayfer Özgür, Rasmus Pagh, Mariana Raykova, Hang Qi, Daniel Ramage, Ramesh Raskar, Dawn Song, Weikang Song, Sebastian U. Stich, Ziteng Sun, Ananda Theertha Suresh, Florian Tramèr, Praneeth Vepakomma, Jianyu Wang, Li Xiong, Zheng Xu, Qiang Yang, Felix X. Yu, Han Yu, and Sen Zhao. Advances and open problems in federated learning. *Foundations and Trends® in Machine Learning*, 14(1), 2021.

[257] Andrej Karpathy, George Toderici, Sanketh Shetty, Thomas Leung, Rahul Sukthankar, and Li Fei-Fei. Large-scale video classification with convolutional neural networks. In *Proceedings of the IEEE Conference on Computer Vision and Pattern Recognition (CVPR)*, June 2014.

[258] Jonathan Katz and Yehuda Lindell. *Introduction to Modern Cryptography.* CRC press, 2020.

[259] Lei Ke, Yu-Wing Tai, and Chi-Keung Tang. Deep occlusion-aware instance segmentation with overlapping bilayers. In *Proceedings of the IEEE/CVF Conference on Computer Vision and Pattern Recognition*, pages 4019–4028, virtual event, June 19–25, 2021.

[260] Chanaka Keerthisinghe, Archie C. Chapman, and Gregor Verbic. Energy management of pv-storage systems: Policy approximations using machine learning. *IEEE Trans. Industrial Informatics*, 15(1):257–265, 2019.

[261] Jiwon Kim, Jung Kwon Lee, and Kyoung Mu Lee. Accurate image super-resolution using very deep convolutional networks. In *Proceedings of the IEEE/CVF Conference on Computer Vision and Pattern Recognition (CVPR)*, pages 1646–1654, 2016.

[262] Volodymyr V. Kindratenko, Jeremy Enos, Guochun Shi, Michael T. Showerman, Galen Wesley Arnold, John E. Stone, James C. Phillips, and Wen-mei W. Hwu. GPU clusters for high-performance computing. In *Proceedings of the IEEE International Conference on Cluster Computing (CLUSTER)*, pages 1–8, 2009.

[263] Diederik P. Kingma and Jimmy Ba. Adam: A method for stochastic optimization. In *Proceedings of the International Conference on Learning Representations (ICLR)*, San Diego, USA, 2015.

[264] Alexander Kirillov, Ross Girshick, Kaiming He, and Piotr Dollár. Panoptic feature pyramid networks. In *Proceedings of the IEEE/CVF Conference on Computer Vision and Pattern Recognition*, pages 6399–6408, 2019.

[265] Atlas 200DK AI Developer Kit. https://e.huawei.com/us/products/cloud-computing-dc/atlas/atlas-200, 2020.

[266] Jetson AGX Xavier Developer Kit. https://developer.nvidia.com/embedded/jetson-agx-xavier-developer-kit, 2021.

[267] Nikita Klyuchnikov, Ilya Trofimov, Ekaterina Artemova, Mikhail Salnikov, Maxim Fedorov, and Evgeny Burnaev. Nas-bench-nlp: neural architecture search benchmark for natural language processing. *arXiv preprint arXiv:2006.07116*, 2020.

[268] Elyor Kodirov, Tao Xiang, and Shaogang Gong. Semantic autoencoder for zero-shot learning. In *Proceedings of the IEEE Conference on Computer Vision and Pattern Recognition*, pages 3174–3183, 2017.

[269] Eleftherios Kokoris-Kogias, Philipp Jovanovic, Linus Gasser, Nicolas Gailly, Ewa Syta, and Bryan Ford. Omniledger: A secure, scale-out, decentralized ledger via sharding. In *2018 IEEE Symposium on Security and Privacy (SP)*, pages 583–598. IEEE, 2018.

[270] Simon Kornblith, Jonathon Shlens, and Quoc V. Le. Do better imagenet models transfer better? In *Proceedings of the IEEE/CVF Conference on Computer Vision and Pattern Recognition (CVPR)*, pages 2661–2671, 2019.

[271] Raghuraman Krishnamoorthi. Quantizing deep convolutional networks for efficient inference: A whitepaper. *arXiv preprint*, abs/1806.08342, 2018.

[272] Alex Krizhevsky. Learning multiple layers of features from tiny images. *University of Toronto*, 2009.

[273] Alex Krizhevsky, Ilya Sutskever, and Geoffrey E. Hinton. Imagenet classification with deep convolutional neural networks. In *Proceedings of the Annual Conference on Neural Information Processing Systems (NeurIPS)*, 2012.

[274] Alex Krizhevsky, Ilya Sutskever, and Geoffrey E Hinton. Imagenet classification with deep convolutional neural networks. *Advances in Neural Information Processing Systems*, 25, 2012.

[275] Alex Krizhevsky, Ilya Sutskever, and Geoffrey E. Hinton. Imagenet classification with deep convolutional neural networks. *Commun. ACM*, 60(6):84–90, 2017.

[276] Alex Krizhevsky, Ilya Sutskever, and Geoffrey E. Hinton. Imagenet classification with deep convolutional neural networks. In *Proceedings of the Advances in Neural Information Processing Systems (NeurIPS)*, pages 1106–1114, Lake Tahoe, USA, 2012.

[277] Abhishek Kumar, Prasanna Sattigeri, Kahini Wadhawan, Leonid Karlinsky, Rogério Schmidt Feris, Bill Freeman, and Gregory W. Wornell. Co-regularized alignment for unsupervised domain adaptation. In *Proceedings of the Annual Conference on Neural Information Processing Systems (NeurIPS)*, pages 9367–9378, 2018.

[278] Aviral Kumar, Justin Fu, George Tucker, and Sergey Levine. Stabilizing off-policy q-learning via bootstrapping error reduction. In *Proceedings of the Annual Conference on Neural Information Processing Systems (NeurIPS)*, 2019.

[279] Thorsten Kurth, Jian Zhang, Nadathur Satish, Evan Racah, Ioannis Mitliagkas, Md. Mostofa Ali Patwary, Tareq M. Malas, Narayanan Sundaram, Wahid Bhimji, Mikhail Smorkalov, Jack Deslippe, Mikhail Shiryaev, Srinivas Sridharan, Prabhat, and Pradeep Dubey. Deep learning at 15pf: supervised and semi-supervised classification for scientific data. In *Proceedings of the International Conference for High Performance Computing, Networking, Storage and Analysis (SC)*, pages 7:1–7:11, 2017.

[280] Liangzhen Lai, Naveen Suda, and Vikas Chandra. Deep convolutional neural network inference with floating-point weights and fixed-point activations. *arXiv preprint*, abs/1703.03073, 2017.

[281] Liangzhen Lai, Naveen Suda, and Vikas Chandra. CMSIS-NN: efficient neural network kernels for arm cortex-m cpus. *arXiv preprint*, abs/1801.06601, 2018.

[282] Shangqi Lai, Sikhar Patranabis, Amin Sakzad, Joseph K Liu, Debdeep Mukhopadhyay, Ron Steinfeld, Shi-Feng Sun, Dongxi Liu, and Cong Zuo. Result pattern hiding searchable encryption for conjunctive queries. In *Proceedings of the ACM SIGSAC Conference on Computer and Communications Security (CCS)*, pages 745–762, 2018.

[283] Wei-Sheng Lai, Jia-Bin Huang, Narendra Ahuja, and Ming-Hsuan Yang. Deep laplacian pyramid networks for fast and accurate super-resolution. In *Proceedings of the IEEE/CVF Conference on Computer Vision and Pattern Recognition (CVPR)*, pages 624–632, 2017.

[284] Christoph H Lampert, Hannes Nickisch, and Stefan Harmeling. Learning to detect unseen object classes by between-class attribute transfer. In *2009 IEEE Conference on Computer Vision and Pattern Recognition*, pages 951–958. IEEE, 2009.

[285] Christoph H Lampert, Hannes Nickisch, and Stefan Harmeling. Attribute-based classification for zero-shot visual object categorization. *IEEE Transactions on Pattern Analysis and Machine Intelligence*, 36(3):453–465, 2014.

[286] Lieven De Lathauwer, Bart De Moor, and Joos Vandewalle. A multilinear singular value decomposition. *SIAM J. Matrix Anal. Appl.*, 21(4):1253–1278, 2000.

[287] Lieven De Lathauwer, Bart De Moor, and Joos Vandewalle. A multilinear singular value decomposition. *SIAM J. Matrix Analysis Applications*, 21:1253–1278, 2000.

[288] Justin Lazarow, Kwonjoon Lee, Kunyu Shi, and Zhuowen Tu. Learning instance occlusion for panoptic segmentation. In *Proceedings of the IEEE/CVF Conference on Computer Vision and Pattern Recognition (CVPR)*, pages 10720–10729, 2020.

[289] Erwan Lecarpentier and Emmanuel Rachelson. Non-stationary markov decision processes, a worst-case approach using model-based reinforcement learning. In *Proceedings of the Annual Conference on Neural Information Processing Systems (NeurIPS)*, pages 7214–7223, 2019.

[290] Y. Lecun, L. Bottou, Y. Bengio, and P. Haffner. Gradient-based learning applied to document recognition. *Proceedings of the IEEE*, 86(11):2278–2324, 1998.

[291] Yann LeCun, Yoshua Bengio, and Geoffrey Hinton. Deep learning. *Nature*, 521(7553):436, 2015.

[292] Yann LeCun, Léon Bottou, Yoshua Bengio, and Patrick Haffner. Gradient-based learning applied to document recognition. *Proceedings of the IEEE*, 86(11):2278–2324, 1998.

[293] Christian Ledig, Lucas Theis, Ferenc Huszár, Jose Caballero, Andrew Cunningham, Alejandro Acosta, Andrew Aitken, Alykhan Tejani, Johannes Totz, Zehan Wang, et al. Photo-realistic single image super-resolution using a generative adversarial network. In *Proceedings of the IEEE/CVF Conference on Computer Vision and Pattern Recognition (CVPR)*, pages 4681–4690, 2017.

[294] Joon-Woo Lee, HyungChul Kang, Yongwoo Lee, Woosuk Choi, Jieun Eom, Maxim Deryabin, Eunsang Lee, Junghyun Lee, Donghoon Yoo, Young-Sik Kim, et al. Privacy-preserving machine learning with fully homomorphic encryption for deep neural network. *IEEE Access*, 2022.

[295] Namhoon Lee, Thalaiyasingam Ajanthan, and Philip H. S. Torr. Snip: single-shot network pruning based on connection sensitivity. In *Proceedings of the International Conference on Learning Representations (ICLR)*, 2019.

[296] Royson Lee, Łukasz Dudziak, Mohamed Abdelfattah, Stylianos I Venieris, Hyeji Kim, Hongkai Wen, and Nicholas D Lane. Journey towards tiny perceptual super-resolution. In *European Conference on Computer Vision*, pages 85–102. Springer, 2020.

[297] Seunghak Lee, Jin Kyu Kim, Xun Zheng, Qirong Ho, Garth A. Gibson, and Eric P. Xing. On model parallelization and scheduling strategies for distributed machine learning. In *Proceedings of the Annual Conference on Neural Information Processing Systems (NeurIPS)*, Canada, 2014.

[298] Yuh-Jye Lee and Olvi L Mangasarian. Ssvm: A smooth support vector machine for classification. *Computational Optimization and Applications*, 20(1):5–22, 2001.

[299] Breiman Leo and Shang Nong. Born again trees. *University of California, Berkeley, Berkeley, CA, Technical Report*, 1(2):4, 1996.

[300] Daliang Li and Junpu Wang. FedMD: Heterogenous federated learning via model distillation. *arXiv*, oct 2019.

[301] Jing Li, Weifa Liang, Mengyu Chen, and Zichuan Xu. Mobility-aware dynamic service placement in d2d-assisted mec environments. In *2021 IEEE Wireless Communications and Networking Conference (WCNC)*, pages 1–6. IEEE, 2021.

[302] Jing Li, Weifa Liang, Meitian Huang, and Xiahua Jia. Providing reliability-aware virtualized network function services for mobile edge computing. In *2019 IEEE 39th International Conference on Distributed Computing Systems (ICDCS)*, pages 732–741. IEEE, 2019.

[303] Jing Li, Weifa Liang, Meitian Huang, and Xiaohua Jia. Reliability-aware network service provisioning in mobile edge-cloud networks. *IEEE Transactions on Parallel and Distributed Systems*, 31(7):1545–1558, 2020.

[304] Jing Li, Weifa Liang, Yuchen Li, Zichuan Xu, and Xiaohua Jia. Delay-aware dnn inference throughput maximization in edge computing via jointly exploring partitioning and parallelism. In *2021 IEEE 46th Conference on Local Computer Networks (LCN)*, pages 193–200. IEEE, 2021.

[305] Jing Li, Weifa Liang, Yuchen Li, Zichuan Xu, Xiaohua Jia, and Song Guo. Throughput maximization of delay-aware dnn inference in edge computing by exploring dnn model partitioning and inference parallelism. *IEEE Transactions on Mobile Computing*, 2021.

[306] Jing Li, Weifa Liang, and Yu Ma. Robust service provisioning with service function chain requirements in mobile edge computing. *IEEE Transactions on Network and Service Management*, 18(2):2138–2153, 2021.

[307] Jing Li, Weifa Liang, Wenzheng Xu, Zichuan Xu, Xiaohua Jia, Wanlei Zhou, and Jin Zhao. Maximizing user service satisfaction for delay-sensitive iot applications in edge computing. *IEEE Transactions on Parallel and Distributed Systems*, 33(5):1199–1212, 2021.

[308] Jing Li, Weifa Liang, Wenzheng Xu, Zichuan Xu, and Jin Zhao. Maximizing the quality of user experience of using services in edge computing for delay-sensitive iot applications. In *Proceedings of the 23rd International ACM Conference on Modeling, Analysis and Simulation of Wireless and Mobile Systems*, pages 113–121, Alicante, Spain, November 16–20, 2020.

[309] Jing Li, Weifa Liang, Zichuan Xu, Xiaohua Jia, and Wanlei Zhou. Service provisioning for multi-source iot applications in mobile edge computing. *ACM Transactions on Sensor Networks (TOSN)*, 18(2):1–25, 2021.

[310] Jing Li, Weifa Liang, Zichuan Xu, and Wanlei Zhou. Service provisioning for iot applications with multiple sources in mobile edge computing. In *2020 IEEE 45th Conference on Local Computer Networks (LCN)*, pages 42–53. IEEE, 2020.

[311] Mu Li, David G. Andersen, Jun Woo Park, Alexander J. Smola, Amr Ahmed, Vanja Josifovski, James Long, Eugene J. Shekita, and Bor-Yiing Su. Scaling distributed machine learning with the parameter server. In *Proceedings of the USENIX Symposium on Operating Systems Design and Implementation (OSDI)*, 2014.

[312] Mu Li, David G. Andersen, Alexander J. Smola, and Kai Yu. Communication efficient distributed machine learning with the parameter server. In *Proceedings of the Annual Conference on Neural Information Processing Systems (NeurIPS)*, 2014.

[313] Mu Li, Tong Zhang, Yuqiang Chen, and Alexander J. Smola. Efficient mini-batch training for stochastic optimization. In *Proceedings of the ACM International Conference on Knowledge Discovery and Data Mining (KDD)*, 2014.

[314] Ruey-Hsia Li and Geneva G Belford. Instability of decision tree classification algorithms. In *Proceedings of the International Conference on Knowledge Discovery and Data Mining (KDD)*, pages 570–575, Edmonton, Alberta, Canada, 2002.

[315] Rundong Li, Yan Wang, Feng Liang, Hongwei Qin, Junjie Yan, and Rui Fan. Fully quantized network for object detection. In *Proceedings of the IEEE/CVF Conference on Computer Vision and Pattern Recognition (CVPR)*, pages 2810–2819, 2019.

[316] Shaofeng Li, Minhui Xue, Benjamin Zhao, Haojin Zhu, and Xinpeng Zhang. Invisible backdoor attacks on deep neural networks via steganography and regularization. *IEEE Transactions on Dependable and Secure Computing*, 2020.

[317] Tian Li, Shengyuan Hu, Ahmad Beirami, and Virginia Smith. Ditto: Fair and robust federated learning through personalization. In *International Conference on Machine Learning*, pages 6357–6368. PMLR, 18–24 July 2021, Virtual Event.

[318] Tian Li, Anit Kumar Sahu, Manzil Zaheer, Maziar Sanjabi, Ameet Talwalkar, and Virginia Smith. Federated optimization in heterogeneous networks. *arXiv preprint arXiv:1812.06127*, 2018.

[319] Tian Li, Maziar Sanjabi, Ahmad Beirami, and Virginia Smith. Fair resource allocation in federated learning. *arXiv preprint arXiv:1905.10497*, 2019.

[320] Yanwei Li, Xinze Chen, Zheng Zhu, Lingxi Xie, Guan Huang, Dalong Du, and Xingang Wang. Attention-guided unified network for panoptic segmentation. In *Proceedings of the IEEE/CVF Conference on Computer Vision and Pattern Recognition*, pages 7026–7035, 2019.

[321] Yiming Li, Tongqing Zhai, Baoyuan Wu, Yong Jiang, Zhifeng Li, and Shutao Xia. Rethinking the trigger of backdoor attack. *arXiv preprint arXiv:2004.04692*, 2020.

[322] Yuchen Li, Weifa Liang, and Jing Li. Profit maximization for service placement and request assignment in edge computing via deep reinforcement learning. In *Proceedings of the 24th International ACM Conference on Modeling, Analysis and Simulation of Wireless and Mobile Systems*, pages 51–55, Alicante, Spain, November 22–26, 2021.

[323] Yuezun Li, Yiming Li, Baoyuan Wu, Longkang Li, Ran He, and Siwei Lyu. Backdoor attack with sample-specific triggers. *arXiv preprint arXiv:2012.03816*, 2020.

[324] Yuhang Li, Xin Dong, and Wei Wang. Additive powers-of-two quantization: An efficient non-uniform discretization for neural networks. In *Proceedings of the International Conference on Learning Representations (ICLR)*, Addis Ababa, Ethiopia, 2020.

[325] Zijun Li, Linsong Guo, Jiagan Cheng, Quan Chen, BingSheng He, and Minyi Guo. The serverless computing survey: A technical primer for design architecture. *ACM Computing Surveys (CSUR)*, 2021.

[326] Xiangru Lian, Ce Zhang, Huan Zhang, Cho-Jui Hsieh, Wei Zhang, and Ji Liu. Can decentralized algorithms outperform centralized algorithms? A case study for decentralized parallel stochastic gradient descent. In *Proceedings of the Annual Conference on Neural Information Processing Systems (NeurIPS)*, 2017.

[327] Xiangru Lian, Wei Zhang, Ce Zhang, and Ji Liu. Asynchronous decentralized parallel stochastic gradient descent. In Jennifer G. Dy and Andreas Krause, editors, *Proceedings of the 35th International Conference on Machine Learning, ICML*, Stockholm, Sweden, July 10–15, 2018.

[328] Jinwen Liang, Zheng Qin, Jianbing Ni, Xiaodong Lin, and Xuemin Shen. Efficient and privacy-preserving outsourced SVM classification in public cloud. In *Proceedings of the IEEE International Conference on Communications (ICC)*, pages 1–6, 2019.

[329] Jinwen Liang, Zheng Qin, Jianbing Ni, Xiaodong Lin, and Xuemin Shen. Practical and secure SVM classification for cloud-based remote clinical decision services. *IEEE Trans. on Computers*, 70(10):1612–1625, 2021.

[330] Jinwen Liang, Zheng Qin, Sheng Xiao, Lu Ou, and Xiaodong Lin. Efficient and secure decision tree classification for cloud-assisted online diagnosis services. *IEEE Trans. on Dependable and Secure Computing*, 18(4):1632–1644, 2021.

[331] Jinwen Liang, Zheng Qin, Liang Xue, Xiaodong Lin, and Xuemin Shen. Efficient and privacy-preserving decision tree classification for health monitoring systems. *IEEE Internet of Things Journal*, 8(16):12528–12539, 2021.

[332] Jinwen Liang, Zheng Qin, Liang Xue, Xiaodong Lin, and Xuemin Shen. Verifiable and secure svm classification for cloud-based health monitoring services. *IEEE Internet of Things Journal*, 8(23):17029–17042, 2021.

[333] Cong Liao, Haoti Zhong, Anna Squicciarini, Sencun Zhu, and David Miller. Backdoor embedding in convolutional neural network models via invisible perturbation. *arXiv preprint arXiv:1808.10307*, 2018.

[334] Bee Lim, Sanghyun Son, Heewon Kim, Seungjun Nah, and Kyoung Mu Lee. Enhanced deep residual networks for single image super-resolution. In *Proceedings of the IEEE Conference on Computer Vision and Pattern Recognition Workshops*, pages 136–144, 2017.

[335] Shiau Hong Lim and Arnaud Autef. Kernel-based reinforcement learning in robust markov decision processes. In *Proceedings of the International Conference on Machine Learning (ICML)*, 97:3973–3981, 2019.

[336] Guosheng Lin, Anton Milan, Chunhua Shen, and Ian Reid. Refinenet: Multi-path refinement networks for high-resolution semantic segmentation. In *Proceedings of the IEEE conference on computer vision and pattern recognition,* pages 1925–1934, 2017.

[337] Ji Lin, Wei-Ming Chen, Yujun Lin, John Cohn, Chuang Gan, and Song Han. Mcunet: Tiny deep learning on iot devices. In *Proceedings of the Advances in Neural Information Processing Systems (NeurIPS),* 2020.

[338] Ji Lin, Wei-Ming Chen, Yujun Lin, Chuang Gan, Song Han, et al. Mcunet: Tiny deep learning on iot devices. *Advances in Neural Information Processing Systems,* 33:11711–11722, 2020.

[339] Ji Lin, Chuang Gan, and Song Han. Tsm: Temporal shift module for efficient video understanding. In *Proceedings of the IEEE/CVF International Conference on Computer Vision,* pages 7083–7093, 2019.

[340] Shouxu Lin, Weifa Liang, and Jing Li. Reliability-aware service function chain provisioning in mobile edge-cloud networks. In *2020 29th International Conference on Computer Communications and Networks (ICCCN),* pages 1–9. IEEE, 2020.

[341] Tao Lin, Lingjing Kong, Sebastian U. Stich, and Martin Jaggi. Ensemble distillation for robust model fusion in federated learning. In *Advances in Neural Information Processing Systems 33: Annual Conference on Neural Information Processing Systems, NeurIPS,* 2020.

[342] Tsung-Yi Lin, Piotr Dollár, Ross Girshick, Kaiming He, Bharath Hariharan, and Serge Belongie. Feature pyramid networks for object detection. In *Proceedings of the IEEE/CVF Conference on Computer Vision and Pattern Recognition (CVPR),* pages 2117–2125, 2017.

[343] Tsung-Yi Lin, Priya Goyal, Ross Girshick, Kaiming He, and Piotr Dollár. Focal loss for dense object detection. In *Proceedings of the IEEE/CVF Conference on Computer Vision and Pattern Recognition (CVPR),* pages 2980–2988, 2017.

[344] Xiaofan Lin, Cong Zhao, and Wei Pan. Towards accurate binary convolutional neural network. In *Proceedings of the Annual Conference on Neural Information Processing Systems (NeurIPS),* pages 345–353, 2017.

[345] Zhouchen Lin and Heung-Yeung Shum. Fundamental limits of reconstruction-based superresolution algorithms under local translation. *IEEE Transactions on Pattern Analysis and Machine Intelligence,* 26(1):83–97, 2004.

[346] Zhouhan Lin, Matthieu Courbariaux, Roland Memisevic, and Yoshua Bengio. Neural networks with few multiplications. In *Proceedings of the International Conference on Learning Representations (ICLR),* 2016.

[347] Boyi Liu, Qi Cai, Zhuoran Yang, and Zhaoran Wang. Neural trust region/proximal policy optimization attains globally optimal policy. In *Proceedings of the Annual Conference on Neural Information Processing Systems (NeurIPS)*, pages 10564–10575, 2019.

[348] Kang Liu, Brendan Dolan-Gavitt, and Siddharth Garg. Fine-pruning: Defending against backdooring attacks on deep neural networks. In *International Symposium on Research in Attacks, Intrusions, and Defenses*, pages 273–294. Springer, 2018.

[349] Wei Liu, Dragomir Anguelov, Dumitru Erhan, Christian Szegedy, Scott Reed, Cheng-Yang Fu, and Alexander C Berg. Ssd: Single shot multibox detector. In *European Conference on Computer Vision*, pages 21–37. Springer, 2016.

[350] Wei Liu, Dragomir Anguelov, Dumitru Erhan, Christian Szegedy, Scott E. Reed, Cheng-Yang Fu, and Alexander C. Berg. SSD: single shot multibox detector. In *Proceedings of the European Conference on Computer Vision (ECCV)*, volume 9905, pages 21–37, 2016.

[351] Xiaoyuan Liu, Hongwei Li, Guowen Xu, Zongqi Chen, Xiaoming Huang, and Rongxing Lu. Privacy-enhanced federated learning against poisoning adversaries. *IEEE Transactions on Information Forensics and Security*, 16:4574–4588, 2021.

[352] Yang Liu, Zhenjiang Li, Zhidan Liu, and Kaishun Wu. Real-time arm skeleton tracking and gesture inference tolerant to missing wearable sensors. In *Proceedings of the Annual International Conference on Mobile Systems (MobiSys)*, pages 287–299, 2019.

[353] Yunfei Liu, Xingjun Ma, James Bailey, and Feng Lu. Reflection backdoor: A natural backdoor attack on deep neural networks. In *European Conference on Computer Vision*, pages 182–199. Springer, 2020.

[354] Yuntao Liu, Yang Xie, and Ankur Srivastava. Neural trojans. In *2017 IEEE International Conference on Computer Design (ICCD)*, pages 45–48. IEEE, 2017.

[355] Ze Liu, Yutong Lin, Yue Cao, Han Hu, Yixuan Wei, Zheng Zhang, Stephen Lin, and Baining Guo. Swin transformer: Hierarchical vision transformer using shifted windows. In *Proceedings of the IEEE/CVF International Conference on Computer Vision*, pages 10012–10022, 2021.

[356] Zhuang Liu, Mingjie Sun, Tinghui Zhou, Gao Huang, and Trevor Darrell. Rethinking the value of network pruning. In *Proceedings of the International Conference on Learning Representations (ICLR)*, 2019.

[357] Ziming Liu, Song Guo, Jingcai Guo, Yuanyuan Xu, and Fushuo Huo. Towards unbiased multi-label zero-shot learning with pyramid and semantic attention. *arXiv preprint arXiv:2203.03483*, 2022.

[358] Jonathan Long, Evan Shelhamer, and Trevor Darrell. Fully convolutional networks for semantic segmentation. In *Proceedings of the IEEE/CVF Conference on Computer Vision and Pattern Recognition (CVPR)*, pages 3431–3440, 2015.

[359] Mingsheng Long, Yue Cao, Jianmin Wang, and Michael I. Jordan. Learning transferable features with deep adaptation networks. In *Proceedings of the International Conference on Machine Learning (ICML)*, volume 37, pages 97–105, 2015.

[360] Christos Louizos, Matthias Reisser, Tijmen Blankevoort, Efstratios Gavves, and Max Welling. Relaxed quantization for discretized neural networks. In *Proceedings of the International Conference on Learning Representations (ICLR)*, 2019.

[361] Bingqian Lu, Jianyi Yang, Lydia Y Chen, and Shaolei Ren. Automating deep neural network model selection for edge inference. In *2019 IEEE First International Conference on Cognitive Machine Intelligence (CogMI)*, pages 184–193. IEEE, 2019.

[362] Xiaoying Lu and Haoyu Wang. Optimal sizing and energy management for cost-effective PEV hybrid energy storage systems. *IEEE Trans. Industrial Informatics*, 16(5):3407–3416, 2020.

[363] Bruce D Lucas, Takeo Kanade, et al. An iterative image registration technique with an application to stereo vision. Vancouver, 1981.

[364] Jianwen Luo and Elisa E Konofagou. A fast normalized cross-correlation calculation method for motion estimation. *IEEE transactions on ultrasonics, ferroelectrics, and frequency control*, 57(6):1347–1357, 2010.

[365] Keyang Luo, Tao Guan, Lili Ju, Yuesong Wang, Zhuo Chen, and Yawei Luo. Attention-aware multi-view stereo. In *Proceedings of the IEEE/CVF Conference on Computer Vision and Pattern Recognition*, pages 1590–1599, 2020.

[366] WANG Luping, WANG Wei, and LI Bo. Cmfl: Mitigating communication overhead for federated learning. In *2019 IEEE 39th International Conference on Distributed Computing Systems (ICDCS)*, pages 954–964. IEEE, 2019.

[367] Diogo C Luvizon, Hedi Tabia, and David Picard. Human pose regression by combining indirect part detection and contextual information. *Computers & Graphics*, 85:15–22, 2019.

[368] Zhihan Lv, Weijia Kong, Xin Zhang, Dingde Jiang, Haibin Lv, and Xiaohui Lu. Intelligent security planning for regional distributed energy internet. *IEEE Trans. Industrial Informatics*, 16(5):3540–3547, 2020.

[369] Lingjuan Lyu, Jiangshan Yu, Karthik Nandakumar, Yitong Li, Xingjun Ma, Jiong Jin, Han Yu, and Kee Siong Ng. Towards fair and privacy-preserving federated deep models. *IEEE Transactions on Parallel and Distributed Systems*, 31(11):2524–2541, 2020.

[370] Yu Ma, Weifa Liang, Jing Li, Xiaohua Jia, and Song Guo. Mobility-aware and delay-sensitive service provisioning in mobile edge-cloud networks. *IEEE Transactions on Mobile Computing*, 21(1):196–210, 2020.

[371] Oisin Mac Aodha, Ahmad Humayun, Marc Pollefeys, and Gabriel J Brostow. Learning a confidence measure for optical flow. *IEEE Transactions on Pattern Analysis and Machine Intelligence (TPAMI), IEEE Trans. Pattern Anal. Mach. Intell.*, 35(5):1107–1120, 2012.

[372] J. MacQueen. Some methods for classification and analysis of multivariate observations. In *Proc. Fifth Berkeley Symposium on Mathematical Statistics and Probability*, volume 1: Statistics, page 281–297, 1967.

[373] Grzegorz Malewicz, Matthew H. Austern, Aart J.C Bik, James C. Dehnert, Ilan Horn, Naty Leiser, and Grzegorz Czajkowski. Pregel: A system for large-scale graph processing. In *Proceedings of the International Conference on Management of Data (SIGMOD)*, 2010.

[374] Moein Manbachi and Martin Ordonez. Intelligent agent-based energy management system for islanded AC-DC microgrids. *IEEE Trans. Industrial Informatics*, 16(7):4603–4614, 2020.

[375] Yishay Mansour, Mehryar Mohri, Jae Ro, and Ananda Theertha Suresh. Three approaches for personalization with applications to federated learning. *arXiv preprint arXiv:2002.10619*, 2020.

[376] Hongzi Mao, Malte Schwarzkopf, Shaileshh Bojja Venkatakrishnan, Zili Meng, and Mohammad Alizadeh. Learning scheduling algorithms for data processing clusters. In *Proceedings of the ACM Conference on Applications, Technologies, Architectures, and Protocols for Computer Communications (SIGCOMM)*, pages 270–288, 2019.

[377] Huizi Mao, Song Han, Jeff Pool, Wenshuo Li, Xingyu Liu, Yu Wang, and William J. Dally. Exploring the regularity of sparse structure in convolutional neural networks. *arXiv preprint*, abs/1705.08922, 2017.

[378] Alberto Marchisio, Andrea Massa, Vojtech Mrazek, Beatrice Bussolino, Maurizio Martina, and Muhammad Shafique. Nascaps: A framework for neural architecture search to optimize the accuracy and hardware efficiency of convolutional capsule networks. In *2020 IEEE/ACM International Conference On Computer Aided Design (ICCAD)*, pages 1–9. IEEE, 2020.

[379] Akhil Mathur, Nicholas D. Lane, Sourav Bhattacharya, Aidan Boran, Claudio Forlivesi, and Fahim Kawsar. Deepeye: Resource efficient local execution of multiple deep vision models using wearable commodity hardware. In *Proceedings of the Annual International Conference on Mobile Systems (MobiSys)*, pages 68–81, 2017.

[380] Akhil Mathur, Nicholas D. Lane, Sourav Bhattacharya, Aidan Boran, Claudio Forlivesi, and Fahim Kawsar. Deepeye: Resource efficient local execution of multiple deep vision models using wearable commodity hardware. *Proceedings of the 15th Annual International Conference on Mobile Systems, MobiSys, Applications, and Services*, 2017.

[381] Bradley McDanel, Sai Qian Zhang, H. T. Kung, and Xin Dong. Full-stack optimization for accelerating cnns using powers-of-two weights with FPGA validation. In *Proceedings of the ACM International Conference on Supercomputing (ICS)*, pages 449–460, 2019.

[382] Brendan McMahan, Eider Moore, Daniel Ramage, Seth Hampson, and Blaise Agüera y Arcas. Communication-efficient learning of deep networks from decentralized data. In *Proceedings of the International Conference on Artificial Intelligence and Statistics (AISTATS)*, volume 54, pages 1273–1282, 2017.

[383] Qi Meng, Wei Chen, Yue Wang, Zhi-Ming Ma, and Tie-Yan Liu. Convergence analysis of distributed stochastic gradient descent with shuffling. *arXiv preprint*, abs/1709.10432, 2019.

[384] Ralph C Merkle. A digital signature based on a conventional encryption function. In *Proceedings of the Conference on the Theory and Applications of Cryptographic Techniques (CRYPTO)*, pages 369–378. Springer, 1987.

[385] Ilya Mironov. Rényi differential privacy. In *Proceedings of the IEEE Computer Security Foundations Symposium*, pages 263–275. IEEE, 2017.

[386] Mehdi Mirza and Simon Osindero. Conditional generative adversarial nets. *arXiv preprint arXiv:1411.1784*, 2014.

[387] Asit K. Mishra, Eriko Nurvitadhi, Jeffrey J. Cook, and Debbie Marr. WRPN: wide reduced-precision networks. In *Proceedings of the International Conference on Learning Representations (ICLR)*, 2018.

[388] Ishan Misra, Abhinav Shrivastava, Abhinav Gupta, and Martial Hebert. Cross-stitch networks for multi-task learning. In *Proceedings of the IEEE/CVF Conference on Computer Vision and Pattern Recognition (CVPR)*, pages 3994–4003, 2016.

[389] Volodymyr Mnih, Adrià Puigdomènech Badia, Mehdi Mirza, Alex Graves, Timothy P. Lillicrap, Tim Harley, David Silver, and Koray Kavukcuoglu. Asynchronous methods for deep reinforcement learning. In Proceedings of the International Conference on Machine Learning (ICML), 2016.

[390] Fan Mo, Hamed Haddadi, Kleomenis Katevas, Eduard Marin, Diego Perino, and Nicolas Kourtellis. Ppfl: Privacy-preserving federated learning with trusted execution environments. In *Proceedings of the 19th Annual International Conference on Mobile Systems, Applications, and Services*, MobiSys '21, page 94–108, New York, NY, USA, 2021. Association for Computing Machinery.

[391] Thomas B Moeslund, Adrian Hilton, and Volker Krüger. A survey of advances in vision-based human motion capture and analysis. *Comput. Vis. Image Underst.*, 104(2-3):90–126, 2006.

[392] Anup Mohan, Harshad Sane, Kshitij Doshi, Saikrishna Edupuganti, Naren Nayak, and Vadim Sukhomlinov. Agile cold starts for scalable serverless. In *11th USENIX Workshop on Hot Topics in Cloud Computing (HotCloud 19)*, 2019.

[393] Payman Mohassel and Yupeng Zhang. Secureml: A system for scalable privacy-preserving machine learning. In *Proceedings of the IEEE Symposium on Security and Privacy*, 2017.

[394] Mehryar Mohri, Gary Sivek, and Ananda Theertha Suresh. Agnostic federated learning. *arXiv preprint arXiv:1902.00146*, 2019.

[395] Aryan Mokhtari and Alejandro Ribeiro. DSA: decentralized double stochastic averaging gradient algorithm. *J. Mach. Learn. Res.*, 17:61:1–61:35, 2016.

[396] Seyed-Mohsen Moosavi-Dezfooli, Alhussein Fawzi, Omar Fawzi, and Pascal Frossard. Universal adversarial perturbations. In *Proceedings of the IEEE/CVF Conference on Computer Vision and Pattern Recognition (CVPR)*, pages 1765–1773, 2017.

[397] Philipp Moritz, Robert Nishihara, Stephanie Wang, Alexey Tumanov, Richard Liaw, Eric Liang, Melih Elibol, Zongheng Yang, William Paul, Michael I. Jordan, and Ion Stoica. Ray: A distributed framework for emerging AI applications. In *Proceedings of the USENIX Symposium on Operating Systems Design and Implementation (OSDI)*, 2018.

[398] Christian Mouchet, Juan Troncoso-Pastoriza, Jean-Philippe Bossuat, and Jean-Pierre Hubaux. Multiparty homomorphic encryption from ring-learning-with-errors. In *Proceedings of the Privacy Enhancing Technologies*, Journal of the Privacy Enhancing Technologies, Priv. Enhancing Technol. 2021.

[399] Franck Multon, Richard Kulpa, Ludovic Hoyet, and Taku Komura. Interactive animation of virtual humans based on motion capture data. *Computer Animation and Virtual Worlds*, 20(5-6):491–500, 2009.

[400] Markus Nagel, Marios Fournarakis, Rana Ali Amjad, Yelysei Bondarenko, Mart van Baalen, and Tijmen Blankevoort. A white paper on neural network quantization. *CoRR*, abs/2106.08295, 2021.

[401] Markus Nagel, Mart van Baalen, Tijmen Blankevoort, and Max Welling. Data-free quantization through weight equalization and bias correction. In *Proceedings of the IEEE/CVF International Conference on Computer Vision (ICCV)*, pages 1325–1334, Seoul, Korea (South), 2019.

[402] Satoshi Nakamoto. Bitcoin: A peer-to-peer electronic cash system. *Decentralized Business Review*, page 21260, 2008.

[403] Moni Naor and Benny Pinkas. Oblivious transfer and polynomial evaluation. In *Proceedings of the ACM Symposium on Theory of Computing (STOC)*, pages 245–254, 1999.

[404] Moni Naor and Benny Pinkas. Oblivious transfer with adaptive queries. In *Annual International Cryptology Conference (CRYPTO)*, pages 573–590. Springer, 1999.

[405] Moni Naor and Benny Pinkas. Efficient oblivious transfer protocols. In *Proceedings of the twelfth annual ACM-SIAM symposium on Discrete algorithms (SODA)*, volume 1, pages 448–457, 2001.

[406] Deepak Narayanan, Aaron Harlap, Amar Phanishayee, Vivek Seshadri, Nikhil R. Devanur, Gregory R. Ganger, Phillip B. Gibbons, and Matei Zaharia. Pipedream: Generalized pipeline parallelism for DNN training. In *Proceedings of the ACM Symposium on Operating Systems Principles (SOSP)*, pages 1–15, 2019.

[407] Milad Nasr, Reza Shokri, and Amir Houmansadr. Comprehensive privacy analysis of deep learning: Passive and active white-box inference attacks against centralized and federated learning. In *Proceedings of the IEEE Symposium on Security and Privacy*, pages 739–753. IEEE, 2019.

[408] Yurii E. Nesterov. Efficiency of coordinate descent methods on huge-scale optimization problems. *SIAM J. Optimization*, 22(2):341–362, 2012.

[409] John Neter, William J. Wasserman, and Michael H. Kutner. Applied linear statistical models : regression, analysis of variance, and experimental designs. 1974.

[410] Alejandro Newell, Kaiyu Yang, and Jia Deng. Stacked hourglass networks for human pose estimation. In *European Conference on Computer Vision*, pages 483–499. Springer, 2016.

[411] Thien Duc Nguyen, Phillip Rieger, Huili Chen, Hossein Yalame, Helen Möllering, Hossein Fereidooni, Samuel Marchal, Markus Miettinen, Azalia Mirhoseini, Shaza Zeitouni, et al. Flame: Taming backdoors in federated learning. In *Proceedings of the USENIX Security Symposium*. USENIX, Cryptology ePrint Archive 2022.

[412] Thien Duc Nguyen, Phillip Rieger, Huili Chen, Hossein Yalame, Helen Möllering, Hossein Fereidooni, Samuel Marchal, Markus Miettinen, Azalia Mirhoseini, Shaza Zeitouni, Farinaz Koushanfar, Ahmad-Reza Sadeghi, and Thomas Schneider. Flame: Taming backdoors in federated learning. In *Proceedings of the USENIX Security Symposium*, 2022.

[413] Tuan Anh Nguyen and Anh Tran. Input-aware dynamic backdoor attack. *Proceedings of the Advances in Neural Information Processing Systems*, 33:3454–3464, 2020.

[414] Hiroaki Niitsuma and Tsutomu Maruyama. Sum of absolute difference implementations for image processing on fpgas. In *2010 International Conference on Field Programmable Logic and Applications*, pages 167–170. IEEE, 2010.

[415] Takayuki Nishio and Ryo Yonetani. Client selection for federated learning with heterogeneous resources in mobile edge. In *ICC 2019-2019 IEEE International Conference on Communications (ICC)*, pages 1–7. IEEE, 2019.

[416] Feng Niu, Benjamin Recht, Christopher Re, and Stephen J. Wright. Hogwild!: A lock-free approach to parallelizing stochastic gradient descent. In *Proceedings of the Annual Conference on Neural Information Processing Systems (NeurIPS)*, 2011.

[417] Mohammad Sohrab Hasan Nizami, Jahangir Hossain, and Edstan Fernandez. Multiagent-based transactive energy management systems for residential buildings with distributed energy resources. *IEEE Trans. Industrial Informatics*, 16(3):1836–1847, 2020.

[418] Huawei Kirin NPU. `https://consumer.huawei.com/en/campaign/kirin980/`, 2020.

[419] NumPy. Numpy. `http://www.numpy.org`, 2019.

[420] Ozan Oktay, Enzo Ferrante, Konstantinos Kamnitsas, Mattias Heinrich, Wenjia Bai, Jose Caballero, Stuart A Cook, Antonio De Marvao, Timothy Dawes, Declan P O'Regan, et al. Anatomically constrained neural networks (acnns): application to cardiac image enhancement and segmentation. *IEEE Transactions on Medical Imaging*, 37(2):384–395, 2018.

[421] Pybind11: Seamless operability between C++11 and Python. `https://pybind11.readthedocs.io/en/stable/index.html`, 2020.

[422] Yosuke Oyama, Naoya Maruyama, Nikoli Dryden, Erin McCarthy, Peter Harrington, Jan Balewski, Satoshi Matsuoka, Peter Nugent, and Brian Van Essen. The case for strong scaling in deep learning: Training large 3d cnns with hybrid parallelism. *IEEE Transactions on Parallel and Distributed Systems*, 32(7):1641–1652, 2020.

[423] MPI Forum: Message Passing Interface (MPI) Forum Home Page. `https://www.mpi-forum.org/`, 2019.

[424] Pascal Paillier. Public-key cryptosystems based on composite degree residuosity classes. In *Proceedings of the International Conference on the Theory and Application of Cryptographic Techniques (EUROCRYPT)*, pages 223–238. Springer, 1999.

[425] Sinno Jialin Pan and Qiang Yang. A survey on transfer learning. *IEEE Trans. Knowl. Data Eng.*, 22(10):1345–1359, 2010.

[426] George Papandreou, Tyler Zhu, Nori Kanazawa, Alexander Toshev, Jonathan Tompson, Chris Bregler, and Kevin Murphy. Towards accurate multi-person pose estimation in the wild. In *Proceedings of the IEEE/CVF Conference on Computer Vision and Pattern Recognition (CVPR)*, pages 4903–4911, 2017.

[427] Nicolas Papernot, Patrick McDaniel, Arunesh Sinha, and Michael P Wellman. Sok: Security and privacy in machine learning. In *Proceedings of the IEEE European Symposium on Security and Privacy*, pages 399–414. IEEE, 2018.

[428] Angshuman Parashar, Minsoo Rhu, Anurag Mukkara, Antonio Puglielli, Rangharajan Venkatesan, Brucek Khailany, Joel S. Emer, Stephen W. Keckler, and William J. Dally. SCNN: an accelerator for compressed-sparse convolutional neural networks. In *Proceedings of the Annual International Symposium on Computer Architecture (ISCA)*, pages 27–40, 2017.

[429] Ankur P Parikh, Oscar Täckström, Dipanjan Das, and Jakob Uszkoreit. A decomposable attention model for natural language inference. *Empirical Methods in Natural Language Processing*, 2016.

[430] Jay H Park, Gyeongchan Yun, M Yi Chang, Nguyen T Nguyen, Seungmin Lee, Jaesik Choi, Sam H Noh, and Young-ri Choi. HetPipe: Enabling Large DNN Training on (Whimpy) Heterogeneous GPU Clusters through Integration of Pipelined Model Parallelism and Data Parallelism. In *2020 USENIX Annual Technical Conference (USENIX ATC 20)*, pages 307–321, Virtual Event 2020.

[431] Jay H. Park, Gyeongchan Yun, Chang M. Yi, Nguyen T. Nguyen, Seungmin Lee, Jaesik Choi, Sam H. Noh, and Young-ri Choi. Hetpipe: Enabling large DNN training on (whimpy) heterogeneous GPU clusters through integration of pipelined model parallelism and data parallelism. In *Proceedings of the USENIX Annual Technical Conference (ATC)*, pages 307–321, Virtual Event 2020.

[432] Wonpyo Park, Dongju Kim, Yan Lu, and Minsu Cho. Relational knowledge distillation. In *Proceedings of the IEEE/CVF Conference on Computer Vision and Pattern Recognition (CVPR)*, pages 3967–3976, 2019.

[433] Romain Paulus, Caiming Xiong, and Richard Socher. A deep reinforced model for abstractive summarization. *arXiv preprint arXiv:1705.04304*, 2017.

[434] Yanghua Peng, Yixin Bao, Yangrui Chen, Chuan Wu, and Chuanxiong Guo. Optimus: an efficient dynamic resource scheduler for deep learning clusters. In *Proceedings of the Thirteenth EuroSys Conference (EuroSys)*, pages 3:1–3:14, 2018.

[435] Yanghua Peng, Yibo Zhu, Yangrui Chen, Yixin Bao, Bairen Yi, Chang Lan, Chuan Wu, and Chuanxiong Guo. A generic communication scheduler for distributed DNN training acceleration. In Tim Brecht and Carey Williamson, editors, *Proceedings of the ACM Symposium on Operating Systems Principles (SOSP)*, pages 16–29, 2019.

[436] Bryan Perozzi, Rami Al-Rfou, and Steven Skiena. Deepwalk: online learning of social representations. In *Proceedings of the ACM International Conference on Knowledge Discovery and Data Mining (KDD)*, pages 701–710. ACM, 2014.

[437] Tomas Pfister, James Charles, and Andrew Zisserman. Flowing convnets for human pose estimation in videos. In *Proceedings of the IEEE/CVF Conference on Computer Vision and Pattern Recognition (CVPR)*, pages 1913–1921, 2015.

[438] Bigi Varghese Philip, Tansu Alpcan, Jiong Jin, and Marimuthu Palaniswami. Distributed real-time iot for autonomous vehicles. *IEEE Trans. Industrial Informatics*, 15(2):1131–1140, 2019.

[439] Krishna Pillutla, Sham M Kakade, and Zaid Harchaoui. Robust aggregation for federated learning. *arXiv preprint arXiv:1912.13445*, 2019.

[440] Antonio Polino, Razvan Pascanu, and Dan Alistarh. Model compression via distillation and quantization. In *Proceedings of the International Conference on Learning Representations (ICLR)*, 2018.

[441] Jin Qi, Lei Liu, Zixin Shen, Bin Xu, Kwong-Sak Leung, and Yanfei Sun. Low-carbon community adaptive energy management optimization toward smart services. *IEEE Trans. Industrial Informatics*, 16(5):3587–3596, 2020.

[442] Junfei Qiu, Qihui Wu, Guoru Ding, Yuhua Xu, and Shuo Feng. A survey of machine learning for big data processing. *EURASIP Journal on Advances in Signal Processing*, 2016(1):1–16, 2016.

[443] Adnan Siraj Rakin, Zhezhi He, and Deliang Fan. Tbt: Targeted neural network attack with bit trojan. In *Proceedings of the IEEE/CVF Conference on Computer Vision and Pattern Recognition*, pages 13198–13207, 2020.

[444] Mohammad Rastegari, Vicente Ordonez, Joseph Redmon, and Ali Farhadi. Xnor-net: Imagenet classification using binary convolutional neural networks. In *Proceedings of the European Conference on Computer Vision (ECCV)*, volume 9908, pages 525–542, 2016.

[445] Sachin Ravi and Hugo Larochelle. Optimization as a model for few-shot learning. In *Proceedings of the International Conference on Learning Representations (ICLR)*, 2017.

[446] Ravindra Parmar. Detection and segmentation through convnets. https://towardsdatascience.com/detection-and-segmentation-through-convnets-47aa42de27ea, 2018.

[447] Ali Sharif Razavian, Hossein Azizpour, Josephine Sullivan, and Stefan Carlsson. CNN features off-the-shelf: An astounding baseline for recognition. In *Proceedings of the IEEE/CVF Conference on Computer Vision and Pattern Recognition (CVPR)*, pages 512–519, 2014.

[448] Joseph Redmon, Santosh Divvala, Ross Girshick, and Ali Farhadi. You only look once: Unified, real-time object detection. In *Proceedings of the IEEE/CVF Conference on Computer Vision and Pattern Recognition (CVPR)*, pages 779–788, 2016.

[449] Joseph Redmon, Santosh Kumar Divvala, Ross B. Girshick, and Ali Farhadi. You only look once: Unified, real-time object detection. In *Proceedings of the IEEE/CVF Conference on Computer Vision and Pattern Recognition (CVPR)*, pages 779–788, 2016.

[450] Shaoqing Ren, Kaiming He, Ross Girshick, and Jian Sun. Faster r-cnn: Towards real-time object detection with region proposal networks. *In Proceedings of the Annual Conference on Neural Information Processing Systems (NeurIPS)*, 28, 2015.

[451] Zhe Ren, Junchi Yan, Bingbing Ni, Bin Liu, Xiaokang Yang, and Hongyuan Zha. Unsupervised deep learning for optical flow estimation. In *Thirty-First AAAI Conference on Artificial Intelligence*, February 4–9, 2017, San Francisco, California, USA 2017.

[452] Herbert E. Robbins. A stochastic approximation method. *Annals of Mathematical Statistics*, 22:400–407, 2007.

[453] Adriana Romero, Nicolas Ballas, Samira Ebrahimi Kahou, Antoine Chassang, Carlo Gatta, and Yoshua Bengio. Fitnets: Hints for thin deep nets. In *Proceedings of the International Conference on Learning Representations (ICLR)*, 2015.

[454] Olaf Ronneberger, Philipp Fischer, and Thomas Brox. U-net: Convolutional networks for biomedical image segmentation. In *Proceedings of the Medical Image Computing and Computer-Assisted Intervention (MICCAI)*, pages 234–241. Springer, 2015.

[455] Daniel Rothchild, Ashwinee Panda, Enayat Ullah, Nikita Ivkin, Ion Stoica, Vladimir Braverman, Joseph Gonzalez, and Raman Arora. Fetchsgd: Communication-efficient federated learning with sketching. *arXiv preprint*, abs/2007.07682, 2020.

[456] Amrita Roy Chowdhury, Chenghong Wang, Xi He, Ashwin Machanavajjhala, and Somesh Jha. Cryptϵ: Crypto-assisted differential privacy on untrusted servers. In *Proceedings of the ACM SIGMOD International Conference on Management of Data*, pages 603–619, 2020.

[457] Linna Ruan, Yong Yan, Shaoyong Guo, Fushuan Wen, and Xuesong Qiu. Priority-based residential energy management with collaborative edge and cloud computing. *IEEE Trans. Industrial Informatics*, 16(3):1848–1857, 2020.

[458] Sanjay Saini, Dayang Rohaya Awang Rambli, Suziah Sulaiman, Mohamed Nordin Zakaria, and Siti Rohkmah Mohd Shukri. A low-cost game

framework for a home-based stroke rehabilitation system. In *2012 International Conference on Computer & Information Science (ICCIS)*, volume 1, pages 55–60. IEEE, 2012.

[459] Mehdi SM Sajjadi, Bernhard Scholkopf, and Michael Hirsch. Enhancenet: Single image super-resolution through automated texture synthesis. In *Proceedings of the IEEE International Conference on Computer Vision*, pages 4491–4500, 2017.

[460] Charbel Sakr, Naigang Wang, Chia-Yu Chen, Jungwook Choi, Ankur Agrawal, Naresh R. Shanbhag, and Kailash Gopalakrishnan. Accumulation bit-width scaling for ultra-low precision training of deep networks. In *Proceedings of the International Conference on Learning Representations (ICLR)*, 2019.

[461] Felix Sattler, Klaus-Robert Müller, and Wojciech Samek. Clustered federated learning: Model-agnostic distributed multi-task optimization under privacy constraints. *arXiv preprint arXiv:1910.01991*, 2019.

[462] Felix Sattler, Simon Wiedemann, Klaus-Robert Müller, and Wojciech Samek. Robust and communication-efficient federated learning from non-iid data. *IEEE Transactions on Neural Networks and Learning Systems*, 2019.

[463] Sinem Sav, Apostolos Pyrgelis, Juan R Troncoso-Pastoriza, David Froelicher, Jean-Philippe Bossuat, Joao Sa Sousa, and Jean-Pierre Hubaux. Poseidon: privacy-preserving federated neural network learning. In *Proceedings of the NDSS Symposium*, 2021.

[464] Johannes Schneider and Michail Vlachos. Personalization of deep learning. *arXiv preprint arXiv:1909.02803*, 2019.

[465] John Schulman, Filip Wolski, Prafulla Dhariwal, Alec Radford, and Oleg Klimov. Proximal policy optimization algorithms. *arXiv preprint*, abs/1707.06347, 2017.

[466] Alexander Sergeev and Mike Del Balso. Horovod: fast and easy distributed deep learning in tensorflow. *arXiv preprint*, abs/1802.05799, 2018.

[467] Pierre Sermanet, David Eigen, Xiang Zhang, Michaël Mathieu, Rob Fergus, and Yann LeCun. Overfeat: Integrated recognition, localization and detection using convolutional networks. *arXiv preprint arXiv:1312.6229*, 2013.

[468] Sean O. Settle, Manasa Bollavaram, Paolo D'Alberto, Elliott Delaye, Oscar Fernandez, Nicholas C Fraser, Aaron Ng, Ashish Sirasao, and Michael Wu. Quantizing convolutional neural networks for low-power high-throughput inference engines. *arXiv preprint*, abs/1805.07941, 2018.

[469] Hossein Shafiei, Ahmad Khonsari, and Payam Mousavi. Serverless computing: A survey of opportunities, challenges and applications. *arXiv preprint arXiv:1911.01296*, 2019.

[470] Mohammad Shahrad, Rodrigo Fonseca, Íñigo Goiri, Gohar Chaudhry, Paul Batum, Jason Cooke, Eduardo Laureano, Colby Tresness, Mark Russinovich, and Ricardo Bianchini. Serverless in the wild: Characterizing and optimizing the serverless workload at a large cloud provider. In *2020 USENIX Annual Technical Conference (USENIX ATC 20)*, pages 205–218, 2020. Virtual Event.

[471] Adi Shamir. How to share a secret. *Communications of the ACM*, 22(11):612–613, 1979.

[472] Virat Shejwalkar and Amir Houmansadr. Manipulating the byzantine: Optimizing model poisoning attacks and defenses for federated learning. In *Proceedings of the NDSS Symposium*, 2021.

[473] Wei Shi, Qing Ling, Gang Wu, and Wotao Yin. EXTRA: an exact first-order algorithm for decentralized consensus optimization. *SIAM J. Optim.*, 25(2):944–966, 2015.

[474] Wei Shi, Qing Ling, Kun Yuan, Gang Wu, and Wotao Yin. On the linear convergence of the ADMM in decentralized consensus optimization. *IEEE Trans. Signal Process.*, 62(7):1750–1761, 2014.

[475] Weisong Shi, Jie Cao, Quan Zhang, Youhuizi Li, and Lanyu Xu. Edge computing: Vision and challenges. *IEEE Internet of Things Journal*, 3:637–646, 2016.

[476] Yutaro Shigeto, Ikumi Suzuki, Kazuo Hara, Masashi Shimbo, and Yuji Matsumoto. Ridge regression, hubness, and zero-shot learning. In *Joint European Conference on Machine Learning and Knowledge Discovery in Databases*, pages 135–151. Springer, 2015.

[477] Neta Shoham, Tomer Avidor, Aviv Keren, Nadav Israel, Daniel Benditkis, Liron Mor-Yosef, and Itai Zeitak. Overcoming forgetting in federated learning on non-iid data. *arXiv preprint arXiv:1910.07796*, 2019.

[478] Reza Shokri, Marco Stronati, Congzheng Song, and Vitaly Shmatikov. Membership inference attacks against machine learning models. In *Proceedings of IEEE Symposium on Security and Privacy (SP)*, pages 3–18. IEEE, 2017.

[479] Patrice Y Simard, David Steinkraus, John C Platt, et al. Best practices for convolutional neural networks applied to visual document analysis. In *Proceedings of the International Conference on Document Analysis and Recognition (ICDAR)*, volume 3, 2003.

[480] Karen Simonyan and Andrew Zisserman. Two-stream convolutional networks for action recognition in videos. In *Proceedings of the Annual Conference on Neural Information Processing Systems (NeurIPS)*, 2014.

[481] Karen Simonyan and Andrew Zisserman. Very deep convolutional networks for large-scale image recognition. *arXiv preprint arXiv:1409.1556*, 2014.

[482] Karen Simonyan and Andrew Zisserman. Very deep convolutional networks for large-scale image recognition. In *Proceedings of the International Conference on Learning Representations (ICLR)*, 2015.

[483] Virginia Smith, Chao-Kai Chiang, Maziar Sanjabi, and Ameet S. Talwalkar. Federated multi-task learning. In *Proceedings of the Annual Conference on Neural Information Processing Systems (NeurIPS)*, 2017.

[484] Jake Snell, Kevin Swersky, and Richard Zemel. Prototypical networks for few-shot learning. In *Proceedings of the Annual Conference on Neural Information Processing Systems (NeurIPS)*, 2017.

[485] Fuyuan Song, Zheng Qin, Qin Liu, Jinwen Liang, and Lu Ou. Efficient and secure k-nearest neighbor search over encrypted data in public cloud. In *ICC 2019 - 2019 IEEE International Conference on Communications (ICC)*, pages 1–6, 2019.

[486] Linghao Song, Jiachen Mao, Youwei Zhuo, Xuehai Qian, Hai Li, and Yiran Chen. Hypar: Towards hybrid parallelism for deep learning accelerator array. In *2019 IEEE International Symposium on High Performance Computer Architecture (HPCA)*, pages 56–68. IEEE, 2019.

[487] Pierre Stock, Armand Joulin, Rémi Gribonval, Benjamin Graham, and Hervé Jégou. And the bit goes down: Revisiting the quantization of neural networks. In *Proceedings of the International Conference on Learning Representations (ICLR)*, Addis Ababa, Ethiopia, 2020.

[488] Ion Stoica, Dawn Song, Raluca Ada Popa, David A. Patterson, Michael W. Mahoney, Randy H. Katz, Anthony D. Joseph, Michael I. Jordan, Joseph M. Hellerstein, Joseph E. Gonzalez, Ken Goldberg, Ali Ghodsi, David Culler, and Pieter Abbeel. A berkeley view of systems challenges for AI. *arXiv preprint*, abs/1712.05855, 2017.

[489] Zhuo Su, Lan Xu, Dawei Zhong, Zhong Li, Fan Deng, Shuxue Quan, and Lu Fang. Robustfusion: Robust volumetric performance reconstruction under human-object interactions from monocular rgbd stream. *arXiv preprint arXiv:2104.14837*, 2021.

[490] Joseph Suarez. Language modeling with recurrent highway hypernetworks. In *Proceedings of the Annual Conference on Neural Information Processing Systems (NeurIPS)*, pages 3267–3276, 2017.

[491] Sainbayar Sukhbaatar, Edouard Grave, Piotr Bojanowski, and Armand Joulin. Adaptive attention span in transformers. *arXiv preprint arXiv:1905.07799*, 2019.

[492] Lichao Sun and Lingjuan Lyu. Federated model distillation with noise-free differential privacy. In Zhi-Hua Zhou, editor, *Proceedings of the Thirtieth*

International Joint Conference on Artificial Intelligence, IJCAI 2021, pages 1563–1570. ijcai.org, 2021.

[493] Qiuye Sun, Yibin Zhang, Haibo He, Dazhong Ma, and Huaguang Zhang. A novel energy function-based stability evaluation and nonlinear control approach for energy internet. *IEEE Trans. Smart Grid*, 8(3):1195–1210, 2017.

[494] Shizhao Sun, Wei Chen, Jiang Bian, Xiaoguang Liu, and Tie-Yan Liu. Slim-dp: A multi-agent system for communication-efficient distributed deep learning. In *Proceedings of the International Conference on Autonomous Agents and MultiAgent Systems (AAMAS)*, pages 721–729, 2018.

[495] Xiao Sun, Jiaxiang Shang, Shuang Liang, and Yichen Wei. Compositional human pose regression. In *Proceedings of the IEEE International Conference on Computer Vision*, pages 2602–2611, 2017.

[496] Niko Sünderhauf, Oliver Brock, Walter J. Scheirer, Raia Hadsell, Dieter Fox, Jürgen Leitner, Ben Upcroft, Pieter Abbeel, Wolfram Burgard, Michael Milford, and Peter Corke. The limits and potentials of deep learning for robotics. *I. J. Robotics Res.*, 37(4-5):405–420, 2018.

[497] Ilya Sutskever, Oriol Vinyals, and Quoc V Le. Sequence to sequence learning with neural networks. *Advances in neural information processing systems*, 27, 2014.

[498] Richard S. Sutton and Andrew G. Barto. *Reinforcement Learning: An Introduction, Second Edition*. Adaptive computation and machine learning. MIT Press, 2017.

[499] Vivienne Sze, Yu-Hsin Chen, Tien-Ju Yang, and Joel S Emer. Efficient processing of deep neural networks: A tutorial and survey. *Proceedings of the IEEE*, 105(12):2295–2329, 2017.

[500] Christian Szegedy, Wei Liu, Yangqing Jia, Pierre Sermanet, Scott Reed, Dragomir Anguelov, Dumitru Erhan, Vincent Vanhoucke, and Andrew Rabinovich. Going deeper with convolutions. In *Proceedings of the IEEE/CVF Conference on Computer Vision and Pattern Recognition (CVPR)*, pages 1–9, 2015.

[501] Canh T Dinh, Nguyen Tran, and Tuan Dung Nguyen. Personalized federated learning with moreau envelopes. *Advances in Neural Information Processing Systems, NeurIPS*, 33, 2020.

[502] Nima Tajbakhsh, Jae Y. Shin, Suryakanth R. Gurudu, R. Todd Hurst, Christopher B. Kendall, Michael B. Gotway, and Jianming Liang. Convolutional neural networks for medical image analysis: Full training or fine tuning? *IEEE Trans. Medical Imaging*, 35(5):1299–1312, 2016.

[503] Mingxing Tan, Bo Chen, Ruoming Pang, Vijay Vasudevan, Mark Sandler, Andrew Howard, and Quoc V Le. Mnasnet: Platform-aware neural architecture

search for mobile. In *Proceedings of the IEEE/CVF Conference on Computer Vision and Pattern Recognition*, pages 2820–2828, 2019.

[504] Rashish Tandon, Qi Lei, Alexandros G. Dimakis, and Nikos Karampatziakis. Gradient coding: Avoiding stragglers in distributed learning. In *Proceedings of the International Conference on Machine Learning (ICML)*, 2017.

[505] Hanlin Tang, Shaoduo Gan, Ce Zhang, Tong Zhang, and Ji Liu. Communication compression for decentralized training. In Samy Bengio, Hanna M. Wallach, Hugo Larochelle, Kristen Grauman, Nicolò Cesa-Bianchi, and Roman Garnett, editors, *Advances in Neural Information Processing Systems 31: Annual Conference on Neural Information Processing Systems 2018, NeurIPS 2018, 3-8 December 2018, Montréal, Canada*, pages 7663–7673, 2018.

[506] Xueyang Tang, Song Guo, and Jingcai Guo. Personalized federated learning with contextualized generalization. In *Proceedings of the Thirtieth International Joint Conference on Artificial Intelligence*, Messe Wien, Vienna, Austria 2022.

[507] Hokchhay Tann, Soheil Hashemi, R. Iris Bahar, and Sherief Reda. Hardware-software codesign of accurate, multiplier-free deep neural networks. In *Proceedings of the Annual Design Automation Conference (DAC)*, pages 28:1–28:6. ACM, 2017.

[508] Antti Tarvainen and Harri Valpola. Mean teachers are better role models: Weight-averaged consistency targets improve semi-supervised deep learning results. In *Proceedings of the Annual Conference on Neural Information Processing Systems (NeurIPS)*, pages 1195–1204, 2017.

[509] Baidu Ring-AllReduce: Bringing HPC techniques to deep learning. https://github.com/baidu-research/baidu-allreduce, 2016.

[510] Apple Face ID Advanced Technology. https://support.apple.com/en-us/HT208108, 2020.

[511] Eigen: A C++ template library for linear algebra. Eigen c++ linear algebra library. http://eigen.tuxfamily.org/, 2020.

[512] Keras: the Python deep learning API. https://keras.io/, 2020.

[513] Lucas Theis, Iryna Korshunova, Alykhan Tejani, and Ferenc Huszár. Faster gaze prediction with dense networks and fisher pruning. *arXiv preprint*, abs/1801.05787, 2018.

[514] Philip Thomas. Bias in natural actor-critic algorithms. In *Proceedings of the International Conference on Machine Learning (ICML)*, 32:441–448, 2014.

[515] Zhi Tian, Chunhua Shen, Hao Chen, and Tong He. Fcos: Fully convolutional one-stage object detection. In *Proceedings of the IEEE/CVF International Conference on Computer Vision (ICCV)*, pages 9627–9636, 2019.

[516] Alexander Toshev and Christian Szegedy. Deeppose: Human pose estimation via deep neural networks. In *Proceedings of the IEEE/CVF Conference on Computer Vision and Pattern Recognition (CVPR)*, pages 1653–1660, 2014.

[517] Hugo Touvron, Matthieu Cord, Matthijs Douze, Francisco Massa, Alexandre Sablayrolles, and Herve Jegou. Training data-efficient image transformers & distillation through attention. In *International Conference on Machine Learning*, volume 139, pages 10347–10357, July 2021.

[518] Hugo Touvron, Matthieu Cord, Matthijs Douze, Francisco Massa, Alexandre Sablayrolles, and Hervé Jégou. Training data-efficient image transformers & distillation through attention. In *International Conference on Machine Learning*, pages 10347–10357. PMLR, 2021.

[519] Du Tran, Lubomir Bourdev, Rob Fergus, Lorenzo Torresani, and Manohar Paluri. Learning spatiotemporal features with 3d convolutional networks. In *Proceedings of the IEEE/CVF International Conference on Computer Vision (ICCV)*, pages 4489–4497, 2015.

[520] Du Tran, Heng Wang, Lorenzo Torresani, and Matt Feiszli. Video classification with channel-separated convolutional networks. In *Proceedings of the IEEE/CVF International Conference on Computer Vision*, pages 5552–5561, 2019.

[521] Nguyen H. Tran, Wei Bao, Albert Y. Zomaya, Minh N. H. Nguyen, and Choong Seon Hong. Federated learning over wireless networks: Optimization model design and analysis. In *Proceedings of the IEEE International Conference on Computer Communications (INFOCOM)*, pages 1387–1395, 2019.

[522] Mineto Tsukada, Masaaki Kondo, and Hiroki Matsutani. A neural network-based on-device learning anomaly detector for edge devices. *IEEE Trans. Computers*, 69(7):1027–1044, 2020.

[523] Chunming Tu, Xi He, Xuan Liu, Zhikang Shuai, and Li Yu. Resilient and fast state estimation for energy internet: A data-based approach. *IEEE Trans. Industrial Informatics*, 15(5):2969–2979, 2019.

[524] Zhigang Tu, Wei Xie, Dejun Zhang, Ronald Poppe, Remco C Veltkamp, Baoxin Li, and Junsong Yuan. A survey of variational and cnn-based optical flow techniques. *Signal Processing: Image Communication*, 72:9–24, 2019.

[525] Ozan Tuncer, Vitus J. Leung, and Ayse K. Coskun. Pacmap: Topology mapping of unstructured communication patterns onto non-contiguous allocations. In *Proceedings of the ACM International Conference on Supercomputing (ICS)*, pages 37–46, 2015.

[526] Frederick Tung and Greg Mori. Similarity-preserving knowledge distillation. In *Proceedings of the IEEE/CVF International Conference on Computer Vision (ICCV)*, pages 1365–1374, 2019.

[527] Alexander Turner, Dimitris Tsipras, and Aleksander Madry. Label-consistent backdoor attacks. *arXiv preprint arXiv:1912.02771*, 2019.

[528] Tõnis Uiboupin, Pejman Rasti, Gholamreza Anbarjafari, and Hasan Demirel. Facial image super resolution using sparse representation for improving face recognition in surveillance monitoring. In *2016 24th Signal Processing and Communication Application Conference (SIU)*, pages 437–440. IEEE, 2016.

[529] Ashish Vaswani, Noam Shazeer, Niki Parmar, Jakob Uszkoreit, Llion Jones, Aidan N Gomez, Łukasz Kaiser, and Illia Polosukhin. Attention is all you need. In *Proceedings of the Annual Conference on Neural Information Processing Systems (NeurIPS)*, 30, 2017.

[530] Swagath Venkataramani, Ashish Ranjan, Subarno Banerjee, Dipankar Das, Sasikanth Avancha, Ashok Jagannathan, Ajaya Durg, Dheemanth Nagaraj, Bharat Kaul, Pradeep Dubey, and Anand Raghunathan. Scaledeep: A scalable compute architecture for learning and evaluating deep networks. In *Proceedings of the Annual International Symposium on Computer Architecture (ISCA)*, 2017.

[531] Alexander Viand, Patrick Jattke, and Anwar Hithnawi. Sok: Fully homomorphic encryption compilers. In *Proceedings of the IEEE Symposium on Security and Privacy*, pages 1092–1108. IEEE, 2021.

[532] Paul Viola and Michael Jones. Rapid object detection using a boosted cascade of simple features. In *Proceedings of the IEEE/CVF Conference on Computer Vision and Pattern Recognition (CVPR) 2001*, volume 1, pages I–I. Ieee, 2001.

[533] Timo Von Marcard, Bodo Rosenhahn, Michael J Black, and Gerard Pons-Moll. Sparse inertial poser: Automatic 3d human pose estimation from sparse imus. In *Computer Graphics Forum*, volume 36, pages 349–360. Wiley Online Library, 2017.

[534] Tung Thanh Vu, Duy T. Ngo, Nguyen H. Tran, Hien Quoc Ngo, Minh N. Dao, and Richard H. Middleton. Cell-free massive MIMO for wireless federated learning. *arXiv preprint*, abs/1909.12567, 2019.

[535] Li Wan, Matthew D. Zeiler, Sixin Zhang, Yann LeCun, and Rob Fergus. Regularization of neural networks using dropconnect. In *Proceedings of the International Conference on Machine Learning (ICML)*, volume 28, pages 1058–1066, 2013.

[536] Bolun Wang, Yuanshun Yao, Shawn Shan, Huiying Li, Bimal Viswanath, Haitao Zheng, and Ben Y Zhao. Neural cleanse: Identifying and mitigating backdoor attacks in neural networks. In *2019 IEEE Symposium on Security and Privacy (SP)*, pages 707–723. IEEE, 2019.

[537] Hao Wang, Zakhary Kaplan, Di Niu, and Baochun Li. Optimizing federated learning on non-iid data with reinforcement learning. In *INFOCOM*, pages 1698–1707. IEEE, 2020.

[538] Hongyi Wang, Kartik Sreenivasan, Shashank Rajput, Harit Vishwakarma, Saurabh Agarwal, Jy-yong Sohn, Kangwook Lee, and Dimitris Papailiopoulos. Attack of the tails: Yes, you really can backdoor federated learning. *arXiv preprint arXiv:2007.05084*, 2020.

[539] Jun Wang, Tanner A. Bohn, and Charles X. Ling. Pelee: A real-time object detection system on mobile devices. In *Proceedings of the Annual Conference on Neural Information Processing Systems (NeurIPS)*, pages 1967–1976, 2018.

[540] Kangkang Wang, Rajiv Mathews, Chloé Kiddon, Hubert Eichner, Françoise Beaufays, and Daniel Ramage. Federated evaluation of on-device personalization. *arXiv preprint arXiv:1910.10252*, 2019.

[541] Kuan Wang, Zhijian Liu, Yujun Lin, Ji Lin, and Song Han. HAQ: hardware-aware automated quantization with mixed precision. In *Proceedings of the IEEE Conference on Computer Vision and Pattern Recognition (CVPR)*, pages 8612–8620, Long Beach, USA, 2019.

[542] Kun Wang, Jun Yu, Yan Yu, Yirou Qian, Deze Zeng, Song Guo, Yong Xiang, and Jinsong Wu. A survey on energy internet: Architecture, approach, and emerging technologies. *IEEE Systems Journal*, 12(3):2403–2416, 2018.

[543] Limin Wang, Yu Qiao, and Xiaoou Tang. Action recognition with trajectory-pooled deep-convolutional descriptors. In *Proceedings of the IEEE/CVF Conference on Computer Vision and Pattern Recognition (CVPR)*, pages 4305–4314, 2015.

[544] Limin Wang, Yuanjun Xiong, Zhe Wang, and Yu Qiao. Towards good practices for very deep two-stream convnets. *arXiv preprint arXiv:1507.02159*, 2015.

[545] Limin Wang, Yuanjun Xiong, Zhe Wang, Yu Qiao, Dahua Lin, Xiaoou Tang, and Luc Van Gool. Temporal segment networks: Towards good practices for deep action recognition. In *Proceedings of the European Conference on Computer Vision (ECCV)*, pages 20–36. Springer, 2016.

[546] Songtao Wang, Dan Li, Yang Cheng, Jinkun Geng, Yanshu Wang, Shuai Wang, Shu-Tao Xia, and Jianping Wu. Bml: A high-performance, low-cost gradient synchronization algorithm for dml training. In *Proceedings of the Annual Conference on Neural Information Processing Systems (NeurIPS)*, 2018.

[547] Xiaolong Wang, Ross Girshick, Abhinav Gupta, and Kaiming He. Non-local neural networks. In *Proceedings of the IEEE/CVF Conference on Computer Vision and Pattern Recognition (CVPR)*, pages 7794–7803, 2018.

[548] Xin Wang, Fisher Yu, Zi-Yi Dou, Trevor Darrell, and Joseph E. Gonzalez. Skipnet: Learning dynamic routing in convolutional networks. In *Proceedings of the European Conference on Computer Vision (ECCV)*, volume 11217, pages 420–436, 2018.

[549] Yuhui Wang, Hao He, Xiaoyang Tan, and Yaozhong Gan. Trust region-guided proximal policy optimization. In *Proceedings of the Annual Conference on Neural Information Processing Systems (NeurIPS)*, pages 624–634, 2019.

[550] Zheng Wang, Ruimin Hu, Chao Liang, Yi Yu, Junjun Jiang, Mang Ye, Jun Chen, and Qingming Leng. Zero-shot person re-identification via cross-view consistency. *IEEE Transactions on Multimedia*, 18(2):260–272, 2015.

[551] Stefanie Warnat-Herresthal, Hartmut Schultze, Krishnaprasad Lingadahalli Shastry, Sathyanarayanan Manamohan, Saikat Mukherjee, Vishesh Garg, Ravi Sarveswara, Kristian Händler, Peter Pickkers, N. Ahmad Aziz, Sofia Ktena, Florian Tran, Michael Bitzer, Stephan Ossowski, Nicolas Casadei, Christian Herr, Daniel Petersheim, Uta Behrends, Fabian Kern, Tobias Fehlmann, Philipp Schommers, Clara Lehmann, Max Augustin, Jan Rybniker, Janine Altmüller, Neha Mishra, Joana P. Bernardes, Benjamin Krämer, Lorenzo Bonaguro, Jonas Schulte-Schrepping, Elena De Domenico, Christian Siever, Michael Kraut, Milind Desai, Bruno Monnet, Maria Saridaki, Charles Martin Siegel, Anna Drews, Melanie Nuesch-Germano, Heidi Theis, Jan Heyckendorf, Stefan Schreiber, Sarah Kim-Hellmuth, Paul Balfanz, Thomas Eggermann, Peter Boor, Ralf Hausmann, Hannah Kuhn, Susanne Isfort, Julia Carolin Stingl, Günther Schmalzing, Christiane K. Kuhl, Rainer Röhrig, Gernot Marx, Stefan Uhlig, Edgar Dahl, Dirk Müller-Wieland, Michael Dreher, Nikolaus Marx, Jacob Nattermann, Dirk Skowasch, Ingo Kurth, Andreas Keller, Robert Bals, Peter Nürnberg, Olaf Rieß, Philip Rosenstiel, Mihai G. Netea, Fabian Theis, Sach Mukherjee, Michael Backes, Anna C. Aschenbrenner, Thomas Ulas, Angel Angelov, Alexander Bartholomäus, Anke Becker, Daniela Bezdan, Conny Blumert, Ezio Bonifacio, Peer Bork, Bunk Boyke, Helmut Blum, Thomas Clavel, Maria Colome-Tatche, Markus Cornberg, Inti Alberto De La Rosa Velázquez, Andreas Diefenbach, Alexander Dilthey, Nicole Fischer, Konrad Förstner, Sören Franzenburg, Julia-Stefanie Frick, Gisela Gabernet, Julien Gagneur, Tina Ganzenmueller, Marie Gauder, Janina Geißert, Alexander Goesmann, Siri Göpel, Adam Grundhoff, Hajo Grundmann, Torsten Hain, Frank Hanses, Ute Hehr, André Heimbach, Marius Hoeper, Friedemann Horn, Daniel Hübschmann, Michael Hummel, Thomas Iftner, Angelika Iftner, Thomas Illig, Stefan Janssen, Jörn Kalinowski, René Kallies, Birte Kehr, Oliver T. Keppler, Christoph Klein, Michael Knop, Oliver Kohlbacher, Karl Köhrer, Jan Korbel, Peter G. Kremsner, Denise Kühnert, Markus Landthaler, Yang Li, Kerstin U. Ludwig, Oliwia Makarewicz, Manja Marz, Alice C. McHardy, Christian Mertes, Maximilian Münchhoff, Sven Nahnsen, Markus Nöthen, Francine Ntoumi, Jörg Overmann, Silke Peter, Klaus Pfeffer, Isabell Pink, Anna R. Poetsch, Ulrike Protzer, Alfred Pühler, Nikolaus Rajewsky, Markus

Ralser, Kristin Reiche, Stephan Ripke, Ulisses Nunes da Rocha, Antoine-Emmanuel Saliba, Leif Erik Sander, Birgit Sawitzki, Simone Scheithauer, Philipp Schiffer, Jonathan Schmid-Burgk, Wulf Schneider, Eva-Christina Schulte, Alexander Sczyrba, Mariam L. Sharaf, Yogesh Singh, Michael Sonnabend, Oliver Stegle, Jens Stoye, Janne Vehreschild, Thirumalaisamy P. Velavan, Jörg Vogel, Sonja Volland, Max von Kleist, Andreas Walker, Jörn Walter, Dagmar Wieczorek, Sylke Winkler, John Ziebuhr, Monique M. B. Breteler, Evangelos J. Giamarellos-Bourboulis, Matthijs Kox, Matthias Becker, Sorin Cheran, Michael S. Woodacre, Eng Lim Goh, Joachim L. Schultze, COVID-19 Aachen Study (COVAS), and Deutsche COVID-19 Omics Initiative (DeCOI). Swarm learning for decentralized and confidential clinical machine learning. *Nature*, 594(7862):265–270, Jun 2021.

[552] Pijika Watcharapichat, Victoria Lopez Morales, Raul Castro Fernandez, and Peter R. Pietzuch. Ako: Decentralised deep learning with partial gradient exchange. In *Proceedings of the ACM Symposium on Cloud Computing (SoCC)*, 2016.

[553] Andrew B Watson and Albert J Ahumada Jr. A look at motion in the frequency domain. Technical report, 1983.

[554] Kang Wei, Jun Li, Ming Ding, Chuan Ma, Howard H Yang, Farhad Farokhi, Shi Jin, Tony QS Quek, and H Vincent Poor. Federated learning with differential privacy: Algorithms and performance analysis. *IEEE Transactions on Information Forensics and Security*, 15:3454–3469, 2020.

[555] Jiasi Weng, Jian Weng, Jilian Zhang, Ming Li, Yue Zhang, and Weiqi Luo. Deepchain: Auditable and privacy-preserving deep learning with blockchain-based incentive. *IEEE Transactions on Dependable and Secure Computing*, 18(5):2438–2455, 2021.

[556] Josh Wills and Serge Belongie. A feature-based approach for determining dense long range correspondences. In *Proceedings of the European Conference on Computer Vision (ECCV)*, pages 170–182. Springer, 2004.

[557] Wai Kit Wong, David Wai-lok Cheung, Ben Kao, and Nikos Mamoulis. Secure KNN computation on encrypted databases. In *Proceedings of the International Conference on Management of Data (SIGMOD)*, pages 139–152, 2009.

[558] Gavin Wood et al. Ethereum: A secure decentralised generalised transaction ledger. *Ethereum Project Yellow Paper*, 151(2014):1–32, 2014.

[559] Bichen Wu, Xiaoliang Dai, Peizhao Zhang, Yanghan Wang, Fei Sun, Yiming Wu, Yuandong Tian, Peter Vajda, Yangqing Jia, and Kurt Keutzer. Fbnet: Hardware-aware efficient convnet design via differentiable neural architecture search. In *Proceedings of the IEEE/CVF Conference on Computer Vision and Pattern Recognition*, pages 10734–10742, 2019.

[560] Chen Wu, Mingyu Wang, Xiayu Li, Jicheng Lu, Kun Wang, and Lei He. Phoenix: A low-precision floating-point quantization oriented architecture for convolutional neural networks. *arXiv preprint*, abs/2003.02628, 2020.

[561] Felix Wu, Angela Fan, Alexei Baevski, Yann N Dauphin, and Michael Auli. Pay less attention with lightweight and dynamic convolutions. *arXiv preprint arXiv:1901.10430*, 2019.

[562] Tianyu Wu, Kun Yuan, Qing Ling, Wotao Yin, and Ali H. Sayed. Decentralized consensus optimization with asynchrony and delays. *IEEE Trans. Signal Inf. Process. over Networks*, 4(2):293–307, 2018.

[563] Xundong Wu, Yong Wu, and Yong Zhao. Binarized neural networks on the imagenet classification task. *arXiv preprint*, abs/1604.03058, 2016.

[564] Xundong Wu, Yong Wu, and Yong Zhao. Binarized neural networks on the imagenet classification task. *arXiv: Computer Vision and Pattern Recognition*, 2016.

[565] Yonghui Wu, Mike Schuster, Zhifeng Chen, Quoc V Le, Mohammad Norouzi, Wolfgang Macherey, Maxim Krikun, Yuan Cao, Qin Gao, Klaus Macherey, et al. Google's neural machine translation system: Bridging the gap between human and machine translation. *arXiv preprint arXiv:1609.08144*, 2016.

[566] Zhanghao Wu, Zhijian Liu, Ji Lin, Yujun Lin, and Song Han. Lite transformer with long-short range attention. *arXiv preprint arXiv:2004.11886*, 2020.

[567] Han Xiao, Kashif Rasul, and Roland Vollgraf. Fashion-mnist: a novel image dataset for benchmarking machine learning algorithms. *arXiv preprint*, abs/1708.07747, 2017.

[568] Wencong Xiao, Romil Bhardwaj, Ramachandran Ramjee, Muthian Sivathanu, Nipun Kwatra, Zhenhua Han, Pratyush Patel, Xuan Peng, Hanyu Zhao, Quanlu Zhang, Fan Yang, and Lidong Zhou. Gandiva: Introspective cluster scheduling for deep learning. In *Proceedings of the USENIX Symposium on Operating Systems Design and Implementation (OSDI)*, pages 595–610, 2018.

[569] Chulin Xie, Keli Huang, Pin-Yu Chen, and Bo Li. Dba: Distributed backdoor attacks against federated learning. In *International Conference on Learning Representations*, Addis Ababa, Ethiopia, April 26–30, 2020.

[570] Enze Xie, Peize Sun, Xiaoge Song, Wenhai Wang, Xuebo Liu, Ding Liang, Chunhua Shen, and Ping Luo. Polarmask: Single shot instance segmentation with polar representation. In *Proceedings of the IEEE/CVF Conference on Computer Vision and Pattern Recognition (CVPR)*, pages 12193–12202, 2020.

[571] Pengtao Xie, Jin Kyu Kim, Yi Zhou, Qirong Ho, Abhimanu Kumar, Yaoliang Yu, and Eric Xing. Lighter-communication distributed machine learning via sufficient factor broadcasting. In *Proceedings of the Conference on Uncertainty in Artificial ntelligence (UAI)*, 2016.

[572] Pengtao Xie, Jin Kyu Kim, Yi Zhou, Qirong Ho, Abhimanu Kumar, Yaoliang Yu, and Eric P. Xing. Distributed machine learning via sufficient factor broadcasting. *arXiv preprint*, abs/1511.08486, 2014.

[573] Pengtao Xie, Jin Kyu Kim, Yi Zhou, Qirong Ho, Abhimanu Kumar, Yaoliang Yu, and Eric P. Xing. Distributed machine learning via sufficient factor broadcasting. *arXiv preprint*, abs/1511.08486, 2015.

[574] Pengtao Xie, Jin Kyu Kim, Yi Zhou, Qirong Ho, Abhimanu Kumar, Yaoliang Yu, and Eric P. Xing. Lighter-communication distributed machine learning via sufficient factor broadcasting. In *Proceedings of the Conference on Uncertainty in Artificial Intelligence (UAI)*, New York, USA, 2016.

[575] Saining Xie, Ross Girshick, Piotr Dollár, Zhuowen Tu, and Kaiming He. Aggregated residual transformations for deep neural networks. In *Proceedings of the IEEE/CVF Conference on Computer Vision and Pattern Recognition (CVPR)*, pages 1492–1500, 2017.

[576] Saining Xie, Ross B. Girshick, Piotr Dollár, Zhuowen Tu, and Kaiming He. Aggregated residual transformations for deep neural networks. In *Proceedings of the IEEE/CVF Conference on Computer Vision and Pattern Recognition (CVPR)*, pages 5987–5995, 2017.

[577] Saining Xie, Chen Sun, Jonathan Huang, Zhuowen Tu, and Kevin Murphy. Rethinking spatiotemporal feature learning: Speed-accuracy trade-offs in video classification. In *Proceedings of the European Conference on Computer Vision (ECCV)*, pages 305–321, 2018.

[578] Eric P. Xing, Qirong Ho, Wei Dai, Jin Kyu Kim, Jinliang Wei, Seunghak Lee, Xun Zheng, Pengtao Xie, Abhimanu Kumar, and Yaoliang Yu. Petuum: A new platform for distributed machine learning on big data. In *Proceedings of the ACM International Conference on Knowledge Discovery and Data Mining (KDD)*, 2015.

[579] Eric P. Xing, Andrew Y. Ng, Michael I. Jordan, and Stuart Russell. Distance metric learning, with application to clustering with side-information. In *Proceedings of the Annual Conference on Neural Information Processing Systems (NeurIPS)*, 2002.

[580] Jingwei Xu, Zhenbo Yu, Bingbing Ni, Jiancheng Yang, Xiaokang Yang, and Wenjun Zhang. Deep kinematics analysis for monocular 3d human pose estimation. In *Proceedings of the IEEE/CVF Conference on Computer Vision and Pattern Recognition (CVPR)*, pages 899–908, 2020.

[581] Zhengjun Xu, Haitao Zhang, Xin Geng, Qiong Wu, and Huadong Ma. Adaptive function launching acceleration in serverless computing platforms. In *2019 IEEE 25th International Conference on Parallel and Distributed Systems (ICPADS)*, pages 9–16. IEEE, 2019.

[582] Tingman Yan, Yangzhou Gan, Zeyang Xia, and Qunfei Zhao. Segment-based disparity refinement with occlusion handling for stereo matching. *IEEE Transactions on Image Processing*, 28(8):3885–3897, 2019.

[583] Lei Yang, Zheyu Yan, Meng Li, Hyoukjun Kwon, Liangzhen Lai, Tushar Krishna, Vikas Chandra, Weiwen Jiang, and Yiyu Shi. Co-exploration of neural architectures and heterogeneous asic accelerator designs targeting multiple tasks. In *2020 57th ACM/IEEE Design Automation Conference (DAC)*, pages 1–6. IEEE, 2020.

[584] Miao Yang, Akitanoshou Wong, Hongbin Zhu, Haifeng Wang, and Hua Qian. Federated learning with class imbalance reduction. *arXiv preprint arXiv:2011.11266*, 2020.

[585] Zhilin Yang, Junbo Jake Zhao, Bhuwan Dhingra, Kaiming He, William W. Cohen, Ruslan Salakhutdinov, and Yann LeCun. Glomo: Unsupervisedly learned relational graphs as transferable representations. *arXiv preprint*, abs/1806.05662, 2018.

[586] Li Yao, Atousa Torabi, Kyunghyun Cho, Nicolas Ballas, Christopher Pal, Hugo Larochelle, and Aaron Courville. Describing videos by exploiting temporal structure. In *Proceedings of the IEEE/CVF International Conference on Computer Vision (ICCV)*, pages 4507–4515, 2015.

[587] Yousef Yeganeh, Azade Farshad, Nassir Navab, and Shadi Albarqouni. Inverse distance aggregation for federated learning with non-iid data. *arXiv preprint arXiv:2008.07665*, 2020.

[588] Minghao Yin, Yongbing Zhang, Xiu Li, and Shiqi Wang. When deep fool meets deep prior: Adversarial attack on super-resolution network. In *2018 ACM Multimedia Conference on Multimedia Conference*, pages 1930–1938. ACM, 2018.

[589] Jason Yosinski, Jeff Clune, Yoshua Bengio, and Hod Lipson. How transferable are features in deep neural networks? In *Proceedings of the Annual Conference on Neural Information Processing Systems (NeurIPS)*, pages 3320–3328, 2014.

[590] Jason Yosinski, Jeff Clune, Yoshua Bengio, and Hod Lipson. How transferable are features in deep neural networks? In *Advances in Neural Information Processing Systems*, pages 3320–3328, 2014.

[591] Cheng Yu, Bo Wang, Bo Yang, and Robby T Tan. Multi-scale networks for 3d human pose estimation with inference stage optimization. *arXiv preprint arXiv:2010.06844*, 2020.

[592] Lei Yu, Ling Liu, Calton Pu, Mehmet Emre Gursoy, and Stacey Truex. Differentially private model publishing for deep learning. In *Proceedings of the IEEE Symposium on Security and Privacy*, pages 332–349. IEEE, 2019.

[593] Peifeng Yu and Mosharaf Chowdhury. Salus: Fine-grained gpu sharing primitives for deep learning applications. *arXiv preprint*, abs/1902.04610, 2019.

[594] Qian Yu, Songze Li, Netanel Raviv, Seyed Mohammadreza Mousavi Kalan, Mahdi Soltanolkotabi, and Amir Salman Avestimehr. Lagrange coded computing: Optimal design for resiliency, security, and privacy. In *Proceedings of the International Conference on Artificial Intelligence and Statistics (AISTATS)*, volume 89, pages 1215–1225, 2019.

[595] Ye Yu, Yingmin Li, Shuai Che, Niraj K Jha, and Weifeng Zhang. Software-defined design space exploration for an efficient dnn accelerator architecture. *IEEE Transactions on Computers*, 70(1):45–56, 2020.

[596] Kun Yuan, Qing Ling, and Wotao Yin. On the convergence of decentralized gradient descent. *SIAM J. Optim.*, 26(3):1835–1854, 2016.

[597] Yuan Yuan, Siyuan Liu, Jiawei Zhang, Yongbing Zhang, Chao Dong, and Liang Lin. Unsupervised image super-resolution using cycle-in-cycle generative adversarial networks. In *Proceedings of the IEEE Conference on Computer Vision and Pattern Recognition Workshops*, pages 701–710, 2018.

[598] Sergey Zagoruyko and Nikos Komodakis. Paying more attention to attention: Improving the performance of convolutional neural networks via attention transfer. In *Proceedings of the International Conference on Learning Representations (ICLR)*, 2017.

[599] Mahdi Zamani, Mahnush Movahedi, and Mariana Raykova. Rapidchain: Scaling blockchain via full sharding. In *Proceedings of the 2018 ACM SIGSAC Conference on Computer and Communications Security*, pages 931–948, Toronto, ON, Canada, October 15-19, 2018.

[600] Matthew D Zeiler and Rob Fergus. Visualizing and understanding convolutional networks. In *Proceedings of the European Conference on Computer Vision (ECCV)*, pages 818–833. Springer, 2014.

[601] Xiaohang Zhan, Xingang Pan, Bo Dai, Ziwei Liu, Dahua Lin, and Chen Change Loy. Self-supervised scene de-occlusion. In *Proceedings of the IEEE/CVF Conference on Computer Vision and Pattern Recognition*, pages 3784–3792, 2020.

[602] Chengliang Zhang, Suyi Li, Junzhe Xia, Wei Wang, Feng Yan, and Yang Liu. {BatchCrypt}: Efficient homomorphic encryption for {Cross-Silo} federated learning. In *Proceedings of the USENIX Annual Technical Conference*, pages 493–506, 2020.

[603] Chengliang Zhang, Junzhe Xia, Baichen Yang, Huancheng Puyang, Wei Wang, Ruichuan Chen, Istemi Ekin Akkus, Paarijaat Aditya, and Feng Yan. *Citadel: Protecting Data Privacy and Model Confidentiality for Collaborative Learning*, page 546–561. Association for Computing Machinery, New York, NY, USA, 2021.

[604] Hao Zhang, Zeyu Zheng, Shizhen Xu, Wei Dai, Qirong Ho, Xiaodan Liang, Zhiting Hu, Jinliang Wei, Pengtao Xie, and Eric P. Xing. Poseidon: An efficient communication architecture for distributed deep learning on GPU clusters. In *Proceedings of the USENIX Annual Technical Conferenc (ATC)*, pages 181–193, 2017.

[605] He Zhang, Vishwanath Sindagi, and Vishal M Patel. Image de-raining using a conditional generative adversarial network. *IEEE Trans. Circuits Syst. Video Technol.*, 30(11):3943–3956, 2019.

[606] Huaguang Zhang, Yushuai Li, David Wenzhong Gao, and Jianguo Zhou. Distributed optimal energy management for energy internet. *IEEE Trans. Industrial Informatics*, 13(6):3081–3097, 2017.

[607] Huaqing Zhang, Jian Wang, Zhanquan Sun, Jacek M. Zurada, and Nikhil R. Pal. Feature selection for neural networks using group lasso regularization. *IEEE Trans. Knowl. Data Eng.*, 32(4):659–673, 2020.

[608] Jianting Zhang, Zicong Hong, Xiaoyu Qiu, Yufeng Zhan, Song Guo, and Wuhui Chen. Skychain: A deep reinforcement learning-empowered dynamic blockchain sharding system. In *49th International Conference on Parallel Processing – ICPP*, ICPP '20, New York, NY, USA, 2020. Association for Computing Machinery.

[609] Jie Zhang, Zhihao Qu, Chenxi Chen, Haozhao Wang, Yufeng Zhan, Baoliu Ye, and Song Guo. Edge learning: The enabling technology for distributed big data analytics in the edge. *ACM Computing Surveys*, 54(7):1–36, 2021.

[610] Michael Zhang, Karan Sapra, Sanja Fidler, Serena Yeung, and Jose M. Alvarez. Personalized federated learning with first order model optimization. In *9th International Conference on Learning Representations, ICLR 2021*. OpenReview.net, Virtual Event, May 3–7, 2021.

[611] Shichao Zhang, Xuelong Li, Ming Zong, Xiaofeng Zhu, and Ruili Wang. Efficient knn classification with different numbers of nearest neighbors. *IEEE Transactions on Neural Networks and Learning Systems*, 29(5):1774–1785, 2017.

[612] Wei Zhang, Suyog Gupta, Xiangru Lian, and Ji Liu. Staleness-aware async-sgd for distributed deep learning. In *Proceedings of the International Joint Conference on Artificial Intelligence (IJCAI)*, pages 2350–2356, 2016.

[613] Xiangyu Zhang, Xinyu Zhou, Mengxiao Lin, and Jian Sun. Shufflenet: An extremely efficient convolutional neural network for mobile devices. In *Proceedings of the IEEE/CVF Conference on Computer Vision and Pattern Recognition (CVPR)*, pages 6848–6856, 2018.

[614] Yulun Zhang, Kunpeng Li, Kai Li, Lichen Wang, Bineng Zhong, and Yun Fu. Image super-resolution using very deep residual channel attention networks. In

Proceedings of the European Conference on Computer Vision (ECCV), pages 286–301, Munich, Germany, September 8–14, 2018.

[615] Yulun Zhang, Yapeng Tian, Yu Kong, Bineng Zhong, and Yun Fu. Residual dense network for image super-resolution. In *Proceedings of the IEEE Conference on Computer Vision and Pattern Recognition*, pages 2472–2481, 2018.

[616] Ziming Zhang and Venkatesh Saligrama. Zero-shot learning via joint latent similarity embedding. In *Proceedings of the IEEE Conference on Computer Vision and Pattern Recognition*, pages 6034–6042, Las Vegas, NV, USA, June 27–30, 2016.

[617] Jun Zhao. Distributed deep learning under differential privacy with the teacher-student paradigm. In *Workshops at the Thirty-Second AAAI Conference on Artificial Intelligence*, New Orleans, Louisiana, USA, February 2–7, 2018.

[618] Yue Zhao, Meng Li, Liangzhen Lai, Naveen Suda, Damon Civin, and Vikas Chandra. Federated learning with non-iid data. *arXiv preprint arXiv:1806.00582*, 2018.

[619] Jianlong Zhong and Bingsheng He. Kernelet: High-throughput gpu kernel executions with dynamic slicing and scheduling. *IEEE Transactions on Parallel and Distributed Systems*, 25:1522–1532, 2014.

[620] Aojun Zhou, Anbang Yao, Yiwen Guo, Lin Xu, and Yurong Chen. Incremental network quantization: Towards lossless cnns with low-precision weights. In *Proceedings of the International Conference on Learning Representations (ICLR)*, 2017.

[621] Lina Zhou, Shimei Pan, Jianwu Wang, and Athanasios V Vasilakos. Machine learning on big data: Opportunities and challenges. *Neurocomputing*, 237:350–361, 2017.

[622] Qiang Zhou, Shiyin Wang, Yitong Wang, Zilong Huang, and Xinggang Wang. Human de-occlusion: Invisible perception and recovery for humans. In *Proceedings of the IEEE/CVF Conference on Computer Vision and Pattern Recognition*, pages 3691–3701, 2021.

[623] Qihua Zhou, Song Guo, Zhihao Qu, Jingcai Guo, Zhenda Xu, Jiewei Zhang, Tao Guo, Boyuan Luo, and Jingren Zhou. Octo: INT8 training with loss-aware compensation and backward quantization for tiny on-device learning. In *2021 USENIX Annual Technical Conference (USENIX ATC 21)*, pages 177–191. USENIX Association, July 2021. Virtual Event.

[624] Qihua Zhou, Zhihao Qu, Song Guo, Boyuan Luo, Jingcai Guo, Zhenda Xu, and R. Akerkar. On-device learning systems for edge intelligence: A software and hardware synergy perspective. *IEEE Internet of Things Journal*, pages 1–1, 2021.

[625] Shuchang Zhou, Zekun Ni, Xinyu Zhou, He Wen, Yuxin Wu, and Yuheng Zou. Dorefa-net: Training low bitwidth convolutional neural networks with low bitwidth gradients. *arXiv preprint*, abs/1606.06160, 2016.

[626] Wenchao Zhou, Yifan Cai, Yanqing Peng, Sheng Wang, Ke Ma, and Feifei Li. *VeriDB: An SGX-Based Verifiable Database*, page 2182–2194. Association for Computing Machinery, New York, NY, USA, 2021.

[627] Yanlin Zhou, George Pu, Xiyao Ma, Xiaolin Li, and Dapeng Wu. Distilled one-shot federated learning. *CoRR*, abs/2009.07999, 2020.

[628] Yiren Zhou, Seyed-Mohsen Moosavi-Dezfooli, Ngai-Man Cheung, and Pascal Frossard. Adaptive quantization for deep neural network. In *Proceedings of the AAAI Conference on Artificial Intelligence (AAAI)*, pages 4596–4604, 2018.

[629] Zhi Zhou, Xu Chen, En Li, Liekang Zeng, Ke Luo, and Junshan Zhang. Edge intelligence: Paving the last mile of artificial intelligence with edge computing. *Proceedings of the IEEE*, 107(8):1738–1762, 2019.

[630] Chunsheng Zhu, Huan Zhou, Victor C. M. Leung, Kun Wang, Yan Zhang, and Laurence T. Yang. Toward big data in green city. *IEEE Communications Magazine*, 55(11):14–18, 2017.

[631] Feng Zhu, Ruihao Gong, Fengwei Yu, Xianglong Liu, Yanfei Wang, Zhelong Li, Xiuqi Yang, and Junjie Yan. Towards unified INT8 training for convolutional neural network. *arXiv preprint*, abs/1912.12607, 2019.

[632] Michael Zhu and Suyog Gupta. To prune, or not to prune: Exploring the efficacy of pruning for model compression. In *Proceedings of the International Conference on Learning Representations (ICLR)*, 2018.

[633] Yi Zhu, Zhenzhong Lan, Shawn Newsam, and Alexander Hauptmann. Hidden two-stream convolutional networks for action recognition. In *Asian Conference on Computer Vision*, pages 363–378. Springer, 2018.

[634] Yizhe Zhu, Mohamed Elhoseiny, Bingchen Liu, Xi Peng, and Ahmed Elgammal. A generative adversarial approach for zero-shot learning from noisy texts. In *Proceedings of the IEEE Conference on Computer Vision and Pattern Recognition (CVPR)*, 2018.

[635] Barret Zoph and Quoc V Le. Neural architecture search with reinforcement learning. *arXiv preprint arXiv:1611.01578*, 2016.

Index

Printed in the United States
by Baker & Taylor Publisher Services